The Forts and Fortifications of Europe 1815–1945: The Neutral States

*To Willy, Junior, Alphie, Bubbles, Stella,
Leo, Jerry and Callie.*

The Forts and Fortifications of Europe 1815–1945: The Neutral States

Netherlands, Belgium and Switzerland

J.E. Kaufmann and H.W. Kaufmann

Pen & Sword
MILITARY

First published in Great Britain in 2014 by
Pen & Sword Military
an imprint of
Pen & Sword Books Ltd
47 Church Street
Barnsley
South Yorkshire
S70 2AS

ISBN 978 1 78346 392 3

Typeset in Ehrhardt by
Mac Style Ltd, Bridlington, East Yorkshire
Printed and bound in the UK by CPI Group (UK) Ltd, Croydon, CRO 4YY

Pen & Sword Books Ltd incorporates the imprints of Pen & Sword Archaeology, Atlas,
Aviation, Battleground, Discovery, Family History, History, Maritime, Military, Naval,
Politics, Railways, Select, Social History, Transport, True Crime, and Claymore Press,
Frontline Books, Leo Cooper, Praetorian Press, Remember When, Seaforth
Publishing and Wharncliffe.

For a complete list of Pen & Sword titles please contact
PEN & SWORD BOOKS LIMITED
47 Church Street, Barnsley, South Yorkshire, S70 2AS, England
E-mail: enquiries@pen-and-sword.co.uk
Website: www.pen-and-sword.co.uk

Contents

Acknowledgements

We would like to thank the following people for their assistance in this project: William Alcorn (documents from the Belgian Archives and other material), Michel van Best (photos of Dutch forts), Norman H. Clark (photos of Dutch forts), Clayton Donnell (photos of Belgian fortifications), Dale Floyd (various articles), Johan Gieske (photos of Dutch forts), Allert M.A. Goossens* (information on Dutch bunker types and strengths), Martyn Gregg (photos of Belgian and Dutch forts), Willy Houet* (information and documents on Belgian forts), Johan Merckel (data on the Belgian forts), Jean-Christophe Moret* (information on Swiss fortifications), Bernard Paich* (his fortification drawings and photos), Ruud Pols (photos of Dutch forts), Jean Pueluiex* (data and photos on Belgian fortifications), Frank Philippart (information on Belgian fortifications), René Ros* (details on Dutch fortifications and photos), David Ross* (information on Dutch artillery and fortifications), Hans Peter Ruch of AFOM (information on Swiss forts at Sargans), Hans Sakkers (Dutch and Belgian fortifications), Andreas Schröder (photos of Belgian weapons), Geoff Snowden (photos), Oswald Schwitter* (information on the Swiss fortifications), Lee Unterborn (internet research and reference books), Dr. Joost Vaesen* – Director Brussels Studies Institute (recent research information on the Eben Emael), John Verbeek (information on Dutch fortifications) and Caspar Vermeulen (Belgian fortifications). Also, other members of Site O https://sites. google.com/site/siteinternational/ who helped locate and provide information. We hope we have not overlooked anyone.

Martin Rupp provided valuable assistance in translating German wartime terms. Additional help in translating some German wartime material came from Jens Andersen, Hans-Rudolf Neumann and Rudi Rolf.

Note on Illustrations
Photos are credited to the individual source. Most wartime photos come from German wartime documents and have been modified for reproduction. Drawings and maps not by the authors either come from non-copyrighted material, most of which has been modified and include changes and additions by the authors, or are from sources noted on them or in the caption.

---

* The asterisk denotes those who the authors relied upon for much information not presently available in books or other sources.

Note to Reader

Due to the scope of the subject of this book, it is impossible to include sufficient illustrative material in a book of this size. We advise the reader to refer to additional maps, from an atlas or on the Internet, to identify many of the locations mentioned that could not be included on the few maps in this book. In addition, a few Internet sites are referenced, but Internet sites often change address or shut down, so we recommend using an Internet search engine to find additional information and illustrative material.

Glossary of Terms

Avant Cuirasse (Fr.)	'Forward Armour', English, 'glacis armour'; armour that surrounds an armoured **turret**
Bastion (Fr.), **Bastione (It.)** **Bollwerk (Ger.)**	Generally the French spelling is used; it refers to a section of the fortifications or **enceinte** of fortifications of a fort or fortress) that projects outward like a salient to give flanking fires. Bastion System refers to a defensive system that uses a line of bastions. The term Bastion can refer more loosely to any strongpoint
Bunker (Ger.)	Generic term that can refer to any type of enclosed position with relatively thick walls
Caponier	Defensive position extending from the **scarp** into the ditch
Carnot Wall	Wall with firing positions built in a fort's moat covering the **scarp**. Although designed by a Frenchman before the Napoleonic Wars, it was favoured by both Germans and Austrians after that war, but never by the French
Casemate **Caserne (Fr.)** **Caserma (It.)** **Kaserne (Ger.)**	Chamber or bombproof vault within a fort or a type of blockhouse Translates to barracks, the French term often refers to a garrison area with the barracks, the kitchens and other facilities
Cloche (Fr.)	Fixed armoured **cupola** or dome
Coffre (Fr.)	Refers to a **counterscarp casemate**, which in modern concrete fortifications replaced the **caponier** for protection of the ditch (or moat)
Counterscarp	Wall on the outside of a ditch or moat of a fortification
Cupola	General term for any type of **turret** including fixed ones (**cloche**)
Crenel	Loophole or embrasure
Dijk (Dutch)	Dike or embankment
Enceinte (Fr.)	Walls and **bastions** surrounding a fortification
Festung (Ger.)	Fortress
Fossé (Fr.)	Ditch or moat of a fort
Fossé Diamant	Angular, concrete ditch usually in front of an embrasure or embrasures of a **casemate** block
Glacis (Fr.)	Sloped and cleared area around a fortification; see **avant cuirasse**

Gorge	Side of a fortification's surrounding ditch furthest from the enemy, i.e. the rear of the fortification
Lunette (Fr.)	Initially, an outwork with a half-moon shape belonging to a larger fortification; in more recent history, a redan with short flanks and open in the rear; generally it has two faces and two short flanks; see **redan**
Meer (Dutch)	Lake
Polder	Land reclaimed from the sea
Position Fortifiée (PF) (Fr.)	Referring to the Position Fortifiée de Liège (PFL) or Namur (PFN) or Antwerp (PFA)
Ravelin	Triangular detached work placed in the main ditch of a fortification
Redan	Small, often 'V' shaped (two flanks) fortification open in the rear
Redoubt	Small strongpoint or outwork. A large area containing many fortifications and serving as a last line of defence for a nation is called a 'National Redoubt'. The term has also been used for small interval works
Reduit	This term when referring to fortifications of the nineteenth century and after refers to a 'last stand' position within a fortification. In the medieval castle it would be a keep, in the modern fortifications of the last two centuries it was referred to as a core work, kernwerk (German) or noyau (French) inside of a fortification. The high-explosive shell of the 1880s made tower-like reduits obsolete, but not structures with a lower profile. In some cases a National Redoubt is referred to as a National Reduit since the purpose is the same
Remise (Fr.)	Term that refers to a shelter or depot for guns, vehicles or munitions. Usually it is not very large
Scarp	Interior wall of a ditch or moat of a fortification; also known as escarp
Stellung (Ger.)	Position, when referring to a defensive position
Tenaille	A low outwork in the ditch between **bastions** protecting the curtain wall
Trace	Outline of a fortification
Traditore (Italian)	Referred to traitor, but became the word for a battery or **casemate** that gave flanking fire. This type of position was located in the flank or **gorge** of a fort out of the direct line of fire for enemy artillery
Traverse:	Earthen wall perpendicular to the front wall serving as a flank shield for a gun position
Turret:	Small tower on old fortifications; since the nineteenth century, the term generally is applied to a revolving dome (usually armoured),

also referred to as a **cupola**. A revolving cupola has gun embrasures in the armoured dome. An eclipsing (retracting) turret was two components: the armoured dome, known as the calotte, cap, or dome and the mantle. The mantle is the armoured wall of the turret upon which the calotte rests and includes the gun embrasures. When the turret retracts, the mantle sinks below the surface. There is no need for a mantle on a non-eclipsing turret, since the calotte rests on the surface

Vaart (Dutch)   Canal or waterway
Weg (Dutch, Ger.)   path (in Dutch also: road)

Introduction: The Guardians of Neutrality

Born out of revolution, three European nations became the symbols of neutrality for most of the nineteenth century and into the twentieth century: Switzerland, the Netherlands and Belgium. However, only Switzerland successfully maintained that status throughout the twentieth century. All three of these countries had once been part of the German Holy Roman Empire that occupied a key central position in Europe, separating East from West and Slavs from Latins. At the end of the Middle Ages, the Empire began a slow decline. The first major region the Empire lost was the Swiss cantons. The Helvetic Celts lost their lands to the Germanic invaders in the Dark Ages. Over 800 years later, the German-speaking cantons of Uri, Schwyz and Unterwalden declared their independence from the empire in 1291. The Habsburg rulers of the Empire tried to re-establish control over the Swiss, but every effort met with defeat in the mountain fastness. Meanwhile, other Swiss cantons joined the first three cantons that had broken away from the Empire. During the Reformation, the region became a bastion of Calvinism. At the end of the Thirty Years War in 1648, the nation was recognized as a neutral state. Only the French Revolution and the Napoleonic Wars impinged on Swiss neutrality.

In the meantime, the Dutch became a bastion of Calvinism and rebelled against the Habsburgs in the sixteenth century. The Netherlands became part of the domain of the Spanish Habsburgs (Philip II of Spain) in 1556. The Eighty Years War of Independence (1568–1648) broke out soon after that. Recognition of Dutch and Swiss independence in 1648 failed to bring about their neutrality. The Dutch, who acquired a large overseas empire in the early seventeenth century,[1] continued their engagement in European wars until the end of the Napoleonic Era. The Southern Netherlands, mainly modern-day Belgium, remained under Spanish control after 1648. At the end of the War of the Spanish Succession, the Treaty of Rastatt of 1714 assigned the remnants of the Spanish Netherlands to Austria. Next, France absorbed the Austrian Netherlands during the French Revolution. The Congress of Vienna in 1814 settled its final status by turning over its Catholic Flemish and Walloon populations to the Protestant Netherlands. However, this situation did not work out and led to a revolution in 1830, which finally ended with the emergence of an independent Belgium and a guarantee of neutrality.

During the period following the Napoleonic Wars, each of these countries strove to maintain their neutrality. The Dutch did not establish their neutrality by treaty, but rather by policy. They were involved in maintaining an empire, but The Hague was the site where conventions establishing the rules of war were held at the turn of the century.[2] All three nations occupied precarious locations where they formed the flanks of the area of operations between the German Second Reich and the French Republic after the Franco-Prussian War. Thus, in any war both the French and Germans would logically consider outflanking each other by either violating Belgian or Swiss neutrality. The indefensible Maastricht Appendage of the Netherlands made a tempting target since it shielded a large section of Belgian territory from Germany.[3] This alone presented a threat to Dutch neutrality. The only answer to this risk was some form of armed neutrality. All three nations had a military tradition that should have kept away invaders. However, their armed forces did not take part in any major conflicts after the Napoleonic Wars. One solution for the three nations was to build fortifications to fend off possible aggression.

The nature of warfare changed with the Napoleonic Wars and especially after the 1850s. During the Napoleonic Wars, large armies organized into corps and divisions became important while the importance of individual regiments declined, except in small campaigns. Napoleon set a new standard for the art of warfare and for much of the nineteenth century many generals tried to emulate his tactical manoeuvres. Small nations like Switzerland, the Netherlands and Belgium did not have the manpower to field large citizen armies to match those of their neighbours. The Spartan-like qualities of the Swiss soldiers could no longer offset the absence of a small army. For these three nations, the only viable option was to prepare for a defensive war.

During the eighteenth century, thanks to industrialization, Great Britain became the leading military power of Europe. It stayed on top throughout the nineteenth century as the remainder of Europe also gradually became industrialized. The Netherlands and Switzerland were slow to industrialize as Belgium moved ahead of them. This affected the development of their military forces. By the 1860s, the musket was replaced with breech-loading and repeating rifles. After the American Civil War, the appearance of more powerful artillery and even the Gatling Gun (the first machine gun), made it no longer practical to arm soldiers with muskets – even if cheaply mass-produced – and to have them stand in lines on the battlefield. Stone and masonry forts could no longer resist the new artillery and crumbled in battle. In addition, on the naval front, armour-clad steam ships presented a new threat. Submarines entered the scene after the tests on Robert Fulton's *Nautilus* in 1800 and 1801 in France. Mass use of many of these new weapons occurred during the Franco-Prussian War in 1870 under the watchful eye of all of Europe. However, the French tactics were sadly outdated, which led to their ignominious defeat. As France prepared to exact revenge and recoup its losses in that war of 1870, Germany strove to stay ahead. This sparked off an era of militarism similar to the arms race of the Cold War. The neutrals caught between these two great military powers had to gird themselves for the coming conflict, which meant they had to modernize or face oblivion. New rifles and modern infantry tactics would not suffice; they had to do what the Germans, French, Austrians, Italians and Russians were doing: fortify their borders facing the great powers or adopt some other defensive alternative that would make it too costly for an enemy to violate their neutrality. The Belgians took the lead in building fortifications, but they neglected to modernize their army at the same time.

A New Era in Fortifications

The Low Countries and Switzerland were no strangers to fortifications. The Romans built forts there at one time or another and during the Middle Ages the local lords built castles. The appearance of cannons led to lower and thicker walled forts and fortresses during the Renaissance. Simon Stevin (1548–1620) of Flanders (in modern-day Belgium) influenced the construction of the new types of fortifications with emphasis on ravelins. Sébastien de Vauban (1633–1707), the leading military engineer of the era followed Stevin. Vauban, who built fortresses all over France, concentrated a number of them in Flanders (present-day French and Belgian Flanders) as part of his *Pré Carré* (square field) concept[4] to block this lowland invasion route. His Dutch contemporary, Menno van Coehoorn (1641–1704), continued Stevin's work. Thus, modern-day Belgium and the Netherlands became the scene of the greatest advances in fortress construction until the end of the eighteenth century. All that changed when brick and stone forts proved vulnerable to the more advanced artillery of the mid-nineteenth century. After the 1860s, military engineers had to resolve this new conundrum.

The curtain walls of castles and the fortresses that followed them were unable to stand up to the new artillery. Even the bastions that largely replaced the medieval towers no longer had the ability to resist these developments. However, moats and some of the older features that went back to ancient times survived well into the twentieth century. During the nineteenth century and even earlier, military engineers devised new features to protect the moats. At first, bastions included flanking positions that fired into the moat. The ravelin and tenaille served to protect the curtain wall. The caponier was placed in the moat to defend it. Although caponiers continued in use after the mid-nineteenth century, it was gradually replaced with the counterscarp casemate or coffre. Since the coffre was built into the counterscarp instead of the scarp, it was not subject to enemy direct or indirect fire. Another addition to some newer forts was the Carnot Wall, which was located in the moat adjacent to the scarp.[5]

The most significant change that took place in the nineteenth century was the replacement of the bastioned trace with the polygonal system. No longer was the bastion the dominant feature for protecting the curtains. The caponier took over that role. The complex bastioned trace based on mathematical calculations was replaced with the polygonal system. Casemated rifle and artillery positions supplanted most open firing positions. These changes appeared in many brick and stone forts built between the early 1800s and the 1860s when the rifled artillery turned the walls of Fort Sumter and Fort Pulaski, two forts with these features, into rubble during the American Civil War.

The Belgian general Henri Alexis Brialmont (1821–1903), led Europe into a new age of fortifications. Across the border, his French counterpart, General Raymond Adolphe Séré de Rivières (1815–95), also helped bring France into the new era. Séré de Rivières advanced the idea of an eighteenth century French engineer to use detached forts to expand the defences beyond the polygonal trace. After 1870, the French, under the direction of Séré de Rivières, tried to fortify their border with a 'Barrier of Iron' even stronger than Vauban's 'Fence of Iron'.[6] Séré de Rivières' barrier surrounded a number of old fortresses with new forts thus creating fortress rings. Brialmont sought to protect his Belgian homeland with a similar series of fortress rings for the major cities.

The Low Countries and Switzerland were at a disadvantage when it came to the arms race and building fortifications because their industrial capacity was limited. Only Belgium had a limited amount of heavy industry that made it possible to build some of their own armoured components required in the new fortifications. All three nations purchased most of their heavy weapons from other countries. Until the Second World War, the Dutch purchased many of their weapons from the Swedish Bofors company, the German Krupp industries, the Danish Madsen company and the British Vickers and Armstrong companies. The Swiss

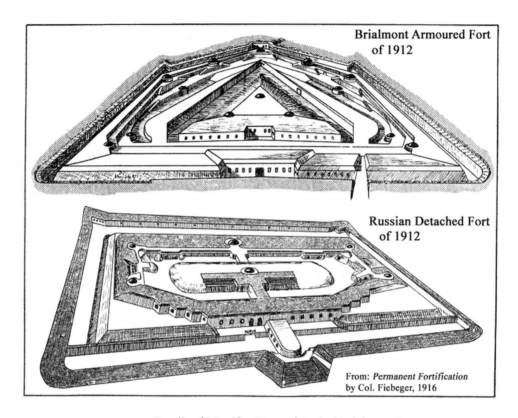

Brialmont Armoured Fort
of 1912

Russian Detached Fort
of 1912

From: *Permanent Fortification*
by Col. Fiebeger, 1916

Details of Massif or Keep of Typical Brialmont Fort

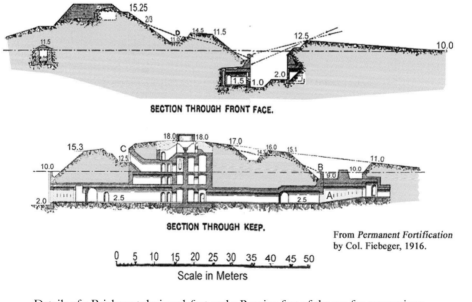

SECTION THROUGH FRONT FACE.

SECTION THROUGH KEEP.

From *Permanent Fortification*
by Col. Fiebeger, 1916.

0 5 10 15 20 25 30 35 40 45 50

Scale in Meters

Details of a Brialmont designed-fort and a Russian fort of the era for comparison.

Fortifications into the Modern Era

From Antiquity through the Middle Ages, the high crenelated wall characterized most permanent fortifications. Most military maps use the crenelated line as a symbol to represent a line of fortifications. Gunpowder and the dawn of the Renaissance brought a major change.

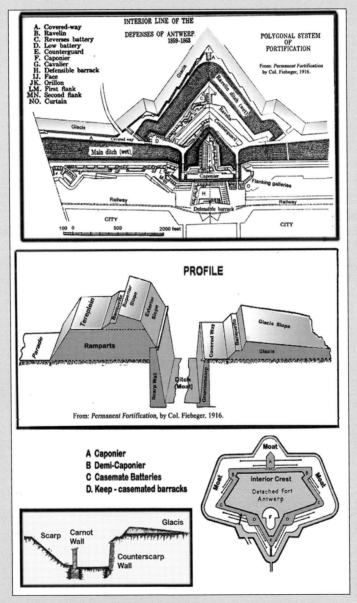

Two drawings from Colonel Fiebeger's book *Permanent Fortifications* (1916) showing parts of fortifications using a Belgian fort of the 1860s as an example.

The walls became thicker, about two-thirds of the height of castle walls, and they were sunk into the moat.[7] The ancient and medieval tower was too high, vulnerable and unsuitable for large cannons. Engineers greatly reduced its height and often enlarged it. This type of tower, called a bastion, continued to protect the curtain walls as the trace of the fortifications became increasingly geometric in the age of Vauban and Coehoorn. Fortifications grew in complexity as additional features, often outworks, were added. The glacis gave the defender a clear field of fire in the bastion-type fort and masked much of the fortification from the view and direct enemy artillery fire at its base. During the latter half of the eighteenth century, René de Montalembert, a French military engineer, suggested replacing the bastion system with a polygonal one and placing the artillery in casemates and even in towers so they could dominate the besiegers' guns. He pointed out that Vauban's bastion system was outdated because the open positions on the ramparts and the interior were exposed to indirect artillery fire. Since a siege was essentially an artillery duel, the guns needed to be protected.[8] His ideas caught the attention of the Prussians who further developed them during the next century. The polygonal system eliminated the need for bastions to protect the moat and the complex mathematical formulas for a trace with the requisite tenailles and accompanying features, which required suitable terrain to be properly sited. Caponiers were devised to protect the ditch and were extended into it or completely across it. This system was more economical and allowed for a greater concentration of artillery against the enemy as the straighter lines replaced the zigzags of the tenaille system.[9] The Prussians added a fortified casemate that served as a barracks or keep and occupied part of the fort's trace. Brialmont liked this idea and used it in the 1860s at Antwerp.

Between the 1860s and early 1880s, new, mostly polygonal fortifications were built throughout Europe. Most were covered with earth to protect them from the heavy artillery being developed. Detached forts, recommended by the French engineers, became important in keeping a city beyond the range of enemy artillery and extending the defences outward. In 1885, the Germans, French and Belgians, who were leading in the development of modern fortifications, faced a new crisis with the appearance of the 'Torpedo Shell',[10] which contained a newly-developed high explosive and could penetrate the newest forts. As a result, the new forts were made concrete and armour and the older ones were reinforced with the same materials.[11]

also bought from some of the same companies, but mainly from Germany's Krupp/Grüson until the First World War. After the war, in 1920, a Swiss company purchased patents from a German weapons producer, which led to the creation of the Oerlikon 20mm anti-aircraft gun. The Swiss Oerlikon company began producing anti-aircraft guns and exported them to many nations until 1940.[12] The Swiss purchased the 7.5mm Maxim Model 1911 produced in Germany and manufactured them under license at Waffenfabrik Bern during the war. These machine guns served in the fortifications built before 1914 and later and remained in service until 1951. The Belgians were able to produce many of their own weapons, but also relied on foreign sources like Hotchkiss machine guns for forts, Maxim machine guns for the field forces and Krupp quick-firing guns.

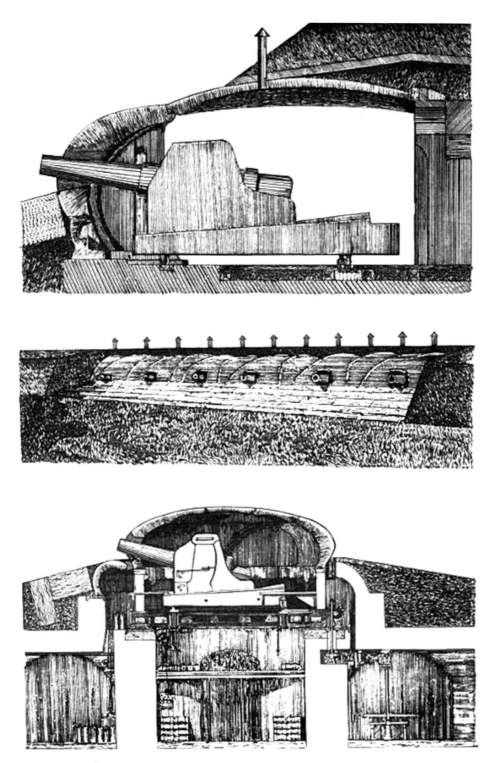

Grüson armoured battery (top) and turret made of chilled iron.

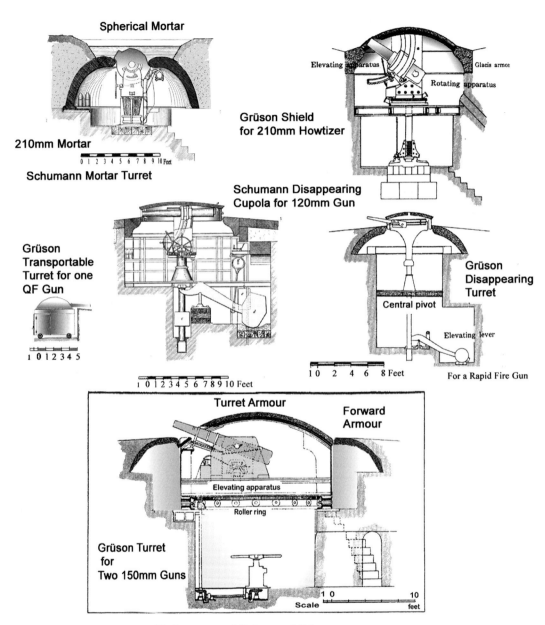

Various types of Grüson and Schumann turrets.

All three countries' ability to meet the requirements for reinforced concrete production was limited. The Netherlands and Switzerland had no iron ore deposits and lacked a large iron and steel manufacturing industry to create the reinforcement rods. They had to import iron and steel from France, Germany and other sources before 1914. All three nations, however, could produce the cement they needed for the concrete. During the First World War, the Dutch and the Swiss were able to continue importing the iron they needed. The Swiss received up to

No. 1—Turret mounting for 21 cm howitzer.
2—Exterior view of turret for 21 cm howitzer.
3—Turret mounting of 21 cm spherical mortar.
4—Disappearing turret for 57 mm automatic gun.
5—Transportable turret for 37 mm automatic gun.
6—Railway turret for 57 mm automatic gun.

Photographs of various types of fortress weapons from Colonel Fieberger's book.

80 per cent of their steel from Germany until 1940, when they had to negotiate to trade their anti-aircraft weapons for German steel. In some of the first forts[13] they built in the 1880s, the Swiss used large granite blocks in response to the new high-explosive shell before they adopted reinforced concrete as a building material.

Although Belgium was in the lead in the development of fortifications under General Brialmont, it lost its edge when its fortifications proved inadequate against the new artillery, which was created after the completion of the last of its forts. The Dutch fell even further behind and by the Second World War, their defences, which relied heavily on inundations, did not stand up well in combat. The Swiss fortifications and defences never had to undergo the test of war.

To wage war successfully and maintain independence the small neutral nations faced more demanding requirements than ever before. Before 1850, field armies of most nations were equal to each other because the main infantry weapon was the musket and the method of firing in ranks remained largely unchanged. Some improvements in artillery had been made, but most navies still relied on wooden sailing warships. Fortifications had begun to change, but the old post-medieval forts and fortresses remained in use while new types of forts were evolving. Logistics improved during the Napoleonic Wars, but since these nations were committed not to take part in aggressive warfare, they maintained the advantage of using interior lines if attacked. Breech-loading and repeating rifles and machine guns drastically changed infantry tactics. The calibre and accuracy of artillery pieces and eventually the high-explosive shell, rendered the cannon, howitzer and mortar more deadly than ever. This not only forced a change in infantry tactics, but also required improved defensive methods. Balloon observation increased the effectiveness of the artillery and offered new methods for the commanders to observe the battlefield. During the next century, aircraft presented a new threat. Railways improved the logistical support and the mobility of field armies. However, the motor vehicle did not become significant until after the First World War. At sea and even on rivers, warships no longer relied on wind, as they became steam-powered and armoured. After the French Revolution, the trend moved toward the creation of massive armies by conscription. The neutrals followed suit, but their populations were too small to match the armies of the great powers while their economies did not allow them to keep up in the arms race between major powers after the Franco–Prussian War of 1870–1. In the last half of the nineteenth century, a military revolution born out of the Industrial Revolution drastically changed the face of warfare.[14]

The neutral nations of Western Europe no longer could consider taking an offensive against France or Germany because they were unable to match their huge conscript armies and lacked the resources to sustain a war. The key option for the Low Countries was to improve their defences so they could act as a shield against invasion. However, they also believed that their small field armies could take the offensive within their own borders to repulse invaders. This was part of the philosophy of the era, which postulated that that the best defence was offence. Neither the rebels during the American Civil War nor the French during the Franco–Prussian War had been able to win on the defensive even though they engaged in limited offensives. The French fought only within their own territory. The Swiss had a more limited and less flexible military during the last half of the century and not even an offensive within their own borders could be considered a viable option. In 1880, unlike the Dutch and Belgians, they had no defensive lines and practically no modern fortifications. The Belgian government, on the other hand, had already decided in 1859 to create a National Redoubt, which was to serve as an entrenched camp for the army at Antwerp. Thus, Brialmont was able to begin the construction of new fortifications. Meanwhile, the Dutch began reassessing some of their older defensive lines, modernizing them and improving their system of inundations to form barriers. The Swiss continued to rely on their mountain barriers and defend a few key access routes. Fortunately for the Swiss, the technological advances were not significant enough to reduce the effectiveness of the mountain barriers. However, the majority of the population lived outside the planned National Redoubt. Nonetheless, the main advantage the Swiss held over the other neutrals was that their country had little of economic value for an invader since most people associated it with the production of cuckoo clocks, umbrellas and watches.[15] Only its strategic position on invasion routes into France, Germany, Austria and Italy gave it some importance, which was mitigated by the presence of the mountains.

Thus, at the dawn of the twentieth century, the best option for these three neutral nations was to attempt to remain neutral. None of the major powers considered any of them a serious threat, unless they teamed up with their adversaries. Before and during the First World War, the Germans prepared plans to invade all three countries while the French set their eyes on Switzerland.

Buffers of Neutrality

In the late nineteenth century, the German Reich and the Austro-Hungarian Empire, with the exceptions of their eastern territories, formed the core of the old Holy Roman Empire. The western borderlands of the old empire – the Netherlands and Switzerland – had been contested between the Empire, France and Burgundy for centuries. Both countries became centres of Calvinism, although the Swiss had broken away from the empire before the Reformation. The Netherlands became virtually independent since the Dutch had revolted against Philip II of Spain in the latter part of the sixteenth century, but they remained at war with the Habsburgs for many more decades. Neither Dutch nor Swiss independence was officially recognized until the Treaty of Westphalia in 1648 ended the Thirty Years War, known to the Dutch as the Eighty Years War of Independence. Eventually, the Netherlands became the main trading centre of Northern Europe and created a vast commercial and colonial empire that included holdings in the Americas and the Dutch East Indies until 1914 and 1940.

Associated with the modern Dutch Republic is Belgium whose population consists of French-speaking Walloons and Germanic-speaking Flemish, a group closely related to the Dutch, which remained largely Catholic during the Reformation. The name of Belgium was derived from the Belgii, a Celtic tribe that according to Julius Caesar occupied the region. The modern-day country is far from being homogeneous either in cultural or topographic terms. During the last half of the Middle Ages, Flanders became a key commercial and cultural centre of Northern Europe thanks to the Flemish weavers who manufactured high quality woolen textiles. Bruges, Ghent and Ypres became the leading cities. Early in the fourteenth century, the French king tried to take control of Flanders, but his armoured knights were defeated by Flemish pikemen at the Battle of Courtrai in 1302. The French retaliated, defeating the Flemish two years later. In 1384, the Duke of Burgundy took over Flanders and the Netherlands. When the Habsburg Holy Roman Emperor married the daughter of the Duke of Burgundy, he inherited all these territories upon the death of the duke. In 1556, Belgium and the Netherlands came under the direct rule of the Habsburg king of Spain, Philip II, after his father abdicated his throne as Holy Roman Emperor and king of Spain. At this time, the city of Antwerp emerged as the leading commercial and cultural centre of the Spanish Netherlands when Bruges' access to the sea silted up earlier in the century. The Dutch Eighty Years War of Independence began after the Reformation came to the Netherlands. During the revolt of 1584, the Spanish army put Antwerp under siege and its defenders resorted to flooding to secure their city. A little over a year later, the city was forced to surrender.

Belgian history was tied to the Netherlands until the Eighty Years War of Independence when the Dutch Protestants fought against Catholic Spain. Belgium, largely Catholic, remained under Spanish rule until 1713 when it was transferred, with Luxembourg, to the Austrian Habsburg family during the War of the Spanish Succession and became known as the Austrian Netherlands. After the Napoleonic Wars in 1815, the Congress of Vienna returned Belgium to the Netherlands. The Belgians revolted in 1830 and crowned their own king in 1831. After eight years of war, the belligerents signed a peace treaty and the major European powers guaranteed the perpetual neutrality of Belgium. Although it was a major economic and industrial centre in Northern Europe, Belgium did not acquire a colonial empire until 1908. The attendees of the Berlin Conference of 1885 awarded King Leopold II the Congo mainly because all the major European colonial powers had been carving up Africa and they wanted to avoid a conflict between those powers expanding into that region. Since the king's administration of the Congo Free State was a disaster, the Belgian government took over in 1908.

At the beginning of the twentieth century, both the Netherlands and Belgium had overseas empires. Germany also had an overseas empire that consisted of holdings in West, East and Southwest Africa and the Pacific. These colonies were a partial factor in turning Germany and the Netherlands into naval powers. Belgium, which took over the king's colony of the Congo only in 1908, had little need for a sizeable navy. Germany's ally, Austria-Hungary, became a naval power with no colonies and its navy had no mission beyond trying to exercise control over the Adriatic. Unlike Belgium, Austria-Hungary was a major power with the resources to acquire a powerful navy to challenge its rival, Italy.

The origins of the nation of Switzerland go back to the confederation of 1291, when, on the death of the Holy Roman Emperor, the three cantons of Uri, Schwyz and Unterwalden broke away from the empire. The Habsburg armies tried to subdue them, but they were beaten back. In the mid-1300s, other cantons joined the confederation. Charles the Bold of Burgundy tried to invade their lands in the 1470s and the Swiss footsoldier proved more of a match for his armoured knights, routing his army. Switzerland later became a bastion of the Reformation, mainly Calvinism. The Treaty of Westphalia in 1648 formally recognized the independence of the Swiss nation. Switzerland was last invaded during the French Revolution. In 1815, the Congress of Vienna restored its independence. Since then, Switzerland had never again been enmeshed in war. In the early 1860s, the work of Henry Dunant led to the creation of the International Red Cross. However, even though for most of the last two centuries Switzerland has been considered a peace-loving nation and stayed out of wars, Swiss mercenaries continued to be recruited by other European powers.

Chapter One

The Dutch Dilemma: The Netherlands and Fortress Holland

Windmills are the quintessential symbol of the Netherlands where they once played a central role in reclaiming a good part of its territory from the sea. Water defences, including intentional inundations, have protected the Dutch for centuries. The Dutch had to leave outlying fortified cities to their own devices and concentrate on the core area where they could create water barriers. These main defences ran from the Zuider Zee to the Rhine/Lek and formed a river line that allowed the Dutch to create a fortress zone with the land area covered by the Old

OLD DUTCH WATERLINE

⌒ Area to be inundated

◎ Fortified Towns

• Fortifications

Fortress Holland in the 19th Century

The Old Dutch Water Line before being replaced by the New Dutch Water Line that moved east of Utrecht in the nineteenth century.

A Confusing Military History

In the seventeenth century, the Dutch had a reputation of having some of the best soldiers in Europe. Their status was similar to the Swiss pikemen and to the burghers of Flanders (modern–day Belgium) a few centuries earlier. The relationship between the Dutch, their allies and their enemies was rather complex, however the French remained their enemy after the Thirty Years War (1618–48) as Louis XIV of France continued to get involved in many conflicts during his long reign. At one point, nonetheless, the Dutch formed an alliance with the French as well.[4] In 1672, the situation changed as Louis allied himself with Charles II after the English engaged in trade wars with the Netherlands that resulted in the Dutch loss of New Amsterdam (New York). In 1672, Louis wanted to conquer the Spanish Netherlands, but could not afford to fight Spain's allies. He decided to avoid Spanish territory and attack the Dutch instead, hoping that this would elicit a reaction from Spain, which would leave it without allies. With Charles II on his side, Louis' army invaded the Netherlands only to be stopped at the Dutch Water Line after taking Utrecht in 1673.[5] Maastricht and several other fortresses were isolated early in the war and fell in 1673. Unable to breach the Water Line and with the Dutch navy beating off an Anglo–French invasion fleet, the French army began to retreat. The Dutch, joined by the armies of the Elector of Brandenburg[6] and the Holy Roman Emperor, went on the offensive. Spain joined the fray and together they captured Bonn. In 1674, the English quit the war. William, the Dutch Stadtholder and his allies even attempted to take Paris. The war, which was fought mostly in modern–day Belgium, finally ended in 1678. After the Glorious Revolution of 1688, Britain and the Netherlands came under the rule of the same man, King William III, who ruled Britain with his wife Mary II and was Stadtholder of the Netherlands.[7]

The next major conflict was the War of the League of Augsburg or the Nine Years War (1688–97). As in an earlier shorter war in the 1680s, much of the fighting took place in Flanders and Luxembourg. The French laid siege to Namur in 1692. The great Vauban conducted the operations while the famous Dutch military engineer Menno van Coehoorn handled the defences (60,000 French vs. 6,000 Dutch). After a month of fighting during which Coehoorn was wounded, on 1 July 1692 the Dutch capitulated accepting terms that allowed them to depart with honours of war. In July 1695, William III marched on Namur, defended by 13,000 Frenchmen and reinforced by Vauban. The 80,000-man Allied army laid siege for two months and the operations were conducted by Coehoorn. The French were forced to surrender in the first week of September.

When the next war, the War of the Spanish Succession, opened the eighteenth century, the Netherlands were still tied to England. The Duke of Marlborough led their combined armies in battle against the French. Once again, Flanders was one of the major battlefields, but the action took place far from Fortress Holland. In the War of Austrian Succession in the 1740s, the French attacked two Dutch fortresses in Belgian Flanders.

Between 1780 and 1784, the Dutch were engaged in a naval war with the British, which led to the decline of the Netherlands. The other European nations no longer considered the Dutch army and navy a major force. In 1795, during the French Revolution, the Dutch Water Line was breached and the Old Dutch Republic came to an end. Dutch forces made their last appearance in a major war at the Battle of Waterloo, when the Netherlands were once again allied with the British with the Duke of Wellington in command. The last European conflict of the nineteenth century in which the Dutch army took part was the Belgian Revolution of 1830. After 1839, their monarchs began to lose power and the politicians strove for a policy of neutrality with a weakened armed force.

Dutch Water Line. This defence line from the sixteenth century ran from the old fortress towns of Muiden on the Zuider Zee to Groinchem on the Merwede River, a branch of the Waal. After the Netherlands freed itself from French domination, the government began work on the New Dutch Water Line (or New Water Line) in 1815.[1]

The Dutch, who had relied on their water defences since the sixteenth century, created the Dutch Water Line (or the Old Dutch Water Line) in the early 1600s. They began working on it in 1629, during the Eighty Years War of independence from the Spanish. After that war, the Dutch became embroiled in wars with the English and later, the French. Louis XIV sent his army into the Netherlands in 1672 but the Dutch water barrier thwarted his plans of conquest. The Dutch cleverly maintained the inundated polders at a level too shallow for boats. Troops became mired in the muddy bottoms of the flooded polders if they tried to wade across neck-deep in water. If the water froze, the Dutch broke the thin ice before it became thick enough to support troops.[2] Amsterdam, the main city in the north,[3] was protected by fortifications that blocked the few crossing points leading to it. The older city walls of Amsterdam had begun to disappear before the seventeenth century. The Dutch had built a number of strongpoints to protect Amsterdam, but few would remain centuries later.

After the end of the Napoleonic Wars and the creation of a Dutch monarchy under King William I, the king and his military leaders had to consider how to protect their nation in the future. The result was the creation of the Amsterdam Position and the New Dutch Water Line. The French had breached the Old Water Line in the winter of 1794–5 when the water froze too hard for the Dutch to crack the ice and prevent enemy troops from crossing.

King William put General Cornelis Rudophus Theodorus Krayenhoff (1768–1840) in charge of organizing new defences. Krayenhoff was a quintessential man of the Enlightenment, not only a general, but also an artist, a physicist and a cartographer. In 1810, he designed the Amsterdam Position. In 1815, he drew up the plans for the New Water Line, which he moved east of Utrecht placing this city inside the defences and creating a wider buffer zone between it and Amsterdam. The general was laying the foundations for the nation's modern defensive system. Another engineer named Jan Blanken (1755–1838) assisted him in creating this new line. Blanken was a civil engineer and after 1808, the Inspector of Public Works who made his mark designing dry docks[8] and the waaiersluis (fan lock) for the New Water Line, a sluice gate that could be easily opened despite different water pressures.[9]

During the Napoleonic Era, General Krayenhoff had already laid out the design for the defences of Amsterdam since little had been left from past centuries. He laid out most of the positions, which consisted of numbered posts on three fronts, between 1799 and 1810. The northern front consisted of Posts #1 to #12, the western front, of Posts #1 to #13 and the southern front, of Posts #1 to #25 – a total of fifty positions. Besides building additional positions, the army modified or eliminated many of the posts later in the century. At the time, large waterways and lakes protected Amsterdam on its northern, western and southwestern sides. During the general's tenure, he had the main work done in the areas northeast and southeast of the city to protect the harbour. Later, Krayenhoff's work became the basis for the Amsterdam Ring in the 1840s when Lake Haarlemmer was drained to create new polder land west to southwest of Amsterdam.[10] This land reclamation project left Amsterdam with a larger exposed land front and began a new period of fortification construction. While this work was underway, the army built the forts of Schiphol, Nieuwe Meer, Liede and Heemsted between

The old fortress of Naarden on the north end of the New Water Line (left). Fort Vechten (right). Top right, looking up at the pulley system for raising cannons to the roof level.

1843 and 1846. Most of these forts were square and had wet moats. Liede and Schiphol had a two-storied casemated reduit.[11]

General Krayenhoff also began working on the New Dutch Water Line, which was to form the main line of defence until early in the next century. He began the line near the Zuider Zee at the old fortress of Naarden. The general included Muiden and several other positions on the Old Water Line in the new line. Between 1810 and 1825, he prepared a system of strips several kilometres wide that could be flooded. The fortifications consisted of a number of redoubts built in the form of bastions blocking routes through the inundated terrain. From the 1840s until 1860, the army incorporated parts of the New Water Line into the Amsterdam Position while it built the new forts of the Amsterdam Position. During this building phase, the government authorized the construction of seven 'Torenforten' or tower forts for the New Water Line. These tower forts consisted of a circular two- or three-floor casemated reduit whose earthworks often had a surrounding wet ditch. A tower fort was added to Weesp and Muiden, two of the old fortresses. The few forts that included a rectangular casemated tower reduit were not considered tower forts. The new forts included Fort Nieuwersluis Honswijk, Fort Everdingen and Fort Vuren. The brick reduits and the Torenforten became obsolete

Medieval castle with seventeenth-century bastions converting it and the town of Muiden into a Fortress. West Battery was a brick tower fort built in the early 1850s. Muizenfort (not shown) was added late in the century as a caserne and caponier. Other smaller positions (not marked) were added by the turn of century. (*Authors*)

with the appearance of rifled cannon in the 1860s, so the army had them reinforced and, in some cases, removed the upper floor. Counterscarp galleries were added to some of the Torenforten in the 1870s. The high-explosive shell of the 1880s left the remaining tower forts virtually useless. Some of the forts like Liede underwent major changes after 1885 to allow them to continue in service. Older fortresses like Muiden and Weesp,[12] remained important for controlling sluices and locks, so the army reinforced them around 1879 by making some positions bombproof. At Muiden, a bombproof caserne was added.

For the Dutch nation, the turning point came with the end of the revolt that resulted in Belgian independence. Until the Belgian revolt, the dilemma the Dutch faced was whether to attempt to return to the status of a major power with a significant armed force, or to become an economic power without the expense of maintaining a significant military force and to take a neutral position. For the Dutch, the debate over government investing in the economy or in defence had raged for centuries with the majority leaning toward the economy and, hopefully, prosperity. Until the end of the previous century, the Netherlands was a major European power with a navy and a large colonial empire that included territory in America, Asia and Africa. The nation's strength rested on its economy and ability to conduct trade, much like Great Britain, but it lacked the resources to become a great industrial power as the nations of Europe began to industrialize during the first half of the nineteenth century. The war of Belgian independence sapped the nation's strength and left it encumbered with huge debts. The size of its army grew so much that the king bankrupted the nation. King William I kept the military ready for nine years before he gave up the idea of retaking Belgium. He also conceded to a new constitution, but after it was written, he objected to it and abdicated. His son, William II, a veteran of Waterloo, took over the reins of power and had a hand in guiding the nation's policy. After 1840, the nation's leaders decided that the best option was to rebuild the economy and join the Belgians in becoming a neutral nation. The new king, deciding that the provinces of Holland and Western Utrecht constituted the economic heart of the country, took a hand in drawing up the future defence plans, which involved the inclusion of the New Dutch Water Line in the projected Fortress Holland where the army could make its last stand. He also concluded that rivers like the Ijssel and the Meuse would form barriers that could be held with fortresses from which the Dutch army could the sally forth. William II apparently still cherished his father's hopes of retaking Belgium. However, according to Dr. V. Bevaart, author of *Nederlandse Defensie: 1839-1874*, the Dutch continued to view France as the potential enemy and allied themselves with Prussia. They considered fighting on Belgian soil to meet a French invasion as they had done in 1815. The new king's grandiose projects were too much for the depleted economy and the opposition called for further military reductions, including the elimination of fortresses. During this decade, all the Dutch military could afford to build were several Torenforten. The liberal unrest that erupted in revolts all over Europe in 1848 reached the Netherlands as well. William died the next year, unhappy with the way a new constitution reduced his powers. As William III took power, the opposition continued to demand that the government tear down many fortresses. William, like his father and grandfather, was a conservative and was interested in restoring Dutch military power. He was dissatisfied with his limited constitutional power, but like his father, he allowed liberal reforms to take place. Despite the demands of the opposition, the commander of the army resisted demolishing the Netherlands' defences for two decades. A government defence committee with members from both sides supported the military leaders' views. The arguing continued through the 1850s and 1860s, with a new related issue: the defence of the Maastricht Appendage. The French or the Prussians could easily isolate the fortified city of Maastricht that required 12,000 troops for its defence, a sizeable force for the Dutch army.[13] A Franco-Prussian war might require the Prussians to pass through this Dutch territory; if it were defended, it could create an embarrassing situation for the Dutch if they wanted to remain neutral. The political opposition's logic was to leave the area undefended and eliminate the fortifications of Maastricht and Venlo.

During the three decades after 1840, the Dutch toyed with the choice of trying to regain the status of a major power or taking the road to neutrality. The weakness of their military led them to maintain a neutral stance for thirty years while the conservatives and liberals heatedly debated whether to build up the military or not. In the 1850s, the Minister of War, Baron H.F.C. Forstner van Dambenoy,[14] tried to get the military budget restored to pre-1848 levels and to rebuild the army to its 1830s strength. However, the politicians continued to debate throughout the 1860s. Funding for the military increased only gradually to modernize equipment, weapons and fortifications. The Franco-Prussian War resolved this dilemma. The government issued a declaration of neutrality. The Dutch army, which mobilized in 1870, was no match for any of the belligerents and the only option it had was to use the water defences of the New Water Line if necessary. In addition, this poorly carried-out mobilization underscored the decline in the armed forces. After the defeat of France, most Dutchmen quickly realized that their army would be unable to face the much larger German forces in the event of war. The Netherlands simply could not form an army large enough to match those of the great European powers with larger populations from which to draw conscripted troops; nor could it meet the demands of modern warfare. Between 1840 and 1870, the Dutch army drew recruits mainly from the lower classes and a military career did not offer attractive prospects. When the Prussians annexed territory in the 1860s, the Dutch became convinced that they might be their next target, which worked in favour of improving the situation for the military. For more than a decade, the new German Reich became the perceived threat. In 1870, the government realized that it was necessary to improve the quality of the troops and to increase their numbers in order to create a more effective deterrent. It authorized a new conscription system and created a Dutch version of the German Landwehr.[15] The modernization of the army's weaponry began before the war. The Dutch gun foundry was still producing bronze weapons when steel artillery began to appear elsewhere. Since Dutch resources were limited, the choice was simple: build up the nation's defences and make the consequences of an invasion unpalatable for any nation considering it. The long dispute and debate that had raged since 1839 over the question of fortifications was resolved with the Fortifications Act of 1874. Fortunately, the Dutch had not invested heavily in brick and stone fortifications, which had become obsolete no sooner than they had been built. The work on the new forts began just before the development of the high-explosive shell, so the Dutch were able to concentrate on building relatively modern defences before 1914. However, they had to depend heavily on foreign sources for armour and artillery.

The Dutch fortifications of the nineteenth century followed somewhat standard layouts unless they were built on pre-existing works. The tower forts of the 1840s were distinctive whereas the later bastioned forts with reduits were less standard. After the 1880s, a polygonal layout became standard; concrete works were added about the turn of the century. The

The Fortifications Act of 1874

The Franco-Prussian War quickly became a cause for concern to the Dutch. Relations with Belgium had not been the best since that nation had won its independence and several possibilities presented themselves. The defeated French empire might rise to take revenge for its defeat and use Belgium as a tool to strike at the Germans, exposing the Dutch to a new war. Likewise, the Germans might use Belgium in the next war, again putting the Netherlands on the flank. In addition, there was the possibility that if the German Reich maintained its superiority established during the 1870 war, it might decide to swallow up the smaller nations if there was no French resurgence. Every modern nation learned from that war, which began a race toward militarization. The Dutch had to prepare for the worst, modernize their defences and create new ones. Thus on 18 April 1874, King William III signed a new law establishing the process for the defence of the nation. It would rest heavily on the old strategy that involved water barriers.

The first article of the law established which sections would be fortified:

A. The New Dutch Water Line from the Zuider Zee to the New Merwede River and running east of Utrecht
B. The Gelderland Valley and the Lower Betuwe (between the Rhine and Waal)
C. The Moerdijk and Volkerak positions
D. The mouth of the Maas and Haringvliet
E. Den Helder position
F. River crossings of the Ijssel, Waal and Maas
G. Amsterdam Position
H. South Waterline (the Maas from St. Andries to Amer to Geertruidenberg)
I. The Western Scheldt.[16]

The second article established priorities:

- 1st Priority: New Water Line, the Den Helder Position and a position of the Amsterdam Position and portions of the crossings of the Ijssel, Waal and Maas
- 2nd Priority: Positions of Moerdijk and Volkerak and the position at the mouth of the Maas and the Haringvliet
- 3rd Priority: The remainder of the Ijssel, Waal and Maas crossings and part of Gelderland
- 4th Priority: The remainder of the Amsterdam Position
- 5th Priority: South Waterline
- 6th Priority: Western Scheldt.

The third article concerned the budget and the fourth specified that the fortifications of Deventer, Zutphen, Grave, Nijmegen – except Fort Kraijenhof – and the forts on the Lent, Hertogenbosch and Breskens had to be razed. The remaining articles concerned the Minister of War on concessions and reporting.

The Minister of War at the time was a former army officer, August Willem Philip Weitzel (1816-1896) who served in two cabinets during this critical time.

appearance of the rifled cannon during the 1860s and the Franco–Prussian War imposed architectural changes. The Dutch government became concerned that its defences were inadequate so King William III signed into law the Fortifications Act of 1874, which outlined the procedure that would be followed during the next several decades. The new law designated the places where the defences were to be built and the order of priority for the positions. Most of the fortified positions in the south no longer served in the nation's defensive scheme and were mostly abandoned or demolished. General August W.P. Weitzel, who served as Minister of War (1873–5), played a major role in the formulation of the act. Since he did not get along very well with the king, it is difficult to determine what input the monarch had. Weitzel[17] also pushed the government to purchase modern breech-loading artillery. It also appears that he decided that the New Dutch Water Line would no longer form part of the National Reduit and that the Amsterdam defences would be expanded to take over that role instead. Thus, before the end of the century, the New Dutch Water Line, which already served as a main line of defence, would no longer serve as the National Reduit. This was necessary since the government was creating more polder land around Amsterdam, which eliminated some older water barriers. The fact that they built few fortifications in 1870s may have saved the Dutch a great deal of money because most of the forts of that period became obsolete by 1885 due to the development of the high-explosive shell.

By 1881, the States-General (Parliament) still had not reached an agreement on the fortifications to be built. It was not until General Weitzel returned as Minister of War in 1883 that the government finally appropriated the funds for the forts of Abcoude and Velsen. As Abcoude neared completion in 1886, the government and the army worried about the high-explosive shells and work ceased until a proper evaluation could be made of the type of protection required. The actual test firings against various types of structures took place in the dune area on the coast near Schoorl. It was concluded that the new forts should be long (or wide) with little depth, reducing the fort's size as a target.[18] This design offered advantages against high-trajectory artillery (howitzers and mortars), which posed the greatest threat to the surface of the fort. Although the fort presented a wider target for direct-fire weapons, its ramparts masked the key positions.

At this time, the government was prompted to do something about Amsterdam's exposed sea front. The navy deemed the Zuider Zee too shallow for large warships to threaten the capital until the German navy built a class of shallow-draft warships mounting one heavy gun in the late 1870s. These *Wespe* class gunboats alarmed Dutch officials who finally allowed Weitzel to begin the construction of Fort Pampus on a man-made island outside of Amsterdam. The German navy removed these new warships – armoured steamers – from service when the fort became operational.[19]

In the 1880s, the work on the Amsterdam Position and the New Water Line was finally underway. By that time, little was left of the Amsterdam Position from the previous centuries. By the time it was completed in 1914, it had a girdle of forts located 10km to 20km from the city with a circumference of about 135km. The key to the defences were the inundations of areas 3km to 5km wide at the right depth to prevent the passage of boats or soldiers on foot. This defence position included thirty-six forts, four batteries and two coastal batteries by 1914.[20] The first forts begun in the 1880s included brick structures for bombproof positions, but their construction stopped after the introduction of the high-explosive shell in 1885. In

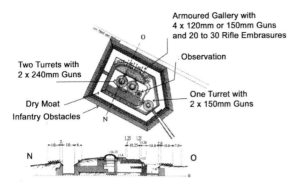

Fort Hoek Van Holland

Fort Ijmuiden

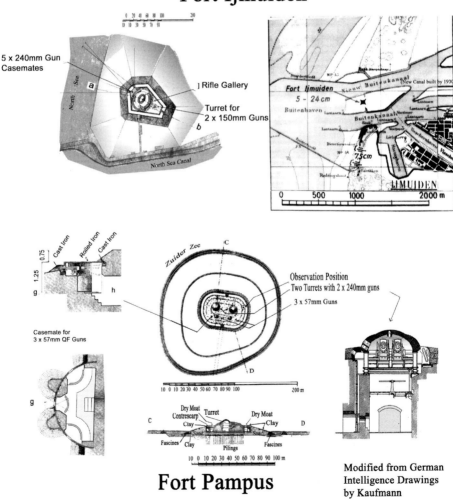

Fort Pampus

Modified from German
Intelligence Drawings
by Kaufmann

Examples of Dutch armoured forts from late in the nineteenth century.

that year, the Dutch army engineers designed and built several types of bombproof structures in the sand dunes on the coast near Schrool for artillery tests. The site remained in use for many years. While the engineers worked on new solutions for bombproof structures, many of the first forts built were mere earthworks, usually with a polygonal shape and surrounded by a ditch. In addition, a number of the sites the army selected for forts were located in areas with a thick layer of peat.[21] To create a stable platform for the concrete structures much of the site had to be excavated and refilled with sand. A layer of clay was added to prevent the sand from washing away. A layer of clay had to be added into the surrounding ditch so it held water making a wet moat possible. Occasionally, this method failed to produce a satisfactory foundation to build upon and the fort became an earthwork position. The forts of the Amsterdam Position began to take shape in the mid-1890s after many years of debate and discussion. Most of the non-turret mounted artillery formed traditore (flanking) batteries in the forts with the guns usually in caponiers or casemates. Dutch military historian René Ros established basic classifications for them in the 1980s.[22] Ros points out that no two forts are identical and that the army established no standard design for them. However, he breaks down their features into three basic types based on the type of concrete positions built in the forts after the mid-1890s.

Type A – built between 1897 and 1907 – included two Grüson 57mm disappearing turrets usually located near the intersection of the right and left flank with the right and left front sections of the ramparts.[23] Earthen ramparts housed firing positions for the infantry and one observation coffre in a structure with seven rooms for the guard unit[24] and storage of ammunition near the front rampart, which had a postern (a covered walkway) connecting to the caserne, usually a gorge caserne. These casernes often had two gorge caponiers, but sometimes a single central one. The bombproof structures were made of non-reinforced concrete.

Type B – built between 1907 and 1912 and similar to Type A – included two Grüson 57mm disappearing turrets. The main difference was that the concrete positions for turrets connected to the caserne, which often had an observation cloche at each end in addition to the one in what the Dutch referred to as the forward or frontal building. Other concrete structures included machine-gun bunkers or casemates on the centre of the front rampart and often one on the left and right front. The frontal building had three rooms instead of seven since there was no need for a large guard position. This frontal building connected to the machine-gun block in front of it. Most of these forts had turret blocks and machine-gun positions often of reinforced concrete.

As the nation began laying down an electric power grid in 1910, the engineers began installing generators in the forts as a source of power for various types of equipment and for electric lighting. Oil lamps remained as a backup. In magazines, these lamps were usually located in niches behind thick panes of glass that often opened from the other side of the wall to prevent accidental sparks from setting off an explosion.

Type C – built between 1912 and 1914 – was similar in layout to the Type B, but it did not have the shelter for a guard unit with an observation cloche near the front rampart, but it had a turret block also linked to the caserne. Four machine-gun blocks occupied positions on the two front walls and the flank walls. Only the forts of Middenweg and Jisperweg belonged to this type and were the result of budget cuts.

Most of the forts built in the low terrain of the Netherlands had to built-up with earth (sand and clay) because of the water table. This resulted in relatively high walls that made them look like small hills. Clay was also used to cover much of the earth used for the fort to help keep it in place and was often used with sand to cover the brick and concrete structures.

Fort Abcoude was the first built on the Amsterdam Position. Its construction began in 1883 and ended in 1887. However, it became obsolete before it was finished because its bombproofs were made of brick and stone. Its two-level caserne was centrally located. Four remises sheltered the guns that fired from open positions on the ramparts where there were traverses and bombproofs to protect the troops. Each of the flanking ramparts mounted two 105mm guns, but they were removed in 1903 leaving only infantry to hold the fort. A wet moat with two bridges surrounded the fort. When the First World War broke out, the badly-needed modernizations were cancelled.

The forts built in the Amsterdam Ring (properly known as the Amsterdam Stellung or Position) occupied four sectors, each divided into subsectors. The forts built by 1914 were:

	Previous Position	*Earthen Fort*	*Bombproofs added*	*Notes*
Sector Ouderkerk (3 subsectors)				
Ft. Pampus			1895	On a man-made island. 2 turrets, each with 2 x 240mm guns
Coast Battery Diemerdam	18th century & 1810		1889–96	3 x 240mm gun coastal battery
Coast Battery Durgerdam	1809		1889–94	3 x 240mm gun coastal battery
Fortress Muiden	13th-century castle			17th-century bastioned fort.* Two modern positions added outside fort
West Battery	1852 tower fort			Northwest of Muiden castle
Muizenfort	1880 barracks		1880–93	Last addition was a caserne and magazine. South of Muiden castle
Ft. Uitermeer		17th century		Tower Fort built 1845 and brick remises added 1878. Outside AP**
Ft. Hinderdam	17th-century fort			1880 brick remise added. Outside AP** & was once part of Water Line.
Fortress Weesp	16th-century fortress			1840s tower fort
Ft. Nigtevecht		1888–95	1903–4	Type A with 4 x 105mm guns
Ft. Abcoude			1884–7	Brick bombproofs. 4 x 105mm guns
Ft. Winkel		1893–4	1908	Type 4 x 105mm guns
Ft. Botschal		1895–6		4 x 105mm guns
Ft. Waver-Amstel		1886–7	1908–12	Type B. 4 x 75mm guns
Ft. Uithoorn		1885–94	1909–11	Type B. 4 x 75mm guns
Ft. Drecht		1884–5	1909–11	Type B. 4 x 75mm guns
Ft. Kwakel		1890–4	1905–6	Type A. 4 x 105mm guns

	Previous Position	Earthen Fort	Bombproofs added	Notes
Sector Sloten (2 subsectors)				
Ft. Kudelstaart		1894	1906–7	Type A
Ft. Schiphol	1844 tower fort			
Ft. Aalsmeer		1894–5	1904	Type A. 4 x 105mm guns
Ft. Hoofddorp		1890–1900	1903–4	Type A. 4 x 105mm guns
Ft. Vifhuizen		1889–94	1897–9	Type A. 4 x 105mm guns
Ft. Liede	1846 tower fort			1914 casemate. 2 x 75mm casemate guns
Ft. Liebrug		1886–95	1898–1900	Type A. 2 x 75mm casemate guns
Ft. Penningsveer		1886–94	1898–1901	Type A. 4 x 75mm casemate guns
Ft. Spaamdam (North & South)		1884–95	1897–1903	Type A. 2 x 105mm guns
Sector Zaandam (2 subsectors)				
Ft. Ijmuiden			1881–8	Outside of AP** on coast. 5 x 240mm casemate guns. Turret with 2 x 150mm
Ft. Velsen		1885	1897–9	Type A. 3 turrets with a 150mm gun. 2 x 105mm guns
Ft Zuidwijkermeer		1894–5	1900–3	Type A. 4 x 105mm guns
Ft. Aagtendijk		1894–5	1897–9	Type A. 4 x 105mm guns
Ft. Veldhuis		1893–5	1897–9	Type A. 4 x 105mm guns
Ft. Ham		1894–8	1900–3	Type A
Ft. Krommeniedijk		1894–8	1900–3	Type A. 4 x 105mm guns
Ft. Marken-Binnen		1890–5	1904	Type A. 4 x 105mm guns
Ft. Spijkerboor		1887–97	1910	2 turrets with a 105mm gun
Sector Ilpendam (2 subsectors)				
Ft. Jisperweg		1889–95	1914	Type C. 4 x 105mm guns
Ft. Middenweg		1889–95	1912–13	Type C. 4 x 105mm guns
Ft. Nekkerweg		1889–97	1912–13	Type B. 4 x 75mm casemate guns
Ft. Purmerend		1886–96	1909–12	Type B. 2 x 75mm casemate guns
Ft. Kwadijk		1888–96	1913	Type B. 4 x 105mm guns
Ft. Edam		1886–95	1909–12	Type B. 4 x 75mm casemate guns

* 17th-century bastioned fort surrounds the castle.

** Considered an extension of the AP (Amsterdam Position) and located on the North Sea.

Source: The information provided by René Ros, based on his system of classification. See his internet site (see bibliography).[25]

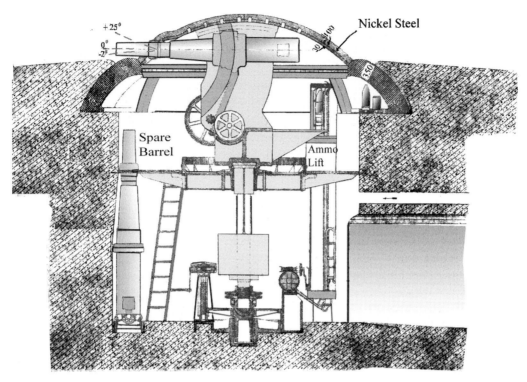

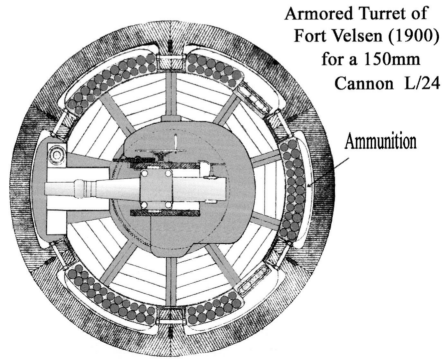

Armored Turret of
Fort Velsen (1900)
for a 150mm
Cannon L/24

Ammunition

The observation cloche and gun turrets of most of the forts were of iron. The older cloche were Grüson chilled cast iron and some could rotate. The newest cloche of steel came from Austria–Hungary and some from Krupp.[26] This was the case for all the forts on the New Dutch Water Line. The older turrets were Grüson cast iron (see Appendix I). Type A and B forts included two 57mm QF guns in Grüson disappearing turrets, many coming from Schneider-Creusot. Forts Spijkerboor and Velsen were the only land forts mounting turrets for guns larger than 57mm. The two coastal forts of Ijmuiden and Pampus also had large gun turrets. Ijmuiden had casemates for 240mm guns. Many of the forts had 75mm or 105mm guns in casemates that served as traditors for flanking fire. In addition, outside some of the forts there were 150mm and 120mm guns in earthen or concrete battery positions for long-range fire and usually 57mm field guns in open positions for close defence.

Some of the remaining representative examples of the Amsterdam Ring forts include Fort Uithoorn and Fort Aalsmeer. Both have a regular shape and comprise structures of unreinforced concrete; Uithoorn is Type B and Aalsmeer Type A. Each had disappearing turrets for 57mm guns and machine-gun casemates on the ramparts. Their wet moats included two gorge caponiers, but at Fort Uithoorn, they mounted a 57mm and two 75mm guns for traditor fire whereas at Fort Aalsmeer, they mounted two 105mm and one 57mm guns each. The caponiers and gorge casemated barracks with additional earthen protection were similar.

During the 1880s and 1890s, the engineers worked on the dikes and sluices to prepare a system of inundations that would be able encircle the position leaving the forts to protect the dry gaps. This required additional work for military engineers on the dikes and canals built to create the polders so that they could flood them as needed to meet the military requirements.

Guns, armour and turrets for the forts came from several sources. The armoured Grüson cast iron casemates at Fort Ijmuiden mounted five Krupp 240mm guns. Fort Pampus also had Grüson turrets with Krupp 240mm guns, like the coastal batteries, but their range was only 8km. The older turrets and cloches[27] in the forts were mainly Grüson chilled cast iron[28] and mounted Krupp guns. A number of 57mm turrets came from the French Schneider-Creusot company, but most were Grüson turrets. The two heavily-armed forts of Velsen and Spijkerboor had Grüson gun turrets and cloches. The newer steel turrets and cloches came from both the Krupp and Skoda factories.[29] The armoured components of the New Dutch Water Line forts were similar.

The New Dutch Water Line and the Amsterdam Ring

By the 1880s, the New Dutch Water Line included over thirty forts, lunettes and batteries between Naarden and the Lek and Waal Rivers. However, most were earthen works with bastioned traces and wet moats with masonry bombproofs. The New Water Line was about 85km long. The Dutch engineers, in reaction to the events of the Franco-Prussian War, planned to prepare four inundation basins for the New Water Line between the Zuider Zee and Lek, three between the Lek and Waal and two south of the Merwede. It was calculated that it would require four to thirteen days to turn the polders into water obstacles by filling these basins. This system was completed in 1890. A short distance from Utrecht, the line comprised four largely earthen forts surrounded with moats and four masonry lunettes with wet ditches on the south bank of the Kromme River[30] near the town of Houtensepad. These were the first fortifications of the New Water Line built in 1824. Circular towers added to the forts in 1860 were to serve as redoubts. When the rifled cannon appeared in the 1860s, the Dutch added earthen ramparts to these positions for additional protection.

Two of the New Water Line's largest forts, Rijnauwen (1867–9) and Vechten (1867–70) and two smaller forts formed a second line in the late 1860s. Fort Rijnauwen, with a slightly irregular shape, had bastions and an arrow-shaped frontal caponier[31] in the 50m wide and 7m deep water-filled moat. It was designed for a garrison of 540 men and 105 artillery pieces making it one of the largest Dutch forts. Fort Vechten was similar but had a more regular pentagonal shape with five bastions. Instead of the frontal caponier, it had a larger, arrow-shaped bastion. Both forts also included a detached redoubt at the rear surrounded by its own water-filled moat. The artillery mounted in open positions included ten guns with earthen traverses at Fort Vechten. After the Franco-Prussian War, bombproofs and large, centrally-located casemated brick barracks were added inside these forts and a couple of smaller ones between 1877 and 1880. Unfortunately, the high-explosive shell of 1885 rendered all these fortifications obsolete. In response to this development, most of the fort artillery was dispersed to the rear of the forts, relegating the strongholds to the role of shelters and depots. The fate of nearby Fort Bilt, built between 1816 and 1819, was not much different. A brick guardhouse was added to it in the 1850s and a casemated barracks in 1875. The fort has a wide moat with two large bastions in the front and half bastions to the rear. A reduit in the rear includes its own moat that occupies the centre and rear of the fort.[32]

Review of the Dutch Fortification System up to the End of the Century

The Dutch, concerned with the developments during the Franco-Prussian War and their own inability to match the huge armies of the great powers, enacted the Dutch Defence Regulations of 18 April 1874 to establish the strategy for the nation's defence. It remained in effect until the 1930s. Fortunately for the Dutch, more debating than work took place before 1880. The two nearly-completed forts of the Amsterdam Position became obsolete when the new technology of 1885 forced the army engineers to develop designs that were more appropriate. The future Fortress Holland was to serve as the main line of defence, protecting the lands lying between the Zuider Zee, the Rhine–Waal–Maas Rivers and the North Sea. The New Water Line, which formed the eastern side of this area, was the main land front. Enclosed in Fortress Holland was the economic heart of the nation. The New Dutch Water Line, which began at the Zuider Zee, stretched southward passing east of Utrecht before it reached the Lek and the Merwede.[33] The Den Helder Position, sections of the Amsterdam Position and some key bridgeheads received first priority.[34] The act called for all work to be completed by January 1883 – an eight-year period. However, construction had barely begun by then. The Dutch Ministry of War had not only failed to meet that deadline but also spent about 80 per cent of the allotted funds by 1885. Only a small amount of construction had begun on the Amsterdam Ring in 1883 and the deadline for completion had long passed. New legislation allowed for six more years, changing the completion date to January 1889. Although few new forts appeared, the army increased the overhead protection of many existing fortifications to counter high-explosive shell. Concrete replaced brick before the end of the century, but the Dutch used it mainly to reinforce brick works, as the French had done, until almost the end of the century. In most cases, the Dutch army built with non-reinforced concrete until the turn of the century. The main mission of the forts was to protect dikes and the few roads that crossed the inundated areas in time of war.

Electricity, which served to provide light or operate turrets in a few of the forts, was not added until late in the first decade of the twentieth century. The water supply came from collected rainwater stored in underground cisterns.

A British intelligence report published by Major J.K. Trotter in 1887 summed up the situation in the Netherlands up to 1886:

The whole country to the west of the line Naarden-Geertruidenberg-Bergen op Zoom and to the north of the West Scheldt, lies below the mean level of Ij at Amsterdam[35] which is the datum level to which all heights are referred and which is designated A.P [Amsterdam level for 0 elevation]. The sole exception is formed by a narrow strip of sand dunes, which extend along the whole of the west coast and have a relative altitude of from 25 to 70 feet [7.5m to 21.0m] above the A.P. East of the line Naarden–Geertruidenberg–Bergen op Zoom and east of the Zuider Zee the ground rises to a maximum altitude of 150-300 feet [45m to 90m] above the A.P., which however, it only attains in a few places, the greater part of the eastern provinces being no more than 75 feet [22m] above A.P. The strip of ground between the south bank of the West Scheldt and the Belgian frontier has a level from A.P. to 3 feet [1m] above A.P.

The greater part of the low-lying country consists of polder land, i.e. land which has been reclaimed and which is kept dry by means of steam pumps and windmills, the water being pumped into canals, protected by large dykes. The surface of the water in these canals is considerably above the level of the surrounding country. In the polders water is always very near the surface of the soil and at certain times of the year the pumps are unable to keep the land dry.

The general appearance of a polder is that of a large field bank, in some cases 20 to 30 feet [6m to 9m] in height and intersected by numerous ditches from 3 to 10 yards [1m to 3m] wide, which cross each other usually at right angles. It would thus be exceedingly difficult for troops to move over such a district, even if it was not inundated, while the dykes around the polders entirely prevent any view being obtained of the surrounding country. The roads run along the tops of the enclosing dykes and it is almost impossible for anyone not a native of the country to cross a polder, or in any way to make a short cut. The roads are of various kinds: a). The 'Straatweg' which is paved road when in repair, but exceedingly trying to the feet and is generally 12 to 15 feet [3.5m to 4.5m] in width; b). Macadamized roads, of which there are few, since in most parts of the country there is no stone; c). 'Grintwegen' or gravel roads, which are fairly good in fine weather, but would soon be destroyed by the passage of artillery; d). 'Landwegen' and 'Kleiwegen' which are merely tracks in sand or clay; these last are as a rule the only roads available between the dykes. Roads are comparatively little used in Holland, the greater part of the passenger traffic being carried on by rail or tramway, while goods are principally transported by the canals.

The polder land can be inundated by stopping the pumps and opening the sluices and either fresh or salt water may be let in, according as the river and canal or sea sluices are opened. [Trotter, p. 123]

This system allowed the inundation of huge tracts of land, which formed the core of the Dutch defences. The earth and masonry fortifications, most of which were obsolete, were relegated to a secondary role when this report was prepared. The flooding could keep enemy artillery out of range of key points. Many of the fortifications protected sluices supplying the water for the inundations and/or were to block the few passages the inundations would leave. However, as the range of big guns increased, the army had to move the main defensive positions and inundations further away from the cities. Although the fortifications became obsolete in 1885, the inundations did not. The water depth in the flooded areas was too shallow for boats and the muddy bottoms and soggy surroundings made it difficult for an enemy to move troops and emplace artillery. The Dutch only needed to concentrate their defences along the narrow non-flooded areas to keep an enemy from advancing into Fortress Holland and to protect the sluices that controlled the water levels. Naturally, these gaps required modern fortifications after 1885.

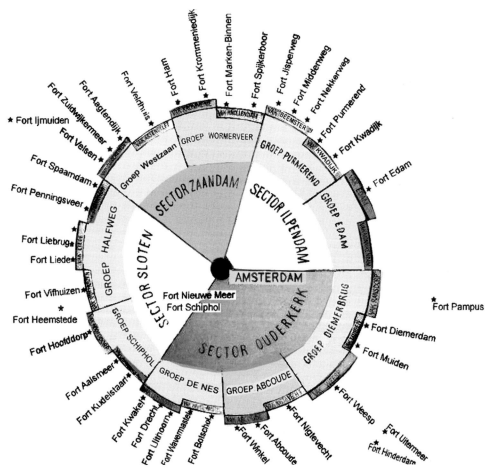

Graphic showing sectors and subsectors of the Amsterdam Ring including the location of forts in service between 1914 and 1918. (*Norman H. Clark, taken of display at Fort Spijkboor*)

The ring of forts at Amsterdam covered a distance of about 130km and served as the last line of resistance. It replaced the New Dutch Water Line as the National Reduit before the end of the century when work on its forts was well underway late in the 1890s. It was created between 1883 and 1914 and it comprised thirty-six forts. During this time, the Amsterdam Position became the National Reduit, although the New Water Line remained the main line of defence. By 1910, the Dutch had perfected the flooding measures that would have created a formidable water barrier around Fortress Holland, including Utrecht.[36]

Fort Spijkerboor mounted a single turret (shown) with two Krupp 105mm guns from 1911. It also had two 57mm gun turrets. (*Norman H. Clark*)

Most of the forts of the Amsterdam Stellung (Position) were built in the late 1890s. Forts Velsen (1896–1905) 16km northwest of Amsterdam on the North Sea Canal (1876) and Spijkerboor (1889–1913), 20km north by northwest of Amsterdam, covered two of the weakest parts of the ring defences. They represented the most heavily-armed forts with turrets mounting guns larger than 57mm. Fort Velsen had three Krupp-Grüson turrets,[37] each of which mounted a Krupp 150mm guns (range of 10.5km) and Fort Spijkerboor had a Grüson turret with two Krupp 105mm guns. Most of the new Dutch forts with concrete positions included a couple of turrets for 57mm guns. Fort Velsen had two long fronts and two very short flanks that formed a salient in accordance with the formula that required a wide front with little depth. Its artillery battery in the front centre was connected to the concrete gorge barracks for the 340-man garrison. The surrounding ditch included two caponiers, which also served as traditors and mounted machine guns and 105mm guns. Each shoulder salient included a disappearing Grüson 57mm gun turret. The entire fort occupies an island-like feature. The Krupp-Grüson turrets were not emplaced until 1910. Fort Spijkerboor, which took longer to complete, received its armour and armament in 1911, but it was not actually ready until 1913. Electric power was added in 1914. It had a two-level concrete gorge barracks for a 300-man garrison. It also had two Grüson 57mm disappearing turrets. The surrounding ditch was water filled and included a two-level caponier attached to the gorge barracks equipped with machine guns and two 57mm guns. When concrete was added to create positions on the forts, the protection became up to 2m thick. A layer of earth covered the structures for additional protection. Fort Pampus, built between 1887 and 1895 on a shoal 3.5km north of Muiden, protected the harbour of Amsterdam. The shoal was turned into a man-made island in 1887. Before construction began, the Minister of War had already intended to purchase Grüson armoured turrets for it. When it was completed, the fort mounted two Grüson turrets, each with two 240mm guns. It also had an armoured observation dome and three Grüson 57mm disappearing turrets. A dry ditch with two caponiers surrounded the fort and a counterscarp gallery with firing positions covered the ditch. The fort was built to protect Amsterdam from German *Wespe* class gunboats although they had been removed from service by the time the fort became operational.[38] When the Afsluitdijk or Great Dike was finished in 1933, it effectively closed the Zuider Zee and the fort was virtually abandoned.[39] Most of the forts of the Amsterdam Position rated as first class fortifications until 1920 when many of them were downgraded to second class.

Fort Ijmuiden, mostly built of brick and ready for service in 1888, is located on the North Sea. Like Fort Pampus, it is located outside the Amsterdam Ring but it was considered part of the position. It was intended to defend the port of Ijmuiden and the entrance to the Nord Sea Canal in conjunction with gunboats and monitors so Amsterdam could maintain access to the sea. It was one of the first Dutch forts to receive an armoured casemate battery with Grüson armoured plates for its five 240mm guns in two casemates and a Grüson cast iron turret with two 150mm guns, which covered the sluices. The Grüson cast iron casemates were 1m thick. The casemate guns covered the coast and the gun turret of 0.7m-thick cast iron and the rifle gallery with steel plates on top of the fort covered the landward side. Fort Ijmuiden with its 300-man garrison served as a bridgehead for the Amsterdam Ring protecting the canal route from the sea to Amsterdam. In the late 1920s, a new channel dug north of the fort transformed the land on which Fort Ijmuiden stood into an island.

Armoured Casemates for 5 x 280mm Guns

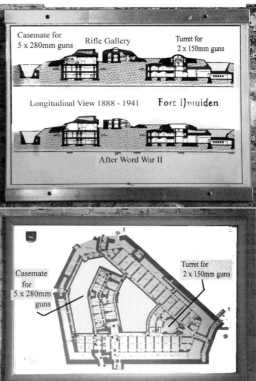

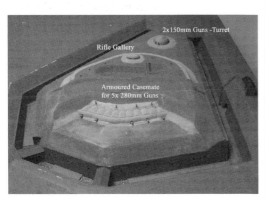

Fort Ijmuiden – photographs of the fort's armoured casemate. Plans of Fort Ijmuiden displayed at the fort. (*Martyn Gregg*)

The forts of the Amsterdam Ring were expanded, modified, or built before 1914. Whereas, about half of approximately forty positions of the New Water Line were erected after 1870, but most were built earlier in the century.

The New Dutch Water Line

	1810–25	*1840–60*	*1867–1880s*
Fortress Muiden	Old fortress	1850 castle used as barracks. 1852 Westbattery–Tower reduit	
Fortress Weesp	Old fortress	Tower reduit	
Ft. Uitermeer	17th-century fort	1845 Torenforten	1878–85 ramparts and remise added
Hinderdam	17th-century fortress	1848 casemated guard house/barrack	1880 additional casemates
Ft. Ronduit	18th-century redoubt		1873–5 bombproof barracks/remise. 1878 crane bridge.**
Ft. Kijkuit	1803 earthwork	1844–7 changed to round earthwork and round guardhouse/barrack	1880 casemated barracks and magazine replace guardhouse
Ft. Spion	1803 redoubt	1844–7 round brick guardhouse/barrack	1880 casemated barracks and magazine
Ft. Tienhoven		1848–50 earthen redoubt and brick guardhouse	1881 entrenchments and additional guardhouse
Ft. Nieuwersluis	1673 bastioned fortress	1849–51 Torenforten	1877 brick barracks 1880–2 fort modified, remises added
Ft. Maarsseveen			1880–1 2-level brick barracks. 80 men
Ft. Gagel	1819–21 redoubt	1850–2 brick guardhouse	1878–80 casemated brick barracks and remises. 4 x 120mm guns and 4 x 150mm howitzers
Ft. Klop	1629–1787 earthwork. Redoubt 1819	1848–50 rectangular shape with gorge blockhouse as reduit	
Ft. Ruigenhoek			1867–70 rectangular bastion and casemated barracks. 1880s remise
Ft. Blauwkapel	1787 redoubt. 1817–18 expanded	1850 brick guardhouse	1874–90 bombproof barracks and remises

	1810–25	1840–60	1867–1880s
Ft. Voordrop			1867–70 brick barracks, magazines, remise. 1878–9 walls modified for more guns and front caponier added. 16 x 90mm guns and 19 x 120mm guns.
Ft. Biltstraat (Ft. Bilt)	1816–19 redoubt	1850–2 brick guardhouse	1875–7 bombproof casemated barracks, remises. 1885 250 men, 34 guns
Ft. Hoofddijk			1877–9 2-level casemated barracks
Ft. Vossegat	1817–19 redoubt	1849 casemated blockhouse	
S. of Utrecht	1822–8 4 x lunettes		
Ft. Rijnauwen			1867–1 5 caponiers. 1877–85 bombproof barracks
Ft. Vechten			1867–70 5 caponiers. 1880 casemated brick barrack and remises. 1880s 514 men and 22 guns of 120mm and 150mm
Ft. Hemeltje			1877–81 bastion and casemated barracks
Ft. Jutphaas	1819–20 redoubt, 2 star-shaped bastions	1846–8 Two bastions connected. Round casemated blockhouse built in gorge.	1871–3 2 remises. 1880s – 128 men and 21 guns.
Ft. Vreeswijk	1672 French redoubt. 1820 restored	1852–5 rebuilt earthwork and formed a lunette.	No bombproof structures
Redoubt of Waalse Wetering			1875–8 earthworks, guard house, bombproof barracks and remise 180 men with 8 guns
Korte Uitweg		1840–50 earthwork	1871–4 earthwork. 1876–9 bombproof barracks and remise 160 men with 12 guns

	1810–25	*1840–60*	*1867–1880s*
Ft. Honswijk		1841–8 earthwork built. 1844–8 Torenforten	1878–88 tower lowered and counterscarp added. Casemated barracks. Rampart – 23 open gun positions. Concrete gun remises.
Fort Spoel	1815 Earthwork	Fort located on the dike	Bombproofs added 1879
Ft. Everdingen		1842–5 earthwork built. 1844–7 Torenforten (single level)	1874 counterscarp added 1877 two bombproof remise
Ft. Asperen		1845–7 Torenforten	1879–80 earthworks and tower added. Gun positions built with Torenforten
Ft. Nieuwe Steeg			1878–80 2-level U-shaped casemated brick barracks (bombproof)
Ft. Vuren		1844–9 Torenforten, lunette-shaped position and 2-level tower	1873–9 tower lowered and counterscarp added. Casemated barrack and gun positions in rampart.
Ft. Altena (Ft. Uppelsche Dijk)		1847 Torenforten	1878–80 Ft. Altena joined with Uppelseche Dijk
Ft. Giessen			1878–81 3 casemates and rampart with gun positions.
Ft. Bakkerskil			1877–9 2-story casemate in gorge and gun positions in rampart
Ft. Steurgat			1880–1 2-story casemate barracks and rampart with gun positions

The redoubts received a casemated reduit to become forts. The reduits were single story and were square or rectangular. Some older forts also received reduits between 1840 and 1860.
The Torenforten above had bastion shaped earthworks and wet ditches.
1867–80 more forts added without reduit towers and soon outdated.
Gorinchem, fortress from 1649 with earthen ramparts and 11 bastions. Served as part of Old Wate Line and then largest fortress city of New Water Line with some 19th century improvements.
*Built on older fortification.
**Crane bridge refers to a special swivel bridge

Fort Ronduit is located north of the enceinte of Fortress Naarden. In 1874, the one-level brick caserne was built which was covered with earth on all but one side to make it bombproof. A few similar earth covered forts had two-level casernes. It accommodated over 120 men and comprised storage areas, including magazines for ammunition and cannons. The artillery was placed in open positions on the ramparts. In forts like Ronduit, rainwater for the troops was collected in tanks. The guardhouse[40] behind the caserne covered the entrance and a cast iron swivel bridge, one of the fort's most interesting features.[41] Before the withdrawal of the bridge, the decking was quickly removed, leaving only the frame of girders supported by triangular supports attached to the abutment of the scarp wall. Next, the remainder of the bridge turned as a hand crank rotated the triangular support to a 90° horizontal angle as the girders attached to the iron supports folded together and rested parallel to the abutment wall leaving an unobstructed view of the gorge moat for defensive fire. This fort is near the coast, on the east side of the water obstacle. Just to the south of Fortress Naarden is Bussum, which consisted of five forts or batteries numbered I to V forming a bridgehead on the east side of the water barrier. These defences include a late eighteenth-century site to the northwest of Bussum to which a bombproof barracks and a remise were added between 1873 and 1875. They were located on either side of the canal and protected the sluice gate. In the area around Bussum there is relatively high ground (although not very high in elevation) that the army found necessary to hold to protect Fortress Naarden. Thus, these battery positions were built east and south of Bussum between 1868 and 1870. The one to the southeast, identified as Bussum Battery or Werk IV, is the only one that still exists. This position has a surrounding brick wall and a dry moat. The battery had a pentagonal shape and included a double caponier on the front and four additional caponiers on the other corners. There were many rifle embrasures in the brick walls. The main armament consisted of three 120mm bronze guns and two howitzers. Two Coehoorn mortars and six machine guns served for close support. Even with the bombproofs, these 'forts' became obsolete in the 1880s.

The bricks used on the structures of the New Water Line and some other positions, are often referred to as 'fortress bricks' because they were thicker than regular bricks and supposedly resistant to the artillery of the time. It was in use in the 1870s and early 1880s, well after the introduction of the rifled cannon, which rendered it obsolete. The solution was to cover it with layers of earth to the sides exposed to enemy artillery fire. The rear face from which it was accessed could not be covered, but it was not exposed to direct or indirect artillery fire that could strike and penetrate its brick wall. The high-explosive shell of the 1880s was able to penetrate the earthen cover and in some countries, a bursting layer consisting of concrete, sand and earth was added for extra protection.

Preparing the Nation for War

During the nineteenth century and later, the War Department of the Netherlands consisted of seven sections that comprised the 1st Section (Secretariat), the 2nd Section (General Staff), the 3rd Section (Personnel), the 4th Section (Artillery), the 5th Section (Engineers), the 6th Section (Quartermaster) and 7th Section (Militia). These sections were, in turn, divided into bureaus. The 2nd Bureau of the 5th Section was Fortresses. This section received and carried out directives from the War Minister concerning policies, defences, construction, improvements and maintenance related to fortifications and inundations. The 3rd Bureau was

The Dutch Army of the 1880s and Later

The Belgian revolt and the years of tension that followed it ended in 1839, leaving the Netherlands heavily in debt. The nation's commitment to maintaining an army and 'defending' its southern border became secondary to rebuilding the economy. During the following era, Dutch military resources were concentrated on defence and the reinforcement of the New Dutch Water Line. At the same time, the Netherlands adopted a policy of neutrality. During the 1880s, the Dutch army was organized into three infantry divisions. The 1st Division had its headquarters at The Hague, the 2nd Division at Arnhem and the 3rd Division at Breda. The Franco-Prussian War had been a cause of concern, leading the Dutch not only to plan for improving their country's defences, but also to reorganize the army, which was divided into the Field Army and the Garrison Army upon mobilization. The Garrison Army was to take up positions in the defences while the Field Army was to operate on the principle that the best defence was offense. Naturally, its offensive operations would be limited to expelling an invader from Dutch territory since it did not have sufficient forces to do much more. One battalion from each of the three regiments of the three infantry divisions was assigned to the Garrison Army, leaving each division with twelve battalions. In addition to artillery batteries, there was a single cavalry brigade.

A colonial army had to be maintained, mainly in the Dutch East Indies, where it consisted of about on-third Dutch troops and the remainder locals. The Dutch West Indies required less from the colonial army. A fleet was necessary not only to maintain the empire but also to defend the coast of the Netherlands.

In the 1880s, most of the artillery had reached obsolescence with the development of high explosives and steel guns. The Dutch inventory in 1885 consisted of both bronze and steel fortress guns. The largest cannons were 76 Krupp 150mm and 159 Krupp 125mm breech-loading rifles. The army also had over 111 older 160mm bronze muzzle-loading rifles, 350 bronze 120mm muzzle-loading rifles and 610 slightly more modern breech-loading 100mm and 120mm rifles.[42] The 150mm and 125mm Krupp guns remained in service until 1940. Other older fortress cannon included over 650 bronze and 79 iron smoothbore cannons unfit for the twentieth century. The coastal artillery included more modern Krupp breech-loading rifles; four of 305mm and 14 of 240mm, but their range was limited to 8km or less. It also included 114 older bronze 160mm muzzle-loading rifles and 57 iron 240mm breech-loaders.

At the end of the century, since the French and British had little interest in helping them, the Dutch purchased artillery from Germany and Sweden until 1914. By that time, the field army had little over 50 modern Swedish Bofors 105mm field howitzers, but the remainder of its 800 guns came from the previous century. The medium artillery – 125mm and 150mm Krupp steel guns from the 1880s – was slow-firing and had a short-range (7–8.5km). The army bought 84mm bronze guns from Switzerland after 1871 and began replacing them with steel Krupp 84mm guns in 1881. Although these weapons became obsolete by 1918 and had a range of only 3.5km, the army modified them in 1927 and kept them in service until 1940. In 1905, the government purchased and put into service about

200 Krupp 75mm quick-firing field guns (range 6.5km). The army added fifty-two new Krupp 120mm howitzers (range 6.1km) at the same time. Although outdated by 1918, these guns remained in service until 1940.

The Dutch armaments industry consisted mainly of a state gun foundry at The Hague that produced bronze guns. The company had to expand in the 1880s and moved to Hembrug, near Amsterdam. It continued to produce military equipment much as it had done since after the Napoleonic Wars. It turned out the bolt-action Mannlicher Mle 1895 rifle[43] for the army. The army was mostly equipped with old machine guns and did not have enough to arm the fortifications as well as the field troops. During the war, the Dutch copied and produced their own version of the Lewis Gun.[44] Simply put, between 1914 and 1918, the Dutch army was not prepared to engage in modern warfare.

Shipyards in the Netherlands built most of the Dutch naval vessels, but much of the large calibre armament for the navy came from the British Armstrong and German Krupp industries. Armstrong sold the Dutch muzzle-loaders while Krupp provided breech-loaders. When some of the ships were scrapped at the turn of the century, their guns went into coast defences. After the 1880s, Dutch guns and ship armour came mainly from Krupp. Until 1880, the navy consisted of a couple of turreted ships, over a dozen monitors and similar large gunboats, as well as other types of vessels, including some with sails. The monitors and gunboats served for coast and river defence. In the 1890s, the Dutch built three coast defence battleships to which they added five additional battleships and a number of torpedo boats and gunboats by 1905. The main calibres of Krupp guns found on Dutch warships before the First World War were 9.4in (239mm), 8.2in (208mm), 6.7in (170mm), 5.9in (150mm) and on a few ships 11in (280mm) guns. By 1914, the Dutch navy was on a par with the army – not ready for war.

Accounts, which included financial matters of the Army Engineers including those related to fortifications. During the period following the Franco-Prussian War, after the Dutch had mobilized and prepared their inundations, the importance of the 2nd Bureau, 5th Section grew because the government pinned its future on a strong defensive policy. Thus, fortifications had a higher status in the government than in most other countries. Despite its position, the 2nd Bureau failed to modernize the Dutch fortifications and keep pace with the neighbouring countries.

Dr. Wim Klinkert, author of *Het Vaderland Verdedigd*, published for the Dutch Army Historical Service, points out that the mid-1880s witnessed a new development in defensive policy when the Dutch no longer felt threatened by German ambitions to annex their country. As that concern evaporated, the army became concerned about the province of Limburg, which was vulnerable to Germany as well as France should these two nations go to war again. The Dutch government decommissioned the fortresses of Venlo and Maastricht in 1867 and decided that funds for fortifications had to be devoted to the main line of defences. This renewed an interest in creating a large, mobile army at the expense of fortifications around the nation's economic core in order to protect the kingdom more effectively. At this time, the Dutch leadership actually considered a policy that would help Belgium, by defending the

Meuse river crossings with the field army. The Belgians were beginning to fortify Liège and Namur along the Meuse. If the two countries coordinated their efforts, they could present a solid front against a German invasion. However, this type of concerted endeavour never actually materialized.

The death of King William III brought about another change to the Netherlands. William's daughter, Wilhelmina (1880–1960 – ruled from 1890–1948) took the throne. According to Dr. Klinkert, the rivalry between the British and German navies after 1905 made the Dutch coast both tempting and vulnerable to both nations, creating additional defensive headaches for the Dutch. By this time, the young queen, who no longer had a regent, came to distrust the British because of their inhumane treatment of the Dutch farmers during the Boer War. The War Ministry, on the other hand, worried about the vulnerability of their coastline, including the Zuider Zee, more than it had done in the past.

The Dutch port of Den Helder and several coastal sites on the North Sea remained vulnerable. During the nineteenth century, the government commissioned work that included several forts to protect Den Helder. The construction at Den Helder had begun under Napoleon, after a British attack in 1799 exposing the vulnerability of the port and a possible threat to Amsterdam. The French built several new forts in the area: Erfprins (French Lasalle), Dirksz Admiraal (French l'Écluse) and Westoever (French Dugommier), which formed a fortified line. They also built Fort Kijkduin (French Morland). Fort Erfprins, one of the largest forts in the country, was built in 1811–13 and it included a wet moat, three bastions and a ravelin. After it underwent major modernization in the late 1870s, it comprised a brick barracks for a thousand men and mounted eighteen 240mm guns mounted on the ramparts. Fort Dirksz Admiraal, also built between 1811 and 1813, received a double caponier armed with two 120mm guns in the 1880s. The Dutch army commissioned Fort Westoever (1828–30) on the Great North Holland Canal opposite the older Fort Oostoever (1792). Westoever, which was modernized in the early 1880s, mounted two 150mm guns and four 120mm guns in open positions on the ramparts. It also had a large bombproof barracks. Construction of Fort Harssens, the most powerful of the forts, began in 1879. Its two large Grüson turrets with two 305mm guns each were installed in 1884 and test fired the next year. The firing is said to have shattered windows in nearby houses so that further tests were restricted. The fort had a brick foundation covered with hard grey stone. It was shaped like a teardrop pointing towards the front.[45] It had a dry moat and a counterscarp gallery with an observation cupola on top of it added at the end of the decade. Unlike other coastal forts, it had no armoured rifle gallery. Like the other new forts, it was equipped with a modern steam engine system to operate its turrets and sundry equipment. Late in the century, like other forts, it received a telegraph link. Its garrison numbered about 250 men.

The work done at Den Helder was part of a larger effort. In 1879, a military commission advised Joseph Reuter, the Minister of War, to build Fort Hasrrens at Den Helder. Plans for the fort had existed since 1875 and passed down from previous war ministers. Reuter approved the construction of the armoured of Forts Pampus, Maasmood (Hoek van Holland) and Ijmuiden at the same time. The plans for these forts called for either Grüson 280mm or 305mm gun turrets. In 1910, the Dutch government pressured the Second House (the House of Representatives)[46] of the States-General for funding to improve the vulnerable coast defences of the nation. Proposals and counterproposals delayed construction until 1912 when

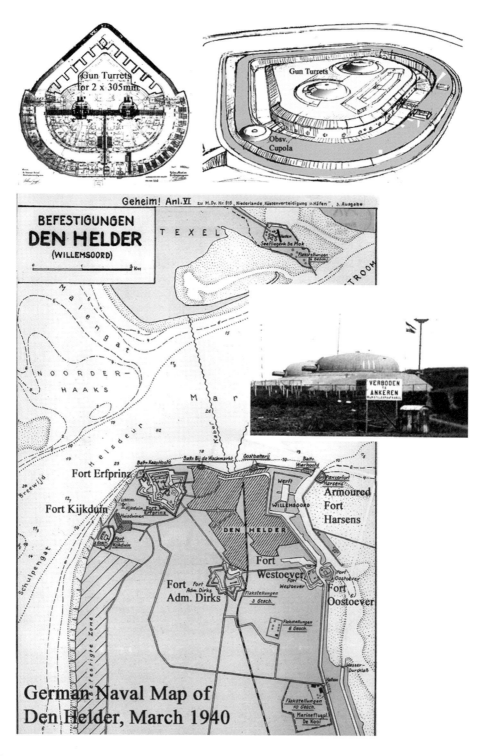

German map of Den Helder in 1940. Old drawings and photo of Fort Harrasens (top) at Den Helder.

the government submitted a more restricted plan hoping to get something done. A translation of a German article in the *Journal of the United States Artillery* reveals that, at the eve of the First World War, the Dutch coastal defences and their obsolete forts were quite vulnerable while the States-General were still bickering over the matter. According to the article, if an enemy took the Den Helder positions, he 'would then be master of the Zuider sea and could with comparative ease capture the position at Amsterdam'. At the time of publication, the Den Helder position was both subject to assault from the sea and the land. The situation in 1911 was as follows:

Fort Kykduin is at the top of a high dune. It principal role is to cover the channel of the Schulpengatts, which at this place is not very broad and lies close to the land. The obsolete 240mm guns are not protected by armored cupolas.

North of Kykduin is Fort Erfpins, which also urgently needs armor protection. It commands the Schulpengatts, Breewyd and Helsdeur. The more easterly fortifications protect the Roads of Helsdeur and Reede. Fort Harssens alone is provided with armored cupolas. What protection the land side has is afforded by the fortifications on the land front of Fort Erfprins, Battery Westover, the connecting line between these works and Battery Admiral Dirks and Fort Oostoever.

The occupation of the harbour of Ymuiden [Ijmuiden] would be very valuable for an enemy attacking Amsterdam. This harbour is protected by Fort Ymuiden, which also protects the North Sea canal locks. The fort has a seacoast battery and a revolving turret. Since the obsolete armament has a very limited range, the government has projected plans for reaching the enemy at long range ...

The armored Fort Pampus in the Zuider sea and the shore batteries Durgerdam and Diemerdam operating with the fleet, protect Amsterdam from attack by the Zuider sea.

The mouth of the Meuse bears very important relations to the interior; this is especially true of the new channel, which offers passage for the largest vessels. Once in possession of Rotterdam, the second city in commercial importance in the land, a landing party could threaten the whole of South Holland to the new water line in the rear, or march without interruption on Amsterdam. With this in mind, there has been erected on the north bank of the new channel the armored fort on Holland Hook [Hoek van Holland]; it defends this channel. The fort is modern. It only lacks some minor details of equipment.

The Haring-Vliet [Haringvliet] is also a waterway of great importance.[47] A landing at Voorne is not very probable, since the enemy would have to cross two bodies of water. However, the fortresses Brielle and Hellevoetsluis are erected here, joined by flooded areas. Hellevoetsluis is, however, of the greater importance since it covers the passage to Haring-Vliet.

These seacoast batteries must be modernized.

The fortifications at these passages will, according to the new budget be considerably strengthened.

The march of an enemy's army across the Holland Diep, that broad arm of water, with its strong currents and barren shallows at low tide, would be an exceedingly hazardous undertaking. Moreover, such a thing would be well-nigh impossible if the troops commissioned with the defense should be supported by a harbor-defense fleet in

Turrets for 2 x 240mm Krupp Guns   **Turret for 2 x 150mm Krupp Guns**

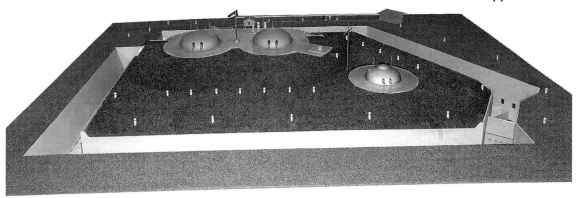

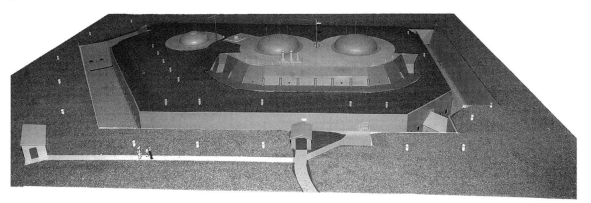

Model (front and rear view) of Fort Hoek van Holland. This was a coastal defence fort, but her guns were obsolete before the First World War. (*Johan Gieske*)

Holland-Diep. The capture or annihilation of this fleet must be first accomplished by the enemy.

In this aspect of the case, it would be of the greatest importance to the attacking force if his ships could be brought in through the Haring-Vliet or the Vokerak to the Holland-Diep, where he could support the landing party in rear during its passage across these meadows.

The object of the fortress at Hellevoetsluis and the position at Holland-Diep and Vokerak is to prevent this. The latter position consists of Fort Willemstad with outlying works and moats, the position of Ooltgensplaat at Overflakke and the fort at Numansdorp in Beierland. Quite reasonable expenditures would bring these works to the highest state of modern equipment.

The works on the West Scheld: Although to this position no political significance applies, it must be stated that in the oft-repeated alarms of the English-French press over the erection of a fort at Vlissingen the essence of the matter is neglected.[48]

The maintenance of Belgian neutrality is always advanced to the foreground, but Holland can only maintain neutrality by directly defending her own territory from an unfriendly attack. If the government of the sovereign Netherlands States deems it necessary to fortify Vlissingen it is no one else's concern.

The West Scheld in Holland is Netherlands territory and it is therefore a matter of the gravest importance that her neutrality be strictly observed. Would the aforementioned press be so vastly perturbed if Holland built blockading forts at Limburg on the Meuse? Moreover, it happens that, although obsolete, forts have already been built on the West Scheld and that Vlissingen [Flushing] was fortified in 1860. Have conditions since then been suddenly changed? Assuredly not. And now, as at any earlier period, the Netherlands dare allow no foreign power to march through her territory and attack of modern battleships and the arrangement of the coast defense batteries is entirely unsatisfactory. [*Journal of the United States Artillery* (1912) translated from an article in the *Internationalen Revue uber die Gesamten Armeen und Flotten, Beihft* No. 130, June 1911].

Typically, armoured forts like Hoek van Holland built for coastal defence in the 1880s became outdated after 1905. Fort Hoek van Holland was built in 1881–9 to guard the newly-finished Nieuwe Waterweg (New Waterway) that led directly to Rotterdam. Two of its caponiers covered the dry ditch, flanking wet moat and casemated barracks. However, its weapons became obsolete before the war ended. Two older Grüson turrets, each with a pair of 240mm guns, stood in the centre of the fort and a turret with two 150mm guns in a front corner. On the landward side, an armoured gallery for thirty-four rifle and six machine-gun positions similar to the one at Fort Ijmuiden provided close support. The 50m long gallery was protected by a roof of iron beams and concrete. The power was supplied by steam engines. The big guns had a range of only about 7,500m and no improvement on their range or the power system happened until after the First World War.

In 1911, the Dutch political leaders proposed putting all coastal defence under the control of the navy because that would help coordinate action between naval vessels and coast defences and allow the army to concentrate on land defences. In 1912, as the States-General and the government continued the debate that had begun in 1910, the government finally reduced its requests to the most important projects. The War Minister pushed for the construction of an armoured fort near Vlissingen on Walchern covering the channel leading into the Scheldt. At Den Helder, the army wanted to transform the old fort of Kijkduin into a powerful fort with armoured cupolas for 280mm guns. Since the guns of the armoured forts of the 1880s were not considered effective against the new warships of the twentieth century, the War Ministry wanted to modify the turret guns at Forts Hoek van Holland, Ijmuiden and Harssens for rapid fire and to improve their ammunition. The ministry also sent a commission to visit the factories of Krupp in Germany, Schneider and St. Chamond in France, Skoda in Austria-Hungary, Armstrong in Great Britain and Bofors in Sweden including. It was particularly interested in the Krupp wedge system for metallic cased ammunition instead of the screw system using cartridge bags. The new request for funds was almost one-quarter of the 1910 petition. Five-eighths of the original budget proposal had been for coast defences and the rest for the support of naval coast defence vessels. The last project was dropped in 1912 so this proposed budget was actually slightly less than half of the amount previously requested for coastal defences. The war ministry also dropped the proposed role of the navy. The ministry of the navy had its own proposals and the needs of the Dutch East Indies had to be weighed when the debate began in the States-General in the spring of 1913.

The Russo-Japanese War (1904–5) signalled the rise of a new great power and the first in the Far East. This alarmed the Dutch whose colonial empire in the East Indies could jeopardize their status as a neutral. Problems had already cropped up in the Dutch East Indies where the army had to deal with social unrest. With the rise of Imperial Japan, the Dutch saw a possible external threat in the East. Governor-General A.W.F. Idenburg wanted a strong Dutch army and navy presence, but the army had barely enough troops for coast defence and the navy consisted of mostly outdated warships from the previous century. The navy leaders argued that without a strong naval force in the Indies the army would be isolated and lost. To make matters worse, in 1906 the British built the first of a new type of all-big-gun battleship – HMS *Dreadnought*[49] – that rendered all other battleships obsolete. Europe was already engaged in an arms race between the major powers and most nations caught in the middle had to join in for self-protection.

At this time, the main symbol of military power was the battleship, especially the dreadnought type after 1906. Every major power and would-be major power had to enter the naval arms race, even if a navy was not critical for their future military operations. The main participants were Great Britain, Germany, France, the USA, Austria-Hungary, Italy, Russia and Japan. Some nations, including Japan, Brazil, Argentina, Chile, Greece and Turkey, had to purchase some or all of their capital ships from other countries. The neutrals such as Sweden, Norway, Denmark and the Netherlands, who did not strive to be a world power, contented themselves with smaller warships designed mainly for coastal defence.

The members of the Dutch States-General did not think that their nation could afford to enter the naval arms race because of the high costs involved and because ships became quickly outdated. As the legislature debated from 1910 through 1914, some pointed out that a single Japanese dreadnought had more firepower than all the large Dutch warships combined. A government commission and the Minister of the Navy pushed for the construction of several dreadnoughts. Initially, they thought nine would be sufficient; five would be assigned to the East Indies and the remainder to home defence. The appropriations requested by the Minister of War for 1910 to improve the coastal defences, including for the construction of new forts, was four-fifths of the estimated cost of a single dreadnought. Neither the army nor the navy got what it wanted since the heated deliberations continued through 1914. The Ministry of the Navy authorized the first battleship in July 1914. The bill for the acquisition of four battleships passed through the States-General in August. However, before the navy order for the construction of the first dreadnought, the war broke out. Only small ships such as torpedo boats were intended for defence of the homeland while the larger elements of the fleet were to be sent overseas. One reason why plans for battleships had to be cancelled was that the Dutch naval shipyards were unable to handle this type of project and in August 1914, none of the major powers would take the contract. In addition, arranging for one of the belligerents to build the battleship could jeopardize the Dutch position of neutrality. The States-General postponed the decision until the end of the war, when they rejected it. The government managed to order three *Java* class cruisers in 1915, two of which the Dutch shipyards actually built. Laid down in 1916 and commissioned in 1925 and 1926, the *Java* and *Sumatra* were ready for the next war.

The war broke out before the Dutch military had the chance to significantly improve the coast defences because the politicians continued in gridlock. The construction of the coastal defence forts had to wait until afte the war. Even then, little was done with regards to their armament, except for close defence. According to Klinkert, the Dutch continued to modernize their forces and defences until 1914, but the pace was too slow so that in 1914, the army did not even have enough machine guns (only 200 modern machine guns and a little over 500 old models) and much of the fortress artillery was obsolete.

The Royal Dutch Navy at the End of the Great War

The Dutch navy did not significantly increase its strength during the war because the Netherlands, even though neutral, still had problems obtaining the necessary materials. Only the Scheldt Naval Shipyards at Vlissingen built warships and it was not capable of producing dreadnoughts. Even before the war began, the navy had relied heavily on Krupp armour and guns for its warships. Furthermore, Germany was having too many problems of its own during the war to supply the Dutch. Several of the Dutch warships were from the previous century yet among the newest, there were several pre-dreadnoughts built after 1906. The *De Zeven Provincien* of 1909 had two turrets each of which mounted a Krupp 11in gun, four 5.9in guns and Krupp armour. The *Jacob van Heemskerck* of 1906 was slightly smaller and mounted two turrets, each with a Krupp 9.4in gun, six 5.9in guns and Krupp armour. The *Marten Tromp* of 1904 was similar to the *Heemskerck* but had only four 5.9in guns. The *Hertog Hendrik* of 1902 was almost identical to the *Tromp*. The light cruiser *Gelderland* of 1898 was rearmed with ten 4.7in guns in 1920 and had Harvey armour. Even though it had been rearmed, it was too outdated and served merely as a training ship in the 1920s. In August 1914, the Dutch navy deployed three pre-dreadnoughts, five submarines and thirty torpedo boats in home waters. The other four obsolete capital ships patrolled the East Indies.

A few destroyers were completed before the war. In addition, over a dozen torpedo boats, a few submarines and smaller vessels were built between 1900 and 1921. The most modern ships to join the fleet were the two *Java* class cruisers with ten 5.9in Bofors guns in single mounts, armour from Coventry and Krupp machinery. *Java* was built at the Flushing shipyards and *Sumatra* at the shipyards in Amsterdam. Before the next World War, the *De Zeven Provincien*, *Heemslerck*, *Hendrik* and *Gelderland* became coast defence ships. Three were stationed in the Netherlands and one in the East Indies. In the 1930s, three new cruisers, also mounting 5.9in guns and a few new destroyers, submarines and smaller vessels joined the two *Java* class cruisers. The Dutch navy of the twentieth century was too weak to protect the homeland or the colonies, only a shadow of the seventeenth-century fleet that had ruled the seas.

Chapter Two

The Dutch Fight for Neutrality

Preparing to Avoid War

At the outbreak of the First World War, the Dutch strove to maintain their neutrality. They mobilized their army, worked on their defences and maintained a high water level in their canals in preparation for defensive inundations. The field army consisted of twenty-four infantry regiments (3,300 men each or just over 79,000 men), several artillery regiments and a cavalry brigade. That was a total of fewer than 90,000 troops, not including the garrison troops for the fortifications. The field army was organized into four divisions. The 1st Division was stationed on the coast, between Ijmuiden and Hoek van Holland to guard against an amphibious assault. The 2nd Division stood along the Ijssel and Rhine river west of Nijmegen. The 3rd Division was in the North Brabant and Zeeland. The 4th Division was the reserve and it was located near Amersfoort. According to Maartje Abbenhuis,[1] author of *The Art of Staying Neutral*, Dutch strategic policy had not changed before 1913 when the object was the defence of the nation's central core. After 1913, General Cornelius Jacobus Snijders (1852–1939) decided that the entire field army would no longer take up positions near the fortifications because the transportation system had improved. The general and his staff concluded that the army now had the ability to manoeuvre more freely and could fall back on the fortifications when necessary. Most of the garrisons of the fortified positions were at about half-strength in 1914. The composition of the fortress battalions had also changed as the number of regular army troops decreased. Now, only twelve out of thirty-five battalions were not Landwehr (Dutch 'Landweer') troops. According to Abbenhuis, fortress battalions, mostly made of older troops – anything but elite – were deployed as follows:

1. The New Dutch Water Line, the main line of defence – 21 battalions.
2. The Amsterdam Ring, the National Reduit – 5 battalions.
3. Hellevoetsluis, on the Haringvliet – 3 battalions.
4. Den Helder Position – 3 battalions.
5. Willemstad – 2¾ battalions.
6. Terneuzen, on the south bank of the Scheld – ¼ battalion.

The Amsterdam Ring with its new forts was ready to take its place as the National Reduit while the New Dutch Water Line, heavily reinforced over the previous fifty years, formed the main land defences. Its forts were manned; barbed-wire fences were setup in some locations, especially on the New Dutch Water Line; trenches were prepared outside the forts; and a number of bombproof shelters were built in some of the interval positions. The army had either abandoned or razed most of the outer fortifications such as Deventer, Doesburg, Arnhem, Nijmegen and the old Grebbe Line after the Act of 1874. Only the barrier fort of Pannerden

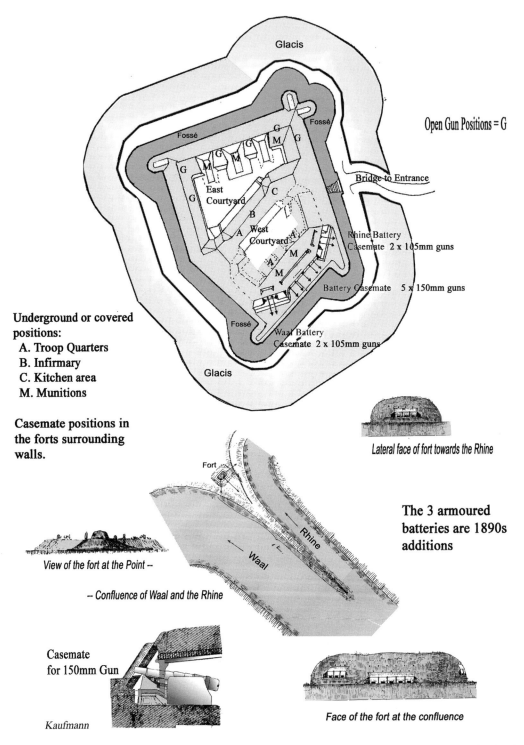

Open Gun Positions = G

Glacis

Fossé

Fossé

East Courtyard

C

B

West Courtyard

A

A

M

M

M

Bridge to Entrance

Rhine Battery
Casemate 2 x 105mm guns

Battery Casemate   5 x 150mm guns

Fossé

Waal Battery
Casemate 2 x 105mm guns

Glacis

Underground or covered positions:
 A. Troop Quarters
 B. Infirmary
 C. Kitchen area
 M. Munitions

Casemate positions in the forts surrounding walls.

Lateral face of fort towards the Rhine

Fort

Rhine

Waal

View of the fort at the Point --

-- Confluence of Waal and the Rhine

The 3 armoured batteries are 1890s additions

Casemate
for 150mm Gun

Kaufmann

Face of the fort at the confluence

Fort Pannerdern, located at the confluence of the Rhine and Waal, was upgraded to an armoured fort in the 1890s with the addition of new batteries.

Guardian of the Scheldt

The Dutch dismantled the fortifications of Flushing on Walchern in 1867 and allowed other defences on the Scheldt at Tenrneuzen and Ellewoutsdijk to decay. These neglected old fortifications became dilapidated well before the end of the century. In 1890, the Belgians were building fortress rings at Antwerp, Liège and Namur to deter possible German or French aggression. The Belgian government was concerned that a German occupation of the Western Netherlands (Zeeland) could close the access to the sea of their main seaport, Antwerp. Consequently, it proposed to the Dutch to refortify the area at Terneuzen and even offered to fund the project. In addition, if war came, the Belgians offered to provide a garrison.

In the early twentieth century, the Dutch rekindled their interest in defending the Scheldt. In 1903, the government was ready to provide the credits for the creation of a new fortress at Flushing. This decision worried the Belgians and drew the disapproval of the French and British. All three nations had come to believe that the Netherlands were falling under the wing of the German Reich. Queen Wilhelmina, who was married to a German, had shown antagonism towards the British because of the Boer War. Flimsy evidence in the form of an alleged letter from Kaiser Wilhelm II to the Queen was made public in 1904 'urging upon her to put Holland in a state of defence against Great Britain and threatening otherwise to occupy, in case of a war, the territory of the kingdom'. The British feared that the German army would overrun the Netherlands and use Flushing as a base for an amphibious invasion of England.[2]

The Dutch did not give up plans for the creation of a new fortress at Flushing. In 1913, construction of the new fort began east of the outer harbour, on the site of the old French Fort Saint-Hilaire, which had been renamed Fort de Ruyter in 1814. The armament was to come from Krupp, but after August 1914, it was impossible to complete the contract. Since the new fort was to be named Fort de Ruyter, another Fort de Ruyter at the Willemstad Position was renamed Fort Sabina Henrica in 1913. Its armament was to consist of four 280mm Krupp guns in cast steel turrets and turrets for two 120mm turrets. Four 75mm guns were also to be included. Early in 1914, articles in the Dutch newspaper *Vlissingsche Courant* described plans for the construction of the fort. One article, titled 'Het fort te Vlissingen', discussed the fort and its functions. According to the author, the fort would not actually protect the harbour, but block access to the Scheldt instead. At the end of the war, no further construction was done. Krupp industries did not deliver the guns, armour and other material ordered in 1913 until June, September and December 1919. Eight 280mm guns and their four turrets had been ordered for both Fort de Ruyter and Fort Kijkduin at Den Helder.[3] Much of the material was stored at the naval shipyard in Amsterdam and was sold off in 1932. On 29 March 1919, the *Vlissingsche Courant* published a notice concerning an auction for barracks and items like two gun installations with ammunition niches at the site of the fort. Finally, on 4 June 1925, another notice mentioned a decree abolishing the fort and decreed its removal. In January 1935, the city of Flushing hired about a dozen labourers to level the remains of Fort de Ruyter. Eventually, the Germans found some limited use for the site in 1944.

at the confluence of the Rhine and Maas remained. The Netherlands relied on the false façade of impregnable fortifications to protect the nation's core. Apparently, most Europeans believed that the Dutch fortifications were up-to-date and modern. In reality, the Dutch fortifications paled in comparison to those of other nations and were only ready to face nineteenth-century weapons. The Dutch army mobilized quickly and more efficiently than it did in 1870 or 1939 and was ready and waiting. Unfortunately, although invaders would not take the Dutch by surprise, their army's ability to resist was limited.

The preparations of the Dutch military were of questionable value. Enemy forces would not face the first major inundation barrier until they reached the New Dutch Water Line. The flooding was not extensive enough to keep the new heavy German artillery, which could smash the outdated Dutch forts like a nutcracker, out of range. Except for 600 new 57mm QF guns, the 2,000 pieces of artillery in the New Dutch Water Line were inadequate and the army deployed two-thirds of them outside the forts. The army's divisional artillery was in no better condition. Furthermore, the Dutch were short of ammunition and were unable to replenish their supplies during the war. Many forts became infantry posts when their guns were transferred to the field forces. The small Dutch air force began with a few aircraft early in the war and grew to about 150 by the end of the war. However, the military had to purchase many planes from France, Sweden and Germany after 1917.

Beginning in July 1914, General C.J. Snijders, the Dutch commander-in-chief, strove effectively to maintain neutrality. However, before the end of the war, when he warned that the army would not be able to resist a German invasion, his opponents accused him of being pro-German. These suspicions stemmed from a lack of understanding that the Dutch forts were unable to resist new enemy artillery, that the army was not equipped to handle gas warfare,[4] and that there were significant shortages of equipment and ammunition. In addition, many of the Dutch troops were not skilled in the duties they were supposed to perform because of their limited training. For instance, a number of soldiers of the cavalry brigade did not know how to ride a horse.

Under General Snijders, the military maintained strict neutrality, treating all belligerents in the same manner. Aircraft that landed in the Netherlands and troops who crossed the border were interned. The population of Zeeland suffered when aircraft of the belligerent nations accidentally bombed several places. In addition, thousands of naval mines washed ashore. The superannuated Dutch navy actively and rather effectively patrolled the waters.

During the war, the relationship between the Dutch and the Germans might be described as cordial. The German army had prepared options for invading the Netherlands, but the Second Reich needed the Dutch to remain neutral out of economic necessity since the war was not going to be a short one after their defeat on the Marne and the onset of trench warfare. Early in the war, the Netherlands offered a point of entry through a British naval blockade for materials the Germans needed. However, that changed when the British imposed restrictions on what could enter Dutch ports in 1915. The Netherlands nonetheless continued to represent a potential food source for Germany. In late 1916, the Germans began to suspect that the Dutch might declare war on them, thus threatening their line of communications to occupied Belgium and the Western Front. As a result, troops returning from the Eastern Front deployed near the Dutch border to build defences. In early 1917, German intelligence sources concluded that the Netherlands did not, in fact, represent any threat.

Later in the war, both Allied and German aircraft used Dutch airspace as a safety zone. However, the Germans had considered giving the Dutch anti-aircraft weapons on condition they would not shoot at German aircraft. The Netherlands also offered safe haven for Belgian citizens and soldiers who escaped from occupied Belgium. The soldiers – if not identified as combatants and interned – and younger Belgians were allowed to proceed to Great Britain where many re-joined the Belgian army still fighting in Western Flanders. In late 1914 and early 1915, both German and Dutch border patrols shot smugglers and suspected spies on sight, but they were unable to stem the tide. The German solution in 1915 was to install an electrified fence that would allow the Germans and the Dutch to reduce the number of men patrolling the border. The fence was partially ready by May and spanned about 300km from the border town of Vaals near Aachen to the Scheldt River. The wire barrier mostly followed the border and waterways where possible, but in places, it cut through Campine, a sandy are of scrubby pine forests and heath vegetation, leaving a gap between the border and the barrier. Sometimes it split villages and crossed over rivers and canals. The barrier consisted of a fence made of electrified copper wire that stood 2–3m above the ground. A number of generators set up near the fence delivered the electrical charge. A guard could shut off a section of the electrified wire for maintenance or removal of the dead. The voltage of the charge is still disputed, but it was sufficient to kill a man. To ensure against accidents, the Germans laid out two additional barriers of barbed wire on either side of the electrified fence. They were lower in height than the lethal fence and served as a warning to people on either side that there was danger.

The Dutch government did not object to this barrier because over a million refugees had flooded into their country before it went up. The refugee camps were a drain on the nation's limited resources. A variety of people, from smugglers to refugees and deserters trying to escape German control, fell afoul of this infamous electric fence. Would-be-escapees tried a variety of methods to breach the barrier and often succeeded. Among others things they tried tunnelling below the wire, short-circuiting it, or pushing barrels under it and crawling through. In 1916, the Germans increased the height of the fence in some areas and added searchlights to observe the wire at night. In 1917, as the war dragged on, the number of German deserters increased. Many of them, like the Belgian refugees, tried to cross the wire. An estimated 2,000 to 3,000 people died from electrocution during the war. The 'Death Wire' in Belgium worked only too well, because it helped reduce the number of refugees who were an added drain on the Dutch economy.

As the war continued, the Dutch tried to strengthen their defences and improve the size and quality of their army. By the end of the war, the army had doubled in size. However, it added little over 300 machine guns and a paltry dozen 120mm guns to its inventory. The rest of the armament remained as outdated as it had been in 1914. Between 1915 and 1918, the Dutch army added some concrete shelters to the New Dutch Water Line. The larger shelters had two entrances instead of one and held sixteen men. Most of the bunkers were smaller, Type 1918. The number of bunkers built during the war was small and it is overshadowed by the large number erected between 1939 and 1940. In 1920, most of the Dutch fortifications and weapons were still obsolete. The war only served to force the Dutch to take stock of their weaknesses. Despite this, the politicians continued to ignore the problem.

**Barrier being strung
across a stream**

Crossing point in barrier

**↑Guards looking at victim
of electrified wire**

Guard standing by the Wire Barrier

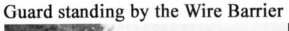

Photos showing the German electrified wire fence set up along the Belgian border with the Netherlands in 1915 to stop the flow of refugees and smuggling.

The Dutch Royal Family

The Republic of the United Provinces ended in 1795 after the invasion of the French who created the Batavian Republic, which became the Kingdom of Holland in 1805 under the reign of Louis Bonaparte, a brother of Napoleon. Louis resisted Napoleon, refusing to support the emperor's Continental System and trading with the British. As a result, the French army invaded the kingdom and he abdicated in 1810. The Congress of Vienna restored the independence of the Netherlands, but kept the nation as a monarchy under William I of Orange (1772–1844), the son of the last Stadtholder of the republic. William had commanded the Dutch army defeated by the French in 1810 when Louis Bonaparte lost his kingdom. He asked General Krayenhoff to strengthen the kingdom's defences. During the Belgian Revolt of 1830, his troops were defeated in Brussels. He later sent a larger army that was stopped by French troops who came to the aid of the defeated Belgian army. William spent the next eight years bankrupting his country to maintain a large army in an effort to retake Belgium. When a new constitution limited his power, he abdicated in 1840 in favour of his son, William II (1792–1849), who had led Dutch forces at Waterloo in 1815. The son was much like his father: ambitious and conservative. He too wanted to rebuild the military, but the economic situation limited his aspirations. Near the end of his reign, a new constitution further curtailed his powers while the politicians argued about whether to build the economy or the military for another twenty years.

In 1849, William III (1817–90) succeeded to his father's throne, continuing a conservative tradition in a country where liberals exerted heavy influence. The Franco-Prussian War worked in favour of William and the supporters of a strong military force. This led to the Fortification Act of 1874, which was followed by almost a decade of argument on what to build. In addition, the military and politicians were divided on the strategy to adopt. William died in 1890 after a long reign leaving his ten-year-old daughter, Wilhelmina (1880–1960), to inherit the throne. Her mother ruled as regent for most of the decade. The Second Boer War (1899–1902), when Dutch and German volunteers went to South Africa to help the Boers, gave the queen an aversion for the British. During this period, the Dutch were afraid that the Anglo-German naval rivalry would lead to either a British or a German invasion because of their country's location on the North Sea. Wilhelmina continued to maintain a position of neutrality, even calling for another international convention at The Hague. Her marriage to a Prussian officer fanned the belief that she might favour Germany even though she showed no signs of partiality for the Kaiser. When the German ruler told her his grenadiers were seven feet tall, she replied that if the dikes were opened, the water would be ten feet deep. Even though her constitutional power was limited, the Dutch were loyal to her and the nation remained neutral. She allowed the Kaiser sanctuary at the end of the war, not for love of Germany, but rather for fear of the spread of Communism. Unlike her predecessors, Wilhelmina maintained some influence on her nation's defence choices in the twentieth century. She kept her country neutral until 1940. When it was overrun by the Germans, she escaped to England to take an active part in keeping up the spirits of her subjects during the enemy occupation.

After the Great War, the government continued to struggle on the issue of fortifications. Both military and political figures realized that many of the nation's fortifications had become too outdated to serve as an effective deterrent in the future. In addition, fortifications are of little value without a properly-trained army to defend them. From 1920 to 1922, the number of army conscripts was reduced by almost half so that until 1936 the number of recruits rose to only about 80 per cent of its 1919 level. The number of professionals declined as well and peacetime formations were eliminated. Initial conscript training dropped from almost six months to six weeks. Minister Colijn in 1936 told the States-General, 'We no longer have an army; it will have to be created at the time of mobilization.' In 1938, a new law increased the number of conscripts and implemented other changes, but there was not enough time for the new system to reach peak performance before the war began. The situation in the Dutch navy was not much better, but the States-General decided after the war not to build any dreadnoughts. The army's funds had to cover expenses for fortifications. Although Krupp delivered some of the arms and armaments for the modernization of Fort Kijkduin at Den Helder and the still unfinished Fort de Ruyter on Walchern, the government decided to cancel the work. Thus, Fort Kijkduin never received its gun turrets, and Fort de Ruyter, having never been completed, was cancelled and parts of it went up for auction. On 4 June 1925, the Dutch newspaper *Vlissingsche Courant* published the following list of fortifications abolished by the government:

1. The Fortresses at Naarden, Willemstad and Woudrichem.[5]
2. Various works of the Grebbe Line in the Neder-Betuwe, near Den Helder, in the Amsterdam Position and portions of Gorinchem's fortifications.
3. Fort De Ruyter, the Breil,[6] Hellevoetsluis and Muiden.

The term 'Fortress Holland' appeared when the Dutch military concentrated their effort on keeping the enemy as far away as possible from Amsterdam, The Hague and Rotterdam. After the Great War, neither the big guns of the fortress ring of Amsterdam nor the New Dutch Water Line were able to offer sufficient protection to the city by keeping an enemy out of range. In 1922, the Dutch military reorganized and formed a united command for the future Fortress Holland whose boundaries, in 1939, would consist of the Zuider Zee, the North Sea, the Lower Rhine and the Waal and Maas Rivers. The army took advantage of the Rhine Delta to create a strong South Front. The East Front relied almost entirely on fortifications and inundations that formed the New Dutch Water Line, which was reinforced during the 1920s and 1930s. Labour was not a problem during the Great Depression, but the States-General continued to be tight-fisted. The fortress area included the provinces of North Holland, South Holland and most of Utrecht.[7] The coastal artillery weapons had not improved either by the end of 1922. An American ordnance officer, Major G.M. Barnes, who visited the Netherlands, sent back the following report:

From conversation with various officers of the Coast Artillery, it was learned that there were no modern Coast Defenses in Holland. The Coast Defense mounts which were installed about 1887 are of the Krupp Cupola type. The guns are all limited to about 15 or 20 degrees elevation and are of short range and of low power. There are a number of 280mm 45 caliber Krupp guns on hand which are now unmounted. The Dutch War

Department are contemplating mounting these guns on railway mounts should the funds become available for the purpose. They are somewhat concerned, however, as to whether or not their present railway bridges will stand the loads.

The Dutch Vertical Base Range Finders of the Coast Defense are repaired at Delft Arsenal. This range finder was of the most primitive type possible and of a very ancient model. It was stated by the officers at the Delft Arsenal that the Coast Defense are now being supplied with 3 meter base self-contained range finders. (2 December 1922 Report #3957)

The 280mm guns Barnes refers to were those ordered for Fort de Ruyter in 1913 and delivered by Krupp in 1919. Apparently, they ended up as scrap and the older Krupp guns remained in service for coast defence. The only improvement for the old gun batteries before 1940 may have been a range finder for the guns that would have probably not been able to engage a naval target successfully in the event of war.

The sea surrounds the province of North Holland on all but one side, which was defended by Fortress Amsterdam whose remaining fronts only required coastal defences with emphasis on the Den Helder Position, the main naval base. The situation changed when the Afsluitdijk (the Enclosing Dike. sometimes referred to as the Great Dike) was built between 1927 and 1933.[8] The 32km dike effectively sealed the Zuider Zee[9] in May 1932, but construction up to the required height continued until the roadway on top of it could be laid out. That road was not finished until a little over a year later. Realizing that the dike was a back door into Fortress Holland, the government had already appropriated funds for the construction of two modern forts on either side of it before the dike was even completed.

The army continued to renovate the New Dutch Water Line until 1936 when the leadership decided they needed a main position further to the east to protect Fortress Holland. The Grebbe Line, an older position abandoned since the Napoleonic Era, was restored as a key feature of the Dutch defences. The Dutch had used the Gelder (Guelder) Valley in the Gelderland for centuries as a defensive line because its land was mostly infertile. In addition, its watercourses, which ran from the Rhine to the Zuider Zee, could flood the valley floor that was already soft with numerous bogs. The Regulations of 1874 gave it only third priority in the plans for national defence. When the Dutch built a railway through Gelderland in 1886, the military required it to pass through Rhenen before turning north and running parallel to the old 'Grebbe Line' so that in the future, assuming new defences were created, troops could easily deploy behind it by rail. Although the Grebbe Line was not part of Fortress Holland, the commander of the army, General Willem Roell, concluded in 1936 that the restored line would prevent a German surprise attack that would quickly overwhelm the Dutch defences. According to historian J.S. van Wieringen, the government ignored Roell in favour of his chief of staff, General Izaak H. Reynders (Reijnders, 1879–1966) who felt that it was better to hold a line along the Ijssel and Maas Rivers to stop or delay a massive German assault. Thus, in 1938, the army worked on the defences of the Ijssel–Maas Line and extended the outer defences southward along the Peel Raam Line.

Of the 2,000 bunkers built in the whole country, 277 were located on the old Grebbe Line. Many of these were not actually erected on the Grebbe Line until 1940. The restored line relied on canals and dams to flood eleven basins. After some debate, construction of a bombproof pumping station began in November 1939. New plans called for two additional basins at the southern end of the valley to make it possible to maintain required inundation levels at times when the water supply might not be adequate. Unfortunately, the project was not finished in time for the Second World War. The advantage of the Grebbe Line, besides keeping the cities of Fortress Holland out of enemy artillery range, was that it had higher relief than most of the country. Unlike most the other Dutch defence lines, it did not rely on dikes for inundation since there were few in the area. This was why more time was needed to complete the inundation system. As a result, a few important weak points remained in the line according to historian Allert Goossens. Both were at the positions with the highest elevations: one at the Grebbeberg and two near Amserfoort. Goossens points out that the Grebbe Line also had a heavier concentration of bunkers than most of the other Dutch positions with about one every 150m. In the vicinity of the Grebbeberg, he wrote, it 'was quite packed with casemates. The sector along the main road alone had about twelve S- and G-type and two PAG casemates to protect the approach to the hill'.[10] To protect the right flank of the Grebbe Line at the river barriers, the army created the Waal–Linge Line that ran back from the Grebbe Line to the New Dutch Water Line using inundated areas and the river to close the gap between the two lines on their south front. The army also created the Ochten de Spees and Puislijk Positions between the Lower Rhine and the Waal and the Waal and the Maas rivers respectively for additional security. These positions made it possible to link up with the Peel–Raam Line. General Reynders had hoped that the Peel–Raam Line could link up to the Belgian positions near the Albert Canal, but that did not happen.

In February 1940, General Reynders resigned after the War Minister, A.Q.H. Dijxhoorn (1889–1953), questioned his strategy. Reynders had planned to meet the Germans in a series of delaying actions and wanted the army to move back through the Grebbe Line to the New Dutch Water Line. General Jan Joseph Godfried Baron van Voorst tot Voorst Jr. (1880–1963), commander of the field army, did not agree with this strategy. Voorst, who was considered an expert strategist, warned that a German invasion would not be preceded by a period of long diplomatic discussion as Reynders thought. He believed that to stop another Polish-type blitzkrieg, the main effort should be to build up the Grebbe Line and its water defences. He also refused to prepare the army for a retreat to the New Dutch Water Line as Reynders had planned. As a result, Dijxhoorn forced Reynders to resign and replaced him with Henri G. Winkelman (1876–1952).[11] Winkelman changed the strategy since he did not believe that the Dutch military could match the German war machine and there was no doubt that the only potential threat the nation faced in the 1930s came from Nazi Germany. He wanted the Peel–Raam Line to link up with the Belgian defences and to build up the Grebbe Line to cover its northern flank to maintain the position.[12] Winkelman and Voorst agreed that the Grebbe Line would be the main line of resistance and this was where the Dutch would fight the Germans. There was not enough time for the army to prepare the Grebbe Line and the government would not allow the forested areas in front of it to be cleared to deny German troops cover. Thus, the situation was not good in the spring of 1940 on the main Dutch front.

In 1940, the Dutch border defences included the Ijssel–Maas Line and the Peel–Raam Line. Fort Pannerden stood near the point where these two lines met. Smaller positions blocked access to the islands of Zeeland. The main eastern defences of Fortress Holland were beyond the fortress and on the Grebbe Line. The Wons Position, a defensive bridgehead, was located

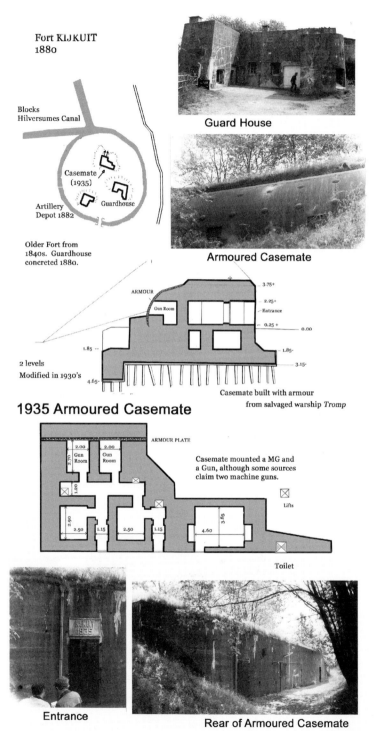

Fort KIJKUIT
1880

Blocks
Hilversumes Canal

Casemate
(1935)

Artillery
Depot 1882

Guardhouse

Older Fort from
1840s. Guardhouse
concreted 1880.

Guard House

Armoured Casemate

ARMOUR

Gun Room

3·75+

2·25+

Entrance

0·25 +

0.00

1·85 --

1·85-

2 levels
Modified in 1930's

4·65-

3·15-

Casemate built with armour
from salvaged warship *Tromp*

1935 Armoured Casemate

ARMOUR PLATE

2.00
Gun
Room

2.00
Gun
Room

2.70

1.20

2.90

2.50   1.15   2.50   1.15   4.60

3.85

Casemate mounted a MG and
a Gun, although some sources
claim two machine guns.

Lifts

Toilet

Entrance

Rear of Armoured Casemate

Fort Kujkuit ('Lookout'), was built in the 1840s and reinforced with concrete in the 1880s. In 1935 armour plate salvaged from a ship was used for an armoured casemate. (*Authors*)

opposite Fort Kornwerderzand, the new fort on the northern end of the Afsluitdijk. Two light defensive lines beyond the Wons Position, the F and Q Lines, served as advanced positions to delay the enemy. It would have taken more troops than the Dutch army had to man all of these positions properly, so Winkelman decided to hold them and the positions in the south with light forces.

The Dutch Fortifications

The Dutch made no major effort to build new forts after the end of the First World War other than the two on the Afsluitdijk. They completed renovations on Fort Kijkuit, an old fort on the New Dutch Water Line modernized in 1880 and reinforced it between 1933 and 1935 with a large casemate that included a large armoured shield 20cm thick with two embrasures for light guns. The shield came from the decommissioned warship *Tromp*.[13] Reinforced concrete was added to strengthen the fort. Fort Kijkuit together with Fort Spion defended a new state

Fort Den Oever, Block IX. This casemate was so large it was built in two segments. The seam between the segments can be seen in the bottom right photo. Concrete trenches on the back on flank of many casemates like this were common (bottom right). This casemate included a machinegun embrasure and an observation cloches. Toilets were normally placed, as seen here, at the rear of the casemate. (*Authors*)

Sluices on Great Dike

Observation Cloche

Ammunition

Machinegun Casemate on 2nd Line of fort
A = Open MG position at rear of casemate
B = Toilets   C = Seam between two sections of the casemate.

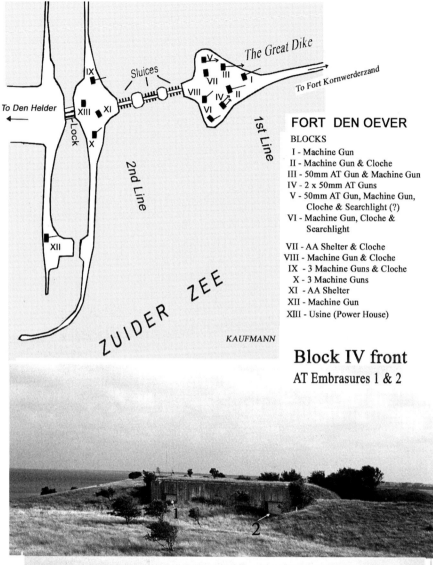

The Great Dike

Sluices

To Fort Kornwerderzand

To Den Helder

Lock

1st Line

2nd Line

ZUIDER ZEE

KAUFMANN

FORT DEN OEVER

BLOCKS

I - Machine Gun
II - Machine Gun & Cloche
III - 50mm AT Gun & Machine Gun
IV - 2 x 50mm AT Guns
V - 50mm AT Gun, Machine Gun,
    Cloche & Searchlight (?)
VI - Machine Gun, Cloche &
    Searchlight

VII - AA Shelter & Cloche
VIII - Machine Gun & Cloche
IX - 3 Machine Guns & Cloche
X - 3 Machine Guns
XI - AA Shelter
XII - Machine Gun
XIII - Usine (Power House)

Block IV front

AT Embrasures 1 & 2

Block II rear

Toilets

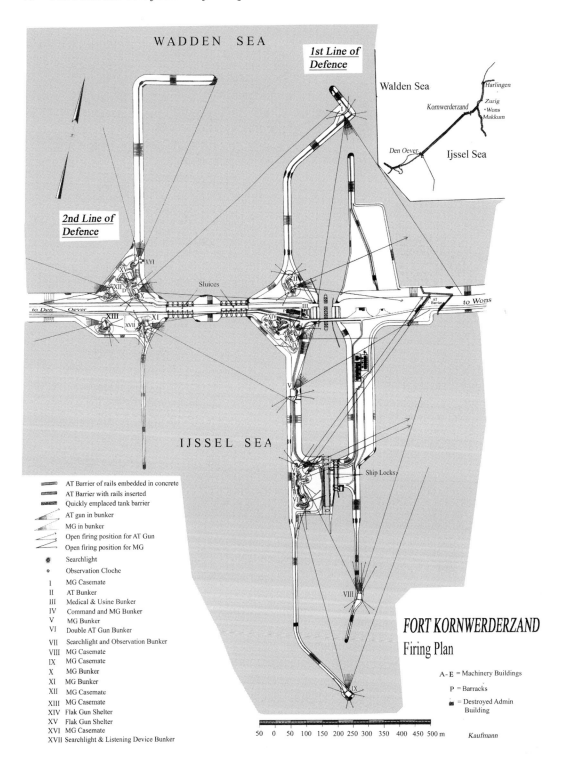

WADDEN SEA

1st Line of Defence

Walden Sea

Harlingen
Zurig
Kornwerderzand
•Wons
Makkum
Den Oever
Ijssel Sea

2nd Line of Defence

XVI
X
XII
XII
L
X
Sluices
II
III
XIII
XVII
XI
XIV
AT Barrier
to Wons
to Den   Oever

IV

V

IJSSEL SEA

VI
VII
Ship Locks

VIII

AT Barrier of rails embedded in concrete
AT Barrier with rails inserted
Quickly emplaced tank barrier
AT gun in bunker
MG in bunker
Open firing position for AT Gun
Open firing position for MG
Searchlight
Observation Cloche
I   MG Casemate
II   AT Bunker
III   Medical & Usine Bunker
IV   Command and MG Bunker
V   MG Bunker
VI   Double AT Gun Bunker
VII   Searchlight and Observation Bunker
VIII   MG Casemate
IX   MG Casemate
X   MG Bunker
XI   MG Bunker
XII   MG Casemate
XIII   MG Casemate
XIV   Flak Gun Shelter
XV   Flak Gun Shelter
XVI   MG Casemate
XVII   Searchlight & Listening Device Bunker

IX

FORT KORNWERDERZAND
Firing Plan

A - E = Machinery Buildings

P = Barracks

= Destroyed Admin Building

50   0   50   100 150 200 250 300 350 400 450 500 m   *Kaufmann*

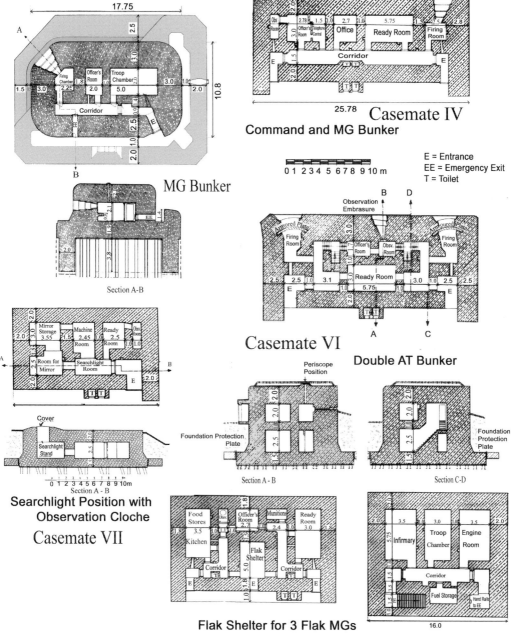

Casemate V

MG Bunker

Section A-B

Searchlight Position with Observation Cloche

Casemate VII

Casemate IV
Command and MG Bunker

E = Entrance
EE = Emergency Exit
T = Toilet

0 1 2 3 4 5 6 7 8 9 10 m

Casemate VI
Double AT Bunker

Flak Shelter for 3 Flak MGs
Casemate XIV

Medical & Power Bunker
Casemate III

Various Types of Blocks at
Fort Kornwerderzand

road that passed through the swampy region of the New Dutch Water Line and ran from Hilversum to Harlem. Fort Spion had been reinforced with concrete as well and in 1939 it received concrete shelters and machine-gun bunkers. Both forts were built on artificial islands in the marshland. Additional casemates of non-reinforced concrete were built along the road. Other positions along the New Dutch Water Line and in other marshy regions of the country had to be built on artificial sand hills that were later planted with trees to hold them in place. Four phases can be identified in the 1930s:

1. Before 1936, adding casemates to old forts.
2. 1936–8, construction of large anti-tank and machine-gun bunkers (the river casemates) built for bridges of Maas-Ijssel.
3. 1939–40, work on bunkers for Grebbe, Maas, Ijssel and Peel–Raam Lines.
4. 1940, improvement of the East and South Fronts of Fortress Holland.

The major fortifications work completed between 1932 and 1936 consisted of the first phase of construction of Fort Kornwerderzand and Fort Den Oever on the artificial islands built to protect the sluices of the Afsluitdijk to close the new back door into Fortress Holland. Each fort formed two lines on each side of the sluices, which were at both ends of the dike. Both forts consisted of several bunkers, but with no subterranean connections between them due to the water table.[14] On both sites, the first line of defence was on the sluices on eastern (or northeastern) side the island; the second was on opposite side of the sluices. Each line ran from one end of these small islands to the other. Both forts included one bunker housing an engine room that provided electrical power. At Fort Den Oever, the first line of defence was on a triangular shaped island with eight bunkers four of which were for machine guns, three for 50mm anti-tank guns and one that served as a shelter for an anti-aircraft gun. The second line, on the island closest to the mainland, had five bunkers. All but one of these were in close proximity to each other and which included three machine-gun bunkers, a shelter for anti-aircraft guns and a bunker with the engine room.

Fort Kornwerderzand also had eight bunkers on its first line which was the island closest to the mainland. They were more dispersed than those of Dan Oever were and included three machine-gun bunkers, two 50mm anti-tank gun bunkers, a command post, a searchlight bunker and a bunker with the engine room and an infirmary. The second line was concentrated on a small island similar to that of Den Oever, with seven bunkers that included five machine-gun bunkers, two anti-aircraft gun shelters and a searchlight bunker. The bunkers were single-level structures with a 2.0m-thick reinforced concrete roof, except for the anti-aircraft gun shelters, which had less. The most vulnerable to enemy weapons had a thickness of 2.5–3.0m.[15] They held ten to twenty men. Each fort consisted of a mixed garrison of artillerymen, infantrymen, engineers and signallers totalling about 200 men. Buried telephone lines linked the various positions to each other to maintain effective communications.

The bunkers of these two forts had to be placed on special heavy foundations so that they could resist heavy artillery. Bunkers in isolated positions, such as the end of a jetty, had their own concrete trench that included firing steps for machine guns in open positions surrounding them. Observation in the bunkers was through roof-mounted periscopes and episcopes in special positions. Some of the bunkers mounted observation cloches. The garrison could install barriers to block the causeway on the dike. The bunkers, usually located in sand hills, were exposed but well protected. An attack on them was difficult and bombing required pinpoint accuracy.

The Wons Position, which provided additional protection for the dike, consisted of about ninety-five bunkers, a third of which only had rifle embrasures and only six of which housed anti-tank guns. Every bridge in the area had an 'S' Type machine-gun bunker. The Wons Position consisted largely of sand and wood structures. The Den Helder Position, with its naval base, on the other side of the dike covered the coast of the province of Northern Holland. It included six old forts one of which, Fort Ersprins, mounted 150mm Krupp guns and ten obsolete 240mm guns. These heavy artillery pieces had a range of about 10km or less which was far too short to support Fort Kornwerderzand. Another of Den Helder's forts was the armoured Fort Harssens, which mounted two ancient iron turrets with a pair of 305mm guns each, also incapable of supporting Kornwerderzand. Warships docked at the naval bases were ready to provide artillery support to the forts on the Afsluitdijk.

The second phase of fortification construction was partially spurred by the Nazi takeover in Germany. The Dutch military commanders like General Roell, doubted that the New Dutch Water Line allowed enough room for manoeuvre and were concerned about a surprise attack. Accordingly, it was decided to push the defences forward by creating an advanced position along the Ijssel and Maas rivers. For this mission, the army designed large multi-storied river casemates to cover the crossings. The additional level was needed to allow the guns to fire over the dikes. These bunkers had two to four levels, no more than two of which were exposed and usually mounted a 50mm anti-tank gun and machine guns for frontal fire. Their walls were 1.5m thick and the roof 0.85m. They held ten to thirteen men. A related single-level anti-tank bunker was also used in some areas and was often built into a river embankment. The Dutch army built about forty of these river casemates to cover bridges on the Ijssel and Maas and added forty more during a third construction phase between 1939 to 1940.

The Dutch military, torn between the opposing opinions of its senior officers, began the third construction phase in 1939. The decision to restore and defend heavily the Grebbe Line was not made until November; over two months after the war had begun. In May 1940, the Grebbe Line was far from being complete and most of its smaller bunkers could not withstand fire from guns heavier than 120mm. Meanwhile, the army filled in the Ijssel–Mass and Peel–Raam lines with additional bunkers. The second line was linked to the Grebbe Line. Fort Pannerden, the largest position, covered the Rhine at the point where it splits to form the Waal.[16] This old pentagonal brick fort built in 1882 included two flanking armoured batteries that mounted two 105mm guns each. Its main armoured battery had five 150mm guns. Other lighter guns and machine guns were mounted in the walls along the dry moat. The wire obstacles were probably the most modern addition. This large fort housed a garrison of 300 men.

Most of the bunkers produced during and after the spring of 1939 were small because they were designed for economy. In addition, according to the Dutch military historian Allert M.A. Goossens, the designs were rather simple because most of the construction was to take place during mobilization and soldiers would have to work under the direction of supervisors with limited training for this. Most of the bunkers had small interiors and no space for latrine facilities or other comforts. Unlike the blocks of the two new forts on the ends of the Afsluitdijk, they were not built for extended occupation. Except under bombardment, the entrances of most of the smaller models had to be left open to allow air to circulate.

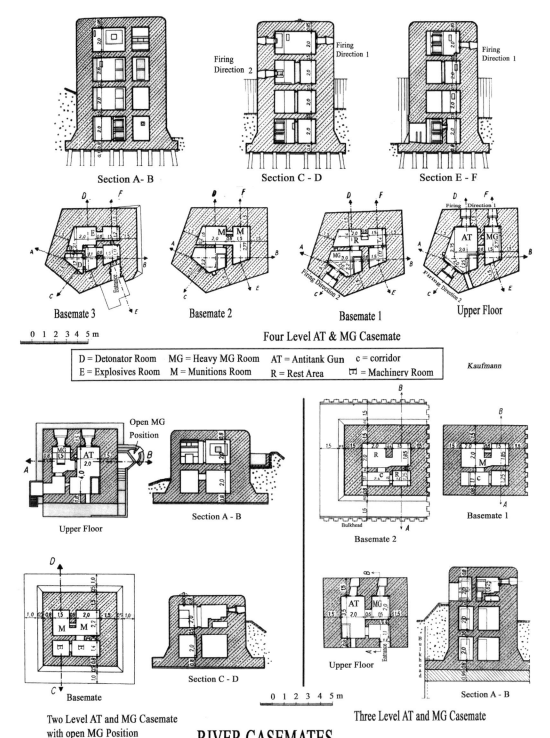

Section A- B   Section C - D   Section E - F

Firing Direction 2   Firing Direction 1   Firing Direction 1

Basemate 3   Basemate 2   Basemate 1   Upper Floor

0 1 2 3 4 5 m   **Four Level AT & MG Casemate**

D = Detonator Room   MG = Heavy MG Room   AT = Antitank Gun   c = corridor
E = Explosives Room   M = Munitions Room   R = Rest Area   ⊞ = Machinery Room

Kaufmann

Open MG Position

Upper Floor   Section A - B   Basemate 2   Basemate 1

Basemate   Section C - D   Upper Floor   Section A - B

Two Level AT and MG Casemate
with open MG Position   0 1 2 3 4 5 m   **Three Level AT and MG Casemate**

RIVER CASEMATES

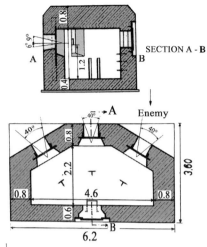

SECTION A - B

Enemy

"S" Type 3 Embrasure Bunker fo Heavy MG

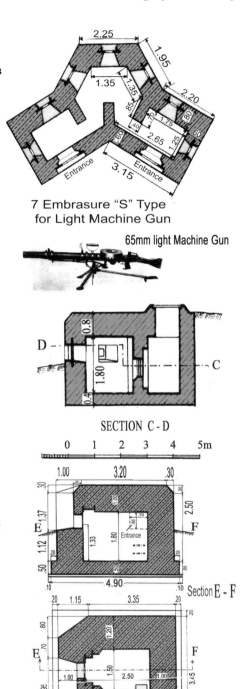

7 Embrasure "S" Type
for Light Machine Gun

65mm light Machine Gun

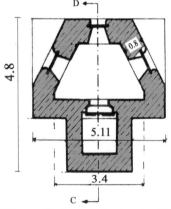

"S" Type 3 Embrasure Bunker for Light MG

SECTION C - D

"S" Type
"Spider" Bunkers
and "B" Type Bunker

Kaufmann

Section E - F

"B" Type for Flanking Fire.
Heavy Machine Gun Casemate

The Dutch built about 215 three-man heavy machine-gun Type B casemates for flanking fire with walls 0.7m to 1.2m and roofs 1.0m thick. The more common three-embrasure bunker for frontal fire with a light machine gun called 'Spider' or 'Porcupine' (Stekelvarken) was found in the most important defence lines and the advanced lines. Its walls were up to 0.8m and its roof, 0.6m thick. It had enough space for a three-man crew. A total of 675 of these bunkers that were built – ninety-nine in the Grebbe Line. The variants of this bunker included positions with one, three and seven embrasures. Another Type S was designed for a heavy machine gun, but the most impressive and least effective was a larger Type S for light machine guns with up to seven embrasures that weakened the walls. Over fifty of this type were found on the coast and in the defences of Fortress Holland, including the New Dutch Water Line.

The Dutch 'G' bunker type was one of the most interesting of the heavy machine-gun positions. It consisted of an armoured turret installed on a concrete foundation and it could shelter three to thirteen men, depending on the variant. Its turret did not rotate, but it was designed so it could be permanently emplaced at one of several possible angles. The lighter 10-ton version had 100mm thick amour and the heavier 15-ton version was 140mm thick. Some of the heavier turrets were used on a concrete foundation that included a ready room for a larger crew. By the time of the invasion in May 1940, over 500 turrets had been installed on the Maas–Ijssel, Peel–Raam and Grebbe Lines, on the South Front, in Zeeland and at some of the old forts of the New Dutch Water Line.

The Dutch also designed armoured turrets for an anti-tank gun that also came in two sizes: one weighing 28 tons with 140mm thick steel armour and the other weighing 35 tons with 170mm thick armour. The first was to mount a 47mm Bohler anti-tank gun and the second, a 50mm Bofors-Hembrok anti-tank gun. Neither was ready in time for the war since the turrets had to be produced in Belgium.

In addition to these turrets, the Dutch designed a troop shelter that also could serve as a command post known as the 'Pyramid' or Type P because of the shape of its 2.15m-thick roof designed to deflect bombs. These bunkers also mounted a roof periscope.[17] This type of shelter often formed lines near roads. Of about the 700 that were built, most were found in the New Dutch Water Line and the South Front.

During the final phase in 1940, work continued on all fronts with greater emphasis on the Grebbe Line and the South Front of Fortress Holland. From 1939 until May 1940, an estimated 2,000 bunkers of the smaller types were completed. Since the Western Front of Fortress Holland did not face danger from the Germans because it was a coastal front, it continued to rely mainly on its old forts, which included the armoured Fort Hoek van Holland from 1888 with two turrets mounting a pair of 240mm guns each and one turret with two 150mm guns. It had a 10m-wide moat and an armoured gallery with rifle embrasures. Fort Ijmuiden, considered obsolete in 1929, had a turret mounting obsolete 150mm guns and five emplacements for old 240mm guns, but the Dutch put it back in service in 1939 after adding two positions for 75mm guns and a few S-type Spider bunkers.

The Moerdijk position included some river casemates (four on the north side of the bridges). A number of Type G and Pyramid bunkers were built in 1940; Type G in the dike and the Pyramid type behind it. This bridgehead to the south of the two bridges over Hollands Diep was defended only lightly with field fortifications and it comprised no concrete bunkers.[18]

Example of Pyramid-type bunkers. Wooden doors were used in many since the steel doors, like the periscopes did not arrive in time. (*Authors*)

In addition to preparing bridges for demolition, the Dutch army defended the main sluices with bunkers and barbed wire and even prepared some of the large sluices for demolition. They also prepared fields of barbed wire and various types of obstacles for blocking roads and possible crossing points, including a Dutch version of Dragon's Teeth, usually in two rows.

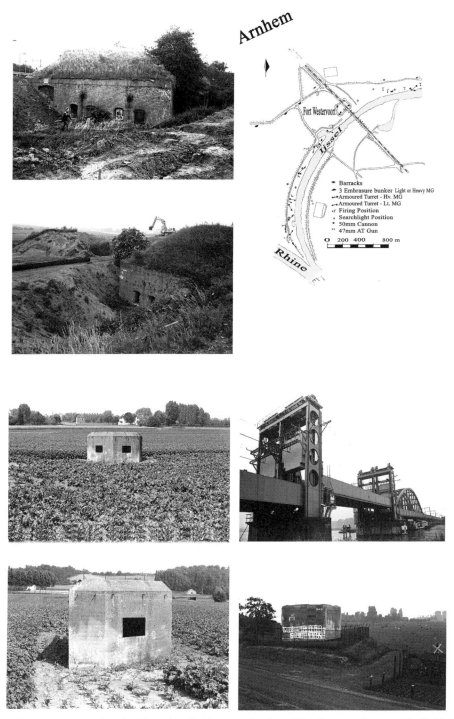

Top: Fort Westervoort covering the Ijssel river bridge near Arnhem. The fort was destroyed in 1982 for road construction. Bottom left (2 photos): Simple S–Type bunker near Maastricht. Bottom right: Ijssel bridge and nearby river casemate. (*Authors*)

Heavy steel gates were prepared to interdict some bridges like those on the Ijssel, but the enemy could easily demolish them if they were not covered by bunkers. Hanging steel gates with embrasures for anti-tank and machine guns were lowered from the trestle of some bridges to close the entrance. A pair of these gates was installed at the Ijssel Bridge, which had two sets of railway tracks. The Dutch also used a few types of mines including a version of the German Tellermine for anti-vehicle use.

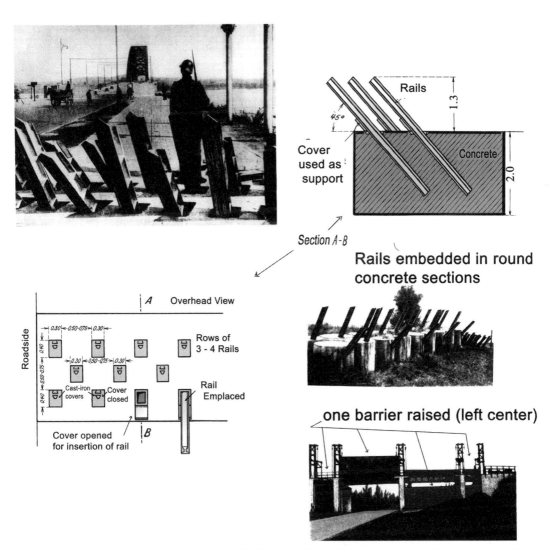

Guillotine Type barrier erected on new road from Utrecht to 's Hertgonbosch.

Examples of Dutch anti-tank Barriers. Top illustrations show rails inserted into prepared positions in roads which was common in other countries such as Switzerland. The guillotine barrier is unique to the Netherlands for it was also intended to seal the dike of which it was part.

Like the Germans, the Dutch were quite effective in camouflaging their bunkers. They made many of the bunkers with high silhouettes appear as normal buildings. However, their efforts were to no avail because the Germans already knew the location of their major concrete positions.

Bunker at Den Helder

AT Pyramids on dike

Bunker and Rail roadblock at Maastricht

German army photos taken during campaign in May 1940. The top photo shows a combat block with an observation cloche built in a style similar to those of the forts on the Great Dike.

Dutch Bunkers and Classifications

In the late 1930s, the Dutch created the *Voorschriften Inrichten Stellingen* (VIS), regulations for the construction of fortifications. The VIS established ten types of reinforced concrete casemates. The VIS system rated the concrete structures based on resistance strength. It was published in several parts between 1928 and 1935.

Part VII *Bouw van Zware Gewapend Beton-Schuilplaatsten*, published in 1928, listed three classifications of W 12-15, W 15-21 and W 21-28 based on the ability to resist high explosive rounds. These three categories of resistance are represented by a letter and two pairs of numbers. The letter W stands for *Weerstand* (resistance), the first set of numbers refers to the calibre of projectile in cm it could resist and the second to the calibre in cm of the projectile it could resist only a few direct hits.

Strength	W 12-15	W 15-21	W 21-28
Roof	0.80m	1.25m	1.50m
Front Wall	1.00m	1.50m	1.80m
Interior Walls	0.40m	0.60m	0.80m

Rear walls were normally thinner than front walls, but thicker than inner walls. The shelters built in 1918 could resist 150mm rounds and they probably could have been classified as W 15-21. The blocks of forts Kornwerderzand and Den Oever were built as W 21-28.

These resistance strengths applied only to high explosive rounds. The Dutch did not test for aerial bombs or armour-piercing rounds. The Dutch referred to the combat bunkers as casemates in 1935–40.

Types of Bunkers

River Casemates – forty-three were built on the Maas, Waal and Ijssel in 1936–7. These W 12-15 strength bunkers usually mounted a 50mm anti-tank gun or light field gun and a heavy machine gun. Type A had a single floor, Type B two to three floors and Type C was a larger version. They included facilities and latrines for the crew and a storage area for demolition charges. They were the only bunkers permanently garrisoned.

P Type Shelter – 'P' stands for pyramid, referring to the shape of its roof. Plans called for 700 of these troop shelters for Fortress Holland. Their construction began mainly in Fortress Holland in October 1939, however in 1940, the work switched to the Grebbe Line. W 21-28 was used for main line defences and W 15-21 for secondary positions. A large version held twelve men and the smaller eight men and included facilities for troops. Many of the steel doors for these bunkers had not been delivered before the invasion.[19]

S Type Casemate – 'S' stands for *Stekelvarken*, Dutch for porcupine, which refers to the protruding metal for attaching camouflage. It was a copy of a German type from the First World War whose walls and roof were only 0.8m thick. They were first built in April 1939.

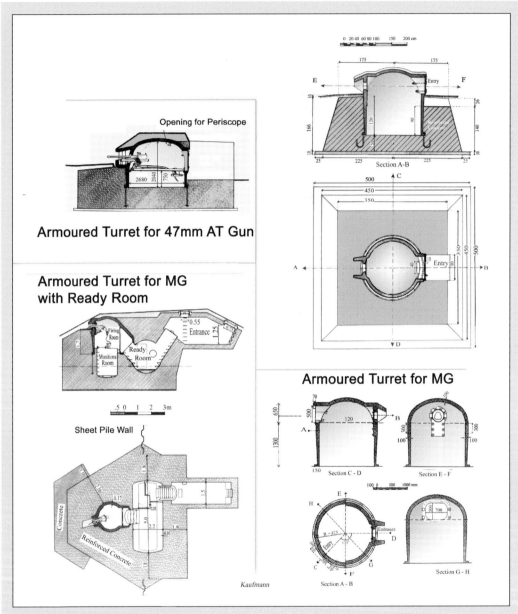

Opening for Periscope

Armoured Turret for 47mm AT Gun

Armoured Turret for MG with Ready Room

Firing Room

Munitions Room

Ready Room

Entrance

Sheet Pile Wall

Concrete

Reinforced Concrete

Section A-B

Entry

Armoured Turret for MG

Section C - D

Section E - F

Embrasure

Entry

Section G - H

Section A - B

Kaufmann

Special Dutch armoured turrets in fixed concrete emplacements. These were for machine guns, those for anti-tank guns were not ready in time.

About 2,000 were built in the Maas–Ijssel, the Peel–Raam and the Grebbe Line. Usually, they mounted a light machine gun. The Szw type mounted a heavy machine gun and smaller embrasures. The three-embrasure type was the most common and it did not have ventilation system. Only a few of the larger five and seven-embrasure types were built.

B Type Flanking Casemate – built in small numbers. It first appeared in June 1939 and mounted either a heavy or a light machine gun in a single embrasure. Strength: W 12-15

G Type for Heavy Machine Gun Casemate – 'G' stands for *Gietstaal*, Dutch term for cast steel. It was a 10cm-thick cast steel cupola. It was designed in 1939 and about 600 complete with the steel turret mounted were built. The fixed steel turret could be set at one of several different angles before it was placed into a concrete bunker. The turret had an automatic exhaust system and could accommodate a maximum of three men.

1937 Steel Casemate – similar to a French Pamard – W 15-21 with steel 14cm or 17cm thick – it mounted heavy machine gun and included a ventilation system. About ninety were built on east and south fronts of Fortress Holland.

PAG Casemate – stands for *Pantserafweergeschut* or anti-tank gun. It mounted a Böhler 47mm-anti-tank gun. Few of these simple, rectangular bunkers were built and of these, even fewer mounted cloches. Strength: W 12-15

All of the Dutch bunkers were supposed to be gas-proof, but the effectiveness of gas-proofing depended on the ventilation system employed.

In 1940, four types of new casemates were part of a plan to reinforce the main lines. They included an observation bunker, two types of personnel shelters and a combat position with a flanking and frontal embrasure for a heavy machine gun. All four types were W 12-15. The project was approved in April, but the invasion happened the next month.

[Source: Allert M.A. Goossens. Personnel correspondence and his internet site: *War Over Holland* www.waroverholland.nl]

Neutrality Ends

During the First World War, the German offensive in the West began quickly and the Dutch managed to mobilize their forces and brace for an assault that never came. The situation was different in 1939 after the war began with the invasion of Poland. The French and British declared war on Germany a few days later. Later in September, this action was followed by a farcical limited French offensive into the German Saar. Although little else happened that year, the Belgians prepared for a violation of their neutrality once again. Several times between the winter of 1939–40 and May 1940, Hitler had to cancel his planned offensive in the West. The Dutch still hoped to remain neutral, but Case Yellow, the German invasion plan for the West, called for the elimination of the Netherlands. As in 1914, the Dutch armed forces mobilized and their leaders continued to formulate a strategy. The change in military leadership, as General Reynders was replaced by Winkelman in February 1940, came too late to implement a new strategy. The Dutch largely abandoned the Peel–Raam Line in March due lack of Belgian cooperation. This move hurt Belgium more than the Netherlands. The Ijssel–Maas Line had never been more than a delaying position and the

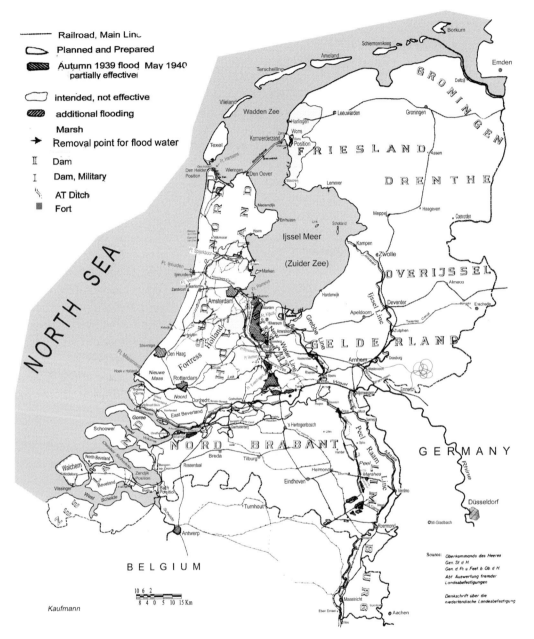

Map of Water Barriers and Defences of the Netherlands from 1939/1940 based on German sources.

fact that the Dutch army did not commit a sizeable force to the defence of Maastricht made it simply too tempting for the Germans not to violate Dutch neutrality to outflank the Belgians. To be sure, the defence of the Maastricht Appendage would have left any Dutch forces in an impossible position unless Belgium was an ally, but the Germans had no other reason to invade that region besides striking at Belgium.

There was no secrecy concerning the Dutch defences. The American military attaché, Major William H. Colbern, who described the Dutch defensive system in reports in February and April 1940, identified the Ijssel–Maas Line and the Peel–Raam Line as delaying positions. He reported that the Grebbe Line was the main position, but he was not aware that it was far from finished even though he was given a tour of it in March. He thought that the line relied heavily on inundation, but that it lacked depth despite its numerous small concrete works. In February, the Major reported that the Dutch frontier fortifications with Germany were 'negligible', that they began at the border and that they had a depth of 15km. The depth might have been impressive, except for the fact that there was not much there. These defences, wrote Major Colbern, were 'mainly to preserve the appearance of neutrality and have little or no defensive value'; they were intended to delay the enemy, but a protracted defence was not contemplated. He apparently included the many obstructions covered by bunkers that blocked bridges already mined for destruction in the 15km depth. Other roadblocks he noted included steel and concrete barricades and preparations for cutting down trees to block roads. He saw that all these bridges had double sentries to prevent a surprise attack. According to Colbern, the bunkers on the frontier mounted either a 47mm anti-tank gun or two heavy machine guns with crews of about six men. To the rear, he observed field fortifications made of trenches and sandbags and troops billeted nearby. The Dutch also planned to remove all road signs and markers up to 75km from the border as a passive defensive measure designed to slow enemy progress. Colbern also felt that the almost level terrain broken by numerous streams and canals would not be suitable for mechanized warfare.

In his report, Major Colbern also highlighted what the Germans in all likelihood already knew about the Dutch defensive system. After the frontier defences, he identified the following positions:

1. The Ijssel–Maas Position formed by much of the two rivers formed the first position. It included a section running from Nijmegen through Huissen and Weurt and along the Maas–Waal Canal, closing the gap between the two rivers. This was not much different from the positions on the frontier except for more solid barriers, including iron gates. The bunkers were supposedly of heavier construction and mounted more anti-tank and machine guns. Colbern was apparently impressed with the multi-level bunkers found near many river crossings. The Dutch had heavily defended and mined the bridges at Zwolle, Deventer, Doesburg, Arnhem, Nijmegen, Venlo and Roermond. Colbern was informed that these lines and the frontier were occupied by from twenty to twenty-five frontier battalions and he suspected only a few of these troops were stationed near the frontier.
2. The Grebbe Line formed the second and main position. This was correct since General Winkelman had replaced Reynders by this time. This line extended from Lake Ijssel (formerly the Zuider Zee until it was sealed by the Afsluitdijk) to the Lower Rhine passing by Spakenburg, Amersfoort and Rhenen. Cobern mentioned that the defended area of the Ochten Spees and Putujk Positions (but not by name) closed the gaps between the Rhine, Waal and Maas Rivers and formed a link to the Peel Line near Grave. These positions south of the Grebbe Line consisted of little more than field fortifications and inundations with small bunkers covering gaps in the flooded areas. Cobern indicated that these positions were of a 'temporary nature' and he was not aware of the condition of the Grebbe Line

itself since he was not allowed to visit it after December. The Dutch army had assigned two corps to the defence of the Grebbe Line between Spakenburg and Rhenen. According to the major, the IV Corps held the front between Spakenburg to Amersfoort and the II Corps from south of Amersfoort to Rhenen. Two reserve divisions labelled as 'A' and 'B', he noted, were in the two positions between the rivers.[20]

3. The Peel Line ran from the Maas River to Weert through Grave, to the Zuid Willems Vaart (Canal), the bogs and marshes of Eastern Brabant, to the Belgian border. It consisted of three lines. The first ran from Grave to Mill, St. Anthonis, Griendsveen, Meijel and Weert using a canal backed with field fortifications and concrete bunkers at about 300-yard (275m) intervals. The second line ran from Grave to Zeeland, Deurne and Meijel where it met the first line and consisted of field works linking the fortified localities. The third line consisting of field fortifications and bunkers ran along the Zuid Willems Vaart (Canal) from s'Hertogenbosch to Nederweert. The first two lines passed through the Peel Marshes, which hampered cross-country movement. The southern section had not yet been inundated in February 1940. The largest bunkers with several heavy machine guns and two anti-tank guns were in the fortified localities supposedly at Grave, Zeeland, Milheeze, Deurne, Meijel, Nederweert, Weert and Handel. Some were concealed in dikes and canal banks and other camouflaged as houses, barns and haystacks. The first line included the non-navigable Grave-St. Anthonis-Griendsvern Canal recently completed to serve as an anti-tank barrier. This line also had land mines. The Zuid Willem Canal, which was meant for two-way navigation, was 18m to 24m wide. Colbern thought the Dutch did not intend to hold the position for long and that its role was only to delay the enemy. He was correct in surmising that the III Corps with its two divisions and the Light Division held about 70km of its front. The province of Limburg south of Roermond and east of Maas River could only be lightly held. Since Colbern was not allowed to visit the Peel Line, he based this information on data he obtained from an American journalist.

4. Fortress Holland was the third and last line of defence. The eastern defences of Fortress Holland ran from Muiden to Utrecht, Vianen, Gorinchem and along the Waal River west to the Hollands Diep. The position (New Dutch Water Line) included the old fortresses of Muiden, Utrecht, Vianen and Gorinchem supplemented by field fortifications and an almost unbroken line of inundation. Roads that entered these fortresses from the east had been rendered impassable by inundation and those that were not were prepared for destruction and covered by defensive positions. Dutch officials allowed Major Colbern to visit the vicinity of Utrecht where he saw field fortifications, barbed wire, trenches and gun emplacements on old earthworks east of the city. They did not appear able to resist artillery or aerial bombs.

A Dutch General Staff officer told Colbern that all the old fortresses at Muiden, Naarden, Utrecht, Vianen and Gorinchem had been modernized with the addition of bombproofs and steel emplacements within the existing brick and earth fortifications. The garrison for the New Dutch Water Line consisted of independent Reserve Divisions 'C' and 'D'. The I Corps was stationed near The Hague and could be used to reinforce the eastern defences.[21] Fortress Amsterdam formed the northern defences of Fortress Holland with its 'ring of obsolete fortresses which connect Muiden and Edam'. The same General Staff officer informed Colbern that the fortifications north of the Nord Zee

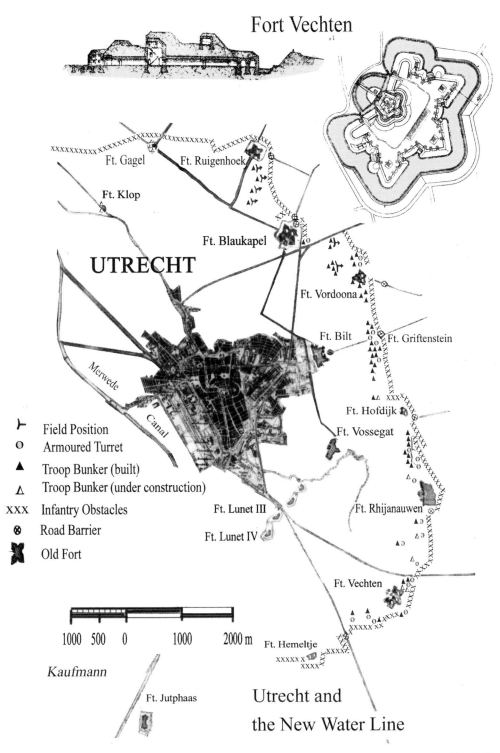

Fort Vechten

UTRECHT

Ft. Gagel
Ft. Ruigenhoek
Ft. Klop
Ft. Blaukapel
Ft. Vordoona
Ft. Bilt
Ft. Griftenstein
Ft. Hofdijk
Ft. Vossegat
Merwede
Canal
Ft. Rhijanauwen
Ft. Lunet III
Ft. Lunet IV
Ft. Vechten

⊢   Field Position
o   Armoured Turret
▲   Troop Bunker (built)
△   Troop Bunker (under construction)
XXX   Infantry Obstacles
⊗   Road Barrier
🛠   Old Fort

1000 500 0   1000   2000 m

Kaufmann

Ft. Hemeltje

Ft. Jutphaas

Utrecht and
the New Water Line

Map showing New Water Line in vicinity of Utrecht with old forts and new positions added by 1940.

Canal that connected Amsterdam to Ijmuiden on the North Sea, had been modernized, but gave no details.

Major Colbern's evaluation of the situation in the Netherlands lacked details on armament and construction in several regions. He did not expect any serious attempt by the Dutch to hold territory east of the Ijssel and Maas since it was an indefensible position. A major German offensive would force the Dutch to fall back on Fortress Holland, which, according to Colbern, would not withstand 'superior German air power'. The only viable obstacle the Dutch had was their system of inundations, which could deny an invading force the element of manoeuvre. The enemy advance would depend on the speed of bridging operations. In short, the situation was not good for the Dutch.

On 20 March, the Dutch General Staff took several military and naval attachés from Belgium, Japan[22] and the United States with several Dutch general staff officers on a tour of the Grebbe Line. According to Major Colbern, the position included a main line protected by inundations and an outpost position. The main position began on the west bank of the Een River on the Zuider Zee and ran south to encircle Amersfoort on its eastern side, along the west bank of the Luntersche Beek to its confluence with the Grebbe near Scherpenzeel and then on the west bank of the Grebbe to the Lower Rhine. The outpost line was from 4–6km east of the main line. The area between them was already partially inundated or prepared for flooding. Colbern was told that the land north of Amersfoort, already at sea level, could be inundated within 4–6 hours. It would take longer south of the town so it was already covered by about 50cm or more of water. Complete inundation was estimated to take about 12 hours, at which point the water would conceal many of the anti-tank ditches and barbed-wire obstacles.

The outpost line consisted of platoon-sized strongpoints placed at intervals of 300–400m. They occupied positions built of sand and wood to rise above the flooded area, but they could only withstand fire from infantry weapons. Both lines incorporated existing farm buildings, but the outpost line had no permanent positions. The main position actually consisted of three lines spaced 500–800m apart. Each included a continuous trench revetted with planks, but without overhead cover. The concrete casemates occupied positions on sand dikes to keep them above water level when inundation took place. The reinforced concrete casemates were about 4m on each side and had walls about 0.4m thick. They mounted three machine guns or two machine guns and an anti-tank gun served by a crew of seven.[23] They included air filters and a hand-operated pump for gas protection. Colbern identified armoured turrets he saw sunk into concrete (actually G Type casemates) as small casemates of cast steel equipped with gas proofing and bulletproof glass. They held three men with a machine gun or anti-tank gun according to his escort. However, the steel-cast casemate for the anti-tank guns were still being cast and none emplaced. The existing casemates were spaced on the dike at about 300–400m apart.

Colbern also observed a range of low sand hills behind the main position that extended from the Zuider Zee to the Rhine with an average elevation of about 40m. The observation posts and artillery were located on its heavily wooded eastern slopes. Four artillery regiments with 105mm Bofors occupied these hills; their range was sufficient to reach the outpost line 7,000–12,000m away.

At the time of this last visit, Major Colbern's escort informed him that all the lines were near completion and all the new work had been camouflaged with sod, bushes and small trees. Wire netting interwoven with burlap painted green covered the trenches. Although he was impressed, Colbern felt that the small bunker positions of the Grebbe Line would not be able to stand up to German artillery or aerial attack even though their location and small size might make them difficult to hit. In his February report, he noted:

At present, the partial inundation of this position has resulted in a broken band of water, about 7km wide (east-west dimension) and deep enough to fill all depressions but not completely covering the surface of the ground. It is understood that complete inundation contemplates a depth of water just sufficient to cover the general level of the fields: too shallow for small boats but deep enough to conceal ditches and obstacles and render fording difficult. I am informed by the General Staff that the present partial inundation in this area is at a stage which would permit complete inundation in twenty-four hours. This would increase the average width of the inundated area to roughly 10km and result in an almost continuous band of water from the Ijssel Meer (Zuider Zee) to the Rhine and in the intervals which lie between the Rhine and Waal and between the Waal and the Maas. Main roads, which are elevated above the normal water level, would not be affected in most cases and are prepared for demolition.

The main problem with the major's report was that he was escorted to selected areas so that the amount of defences he could see was limited. In addition, he relied on descriptions given by his escort. The Dutch army had restricted the areas that could be visited after early 1940 so that Colbern's report can only be compared with what is actually known today.

The Dutch had almost eight months to prepare for war after 1 September 1939, but their mobilization was apparently slower and less effective than it had been in 1914. This may be due to financial reasons. Before 1914, the Dutch had already run up large deficits, which increased when their army stood at the ready during the war. They probably did not want a repeat performance in 1940. In any case, since the leaders expected Dutch troops to build most of the fortifications, this did not help the situation. During the winter months, more time was lost as the Dutch military and political leaderships disagreed with each other until Reynders resigned and Winkelman took command of the armed forces in February 1940. Before he took over, on 12 November 1939 and again on 13 January 1940, the Dutch expected the Germans to launch their invasion. With the spring still ahead of them Winkelman switched the main defensive work from Fortress Holland and the New Dutch Water Line to the Grebbe Line where the higher terrain gave the defenders a slight advantage and German artillery would be well out of range of the cities of Fortress Holland.

When the Germans invaded the Netherlands, they caught the Dutch off balance. Even though the Dutch had had many months to prepare between 1 September 1939 and 10 May 1940, it made little difference. The Belgians had left an 18km gap between their own defences and those of the Dutch whose command wavered between defending the extended line near the border and concentrating on Fortress Holland. When the alert went out in January that the invasion was imminent, the Dutch did not reinforce their southern front, which gave observers an indication that they were not planning to make a determined stand on the

Peel–Raam Line. Once Winkelman took command in February, the strategy had changed to moving the main line forward to the Grebbe Line giving the army only about three months to make the necessary changes and increase the defences. The Dutch maintained their border positions in readiness, after the attack on Denmark and Norway showed them the Germans would strike without warning. Reports of that campaign, which exaggerated the number of paratroopers and seaborne landing parties, should have spurred the Dutch to improve their preparations. As it is, the Germans still managed to catch them off-guard.

Both the Dutch and the Belgians had had advanced warning of Germany's plans thanks to Major G.J. Sas, the Dutch military attaché to Berlin, who was warned by Colonel Hans Oster, second in command of the German Abwehr and an anti-Nazi. Oster had been passing information to his Dutch friend since before the war and supposedly warned of the attack in the West at least twenty times, although time after time 'A Day' was cancelled. According to some historians, Major Sas passed his information to the Minister of War or the Queen who sent it on directly to General Reynders. Apparently, the general had little confidence in Sas' information. It also may have been a matter of 'crying wolf' too many times. Colonel Oster had access to the Führer's war directives that clearly stated that the Netherlands were a target. On 4 November, as German troops began moving into position along their border, the British ambassador warned the Dutch of an impending assault. In response to the warning, Queen Wilhelmina of the Netherlands and King Leopold of Belgium issued a joint peace statement on 7 November. However, the Dutch army cancelled all leave for the troops on 10 November.

Beginning with his war directives of October, Hitler made it clear that the Netherlands were to be part of the invasion plan. The directives of 9 October 1939 clearly show his reasoning; in his mind, both the Netherlands and Belgium presented a major threat to the industrial Ruhr. He claimed that 'both countries are interested in keeping their neutrality, but they are incapable of resisting lasting pressure by Britain and France' and that the Allies would find a way into those countries through propaganda and whatever other means. The two countries would give the Allied air forces bases from which to strike at the Ruhr. In addition, he reasoned, Allied armies would build up on the border and launch an attack into the Ruhr. Many directives emphasized what would happen if the Low Countries were brought into the war and what the German military must do. The plans for the Netherlands changed. In one directive, Hitler wrote that the cities of Fortress Holland must be taken quickly, in another one he ordered his generals to bypass the fortress area and move through the southern part of the country to strike at Belgium. Not long before the actual 'A Day' in May 1940, Hitler's directives made it clear he was not expecting an overwhelming victory like in Poland. Instead, he expected his armies to inflict a major defeat on the Allies, occupy as much Dutch and Belgian territory as possible and advance deep into Northern France. After that, he expected his air and naval forces to strike at Great Britain from bases in the Low Countries while he prepared for a new offensive in the West. However, the operation in May 1940 went much faster than he expected.

Both the Belgians and the Dutch got irrefutable evidence of Hitler's plans after the Mechelen Incident of 10 January 1940. Luftwaffe Major Helmut Reinberger was making slow progress on his way to a conference in Cologne when a pilot offered to fly him there in an Me-108. Reinberger, against orders, was carrying the plans for Fall Gelb (Case Yellow), the offensive in the West. They took off in inclement weather, went off course and came down near the Belgian town of Mechelen. Reinberger tried to destroy the documents, but failed. Hitler and his generals were not sure if their schemes had been compromised or not, but went ahead nonetheless with their preparations in January. However, the weather never cleared up that month. There could be no question now that the Germans had planned to invade both Belgium and the Netherlands, but Major Sas' warnings were ignored. His last alert indicated that the date for 'A Day' would be 8 May 1940. The Dutch military intelligence had already identified ten German divisions on the border north of the Rhine, nine between Cleves and Düsseldorf and thirty along the border of South Limburg to Monschau (Belgium). The military cancelled all leave on 7 May and stood ready for the attack that did not come on that day but two days later, when they relaxed their guard.

There had been other warnings that the Dutch failed to heed. According to Wilhelmina Steenbeek, the author of *Rotterdam: Invasion of Holland*, the Germans had tried to purchase Dutch uniforms for their special forces, the Branderburgers, to wear in order to take some river crossings by surprise. German agents had purchased uniforms in Amsterdam, but they were caught before they could cross the border. Dutch authorities, however, seemed unconcerned. It seems that none of those responsible for providing the uniforms for the Brandenburgers realized that many were actually made in Germany and that the Dutch sold worn-out uniforms to Germany for use as rags. They eventually got their uniforms and on the day of the invasion, one group successfully captured the bridge over the Maas at Gennep. At another bridge, however, Dutch guards captured a Brandenburger team in Dutch uniforms and shot them as spies.[24]

As no offensive was possible in January 1940, Hitler learnt of a plan proposed by General Erich von Manstein to launch the main thrust through the Ardennes where the Allies did not expect a major armoured offensive because of the terrain. The Netherlands was still targeted for invasion and the German navy was authorized to blockade the ports with U-boats the night before the invasion. Later, the navy was given permission to mine the harbours. In these directives, Hitler cautioned against attacking industrial or civilian targets only in the Netherlands. In Directive #8 of 20 November 1939, he stated, 'the attitude of the Dutch Armed Forces cannot be predicted. Where no resistance is met, the invasion is to be given the character of a peaceful occupation.' He seems to have believed that this was the only country that might not offer any resistance, but he was proved wrong.

In mid-November, the Allied command adopted Plan D (Dyle). They had decided that once the German invasion began, British and French forces would race to the Dyle River Line instead of the Escaut (Scheldt).[25] The importance of the change in strategy was that Plan D also included an option where a French army would race along the coast and by sea to the Netherlands with the objective of linking up with the Dutch at Breda. The only problem with the plan was that the Belgians refused to coordinate their operations with the Dutch and the Dutch were not aware of the plan and their troops in Limburg and Zeeland would mainly perform a delaying action.

The first operations of the German offensive in the West on the morning of 10 May 1940 took place in Belgium when the airborne assault on the Eben Emael fortress followed shortly by other border crossings in Belgium and the Netherlands. In the Netherlands, the Germans used armoured trains loaded with troops disguised in Dutch uniforms to capture key bridges. The trick worked in some cases. There was not much time to alert the Dutch who faced not a single battalion of the elite airborne troops, but almost the entire 7th Airborne Division

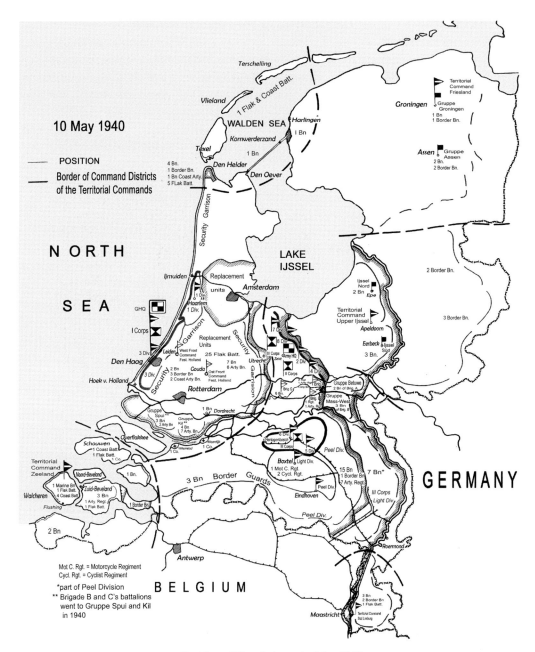

Position of Dutch Army in May 1940.

reinforced by the 22nd Air Landing Division in the largest airborne operation to date. Soon after the start of the border operations, German aircraft struck at seven Dutch airfields, but not the ones they intended to capture. Next, the elite troops descended into Fortress Holland near The Hague to secure three airfields. They succeeded between 6:00 am and 7:30 am. Some of the airborne troops captured the key bridges leading through the South Front of Fortress

Holland because Dutch guards had disconnected the demolition charges on the two bridges at Moerdijk on the order of General Winkelman, who had feared that a nervous soldier might accidentally destroy bridges the Allies would need to rescue the Dutch. In order to take these bridges, two German companies of paratroopers landed northeast of the railway bridge where the Dutch river casemates had no rear-facing embrasures. This German airborne battalion

AIR DROP into FORTRESS HOLLAND at Rotterdam

10 May 1940

ARIAL PHOTO of Dutch Airfield near Rotterdam

1. Where paratroopers landed

2. JU-52 transports on Dutch Airfield where they landed troops

3. JU-52 Transports arriving

Landed by seaplane these troops paddle towards bridge

(Below) Drawing depicting capture of airfield

Germans described this operation to capture Fortress Holland as what the world knows as the concept of Blitzkrieg

German Paratroopers drop into Fortress Holland capturing airfields and key bridges. Photos from *Die Wehrmacht: Der Freiheitskampf der großdeutschen Volkes*, a propaganda book published by the Wehrmacht.

overcame most resistance shortly after landing, at about 5:00 am. Meanwhile, two other companies dropped inside the southern bridgehead. They quickly overcame Dutch resistance with the exception of a few small groups that continued to fight, including one in a river casemate that inflicted a few casualties and had to be attacked. The German paratroopers had to threaten the bunker's garrison with blowing it up with charges taken from one of the bridges before the defenders surrendered. Meanwhile, other paratroopers landed near Dordrecht and eventually captured the road bridge.

At Rotterdam, ninety German troops landed in seaplanes at about 4:50 am and captured key bridges. The German paratroopers, who faced Dutch counterattacks during the day, suffered about 30 per cent losses, but managed to hold their positions. The Dutch had been unprepared to handle a vertical envelopment by airborne troops and Winkelman and his staff were concerned.

The 480 machine-gun bunkers, 352 armoured turrets and 22 anti-tank gun bunkers of the Ijssel–Maas Lines proved to be no match for the Germans even though they defeated all attempts but one to capture the bridges. At Gennep, Brandenburgers successfully took the bridge at Maas. At 4:00 am they were followed by an armoured train and a troop train that broke through the Dutch lines. Before long, the 9th Panzer Division raced across the Netherlands to relieve the paratroopers holding key bridges that opened a back door into Fortress Holland at Moerdijk. Meanwhile, the Germans became tied up for most of the morning trying to eliminate Dutch resistance centred mainly on the casemates all along the Maas Line. On 12 May, the panzer units reached the Moerdijk Bridge and entered Fortress Holland to relieve the embattled airborne forces fighting around Rotterdam and Dordrecht. The fall of the Gennep Bridge virtually secured German victory because without the panzer division, the German air-head might have eventually collapsed. The Germans had intended to capture the airfields of Valkenburg, Ypenburg and Ockenburg the first day and fly in Ju-52 transports with troops and supplies. The aircraft were then to return to German airfields to continue to support the operation. Valkenburg turned out to be still under construction and Ju-52s that landed became mired in the soft earth making take-off impossible. At the other two airfields, the Dutch fiercely attacked, destroying some aircraft and blocking the airfields to prevent additional landings. Even though the Germans secured the airfields by 7:30 am, the Dutch counterattacked. A Dutch battalion drove the enemy off the Valkenburg airfield and into the town by 5:30 pm. Earlier, by 1:30 pm, a reinforced Dutch Grenadier battalion and a Chasseur battalion had driven the Germans from Ockenburg airfield. Two Grenadier battalions had also retaken Ypenburg airfield. At Rotterdam, 1,500 Dutch Royal Marines surrounded the Germans. Airborne reinforcement and supply became limited until the panzer division showed up on day three.

In the south, German formations, including a panzer division, sped toward Maastricht to relieve the airborne troops that had assaulted Eben Emael. Their advance posed a problem to the Belgians because the Dutch were unable to commit significant troops to South Limburg due to its location and Belgium's lack of cooperation. Dutch troops had to abandon the Maas and Peel–Raam Lines after the first day, but most of the casemates on the line held out for as long as possible performing their intended mission. As the panzer division opened a corridor for the airborne troops, it was only a matter of time before the Dutch surrendered. This combined operation was the deathblow rendering the efforts of the Dutch II and IV Corps to hold the Grebbe Line futile.

German troops approach the line of obstacles on the roadway passing through Fort Kornerwerderzand when the fort surrendered.

An unnamed camouflaged bunker of Fort Kornwerderzand.

A river bunker in the harbour of Rotterdam captured by paratroopers of the 1st Regiment.

A Dutch entrenchment at Dordrecht hold by German paratroopers for 3 days.

Trenches of the Grebbe Line

The surrender of Ft. Kornwerderzand at the end of the campaign, and positions taken early in campaign.

Of about 1,000 bridges prepared for demolition before the war, the Dutch only blew up about 200. Among the bridges they brought down were the large steel bridges of the Maas River except the one captured at Gennep. A large part of one Dutch division (the Peel Division retreating from the Brabant) was lost because the bridges were destroyed too soon. The Germans overpowered the Dutch defences in less than three days even though their attempt to storm through the Grebbe Line was unsuccessful because the Brandenburgers had failed to seize two key bridges. If they had succeeded, two armoured trains carrying a battalion each could have raced through to the Grebbe Line. However, the bridges needed on the Ijssel were destroyed. It took the entire day of 10 May for the German Eighteenth Army's X Corps, the 207th and 227th Infantry Divisions and two SS regiments to breach the Ijssel Line and press on. On 11 May, the 207th Division and an SS regiment launched an attack on the southern part of the Grebbe Line and cleared the outpost line that same day. They broke through the front line the next day. The 227th Division, in the meantime, was beaten back at the outpost line near Asschat. The 207th took the second line on 13 May after three days of heavy fighting whereas Dutch held the 227th in the north at bay. The field army was ordered back to the New Water Line, which it reached on the morning of 14 May. The troops of the German X Corps did not realize that it had departed because of the previous days of heavy fighting.

The only bright spot for the Dutch was Fort Kornwerderzand. The German 1st Cavalry Division had easily penetrated the border and the Q and F Lines and then broke through the Wons Position before laying siege to the fort. The 225-man garrison repelled the first attack on 12 May with the help of a Dutch gunboat with 150mm guns, inflicting many casualties. The Germans returned to the attack on 14 May, but failed once more to take the fort or destroy the gunboat.

Dutch resistance was not ending fast enough as far as Hitler was concerned, so on 14 May 1940 he issued Directive # 11, which stated,

> On the northern flank the Dutch army has shown greater power of resistance than was expected. Political as well as military considerations require that this resistance be speedily broken. It is the Army's task to bring about the quick collapse of 'Fortress Holland' by a sufficiently strong offensive form the south in conjunction with the attack from the east.

Rotterdam became the target of the first terror bombing in the West on that day, even though the Germans attempted to recall the aircraft when General Winkelman announced the surrender of Fortress Holland early that evening. The Queen, the royal family and the government had already escaped to England, evading the German paratroopers part of whose mission had been to capture them on the first day. The fighting continued in Zeeland where French forces had finally arrived. All hostilities ended on 18 May when the Allies withdrew their forces. It took the Germans five days to end over a hundred years of Dutch neutrality. The great water barriers that had protected the Dutch for centuries had proved useless. Dutch resistance was fierce, despite the intervention of the 'Fifth Column',[26] which, except for disrupting some Dutch operations and some adverse effect on Allied morale, failed to achieve much. The Dutch fortifications were hardly the strongest in Western Europe and the defence lines were incomplete, but they were not the cause of defeat for the Dutch. The only mobile division in the Dutch army consisted of bicycle and motorcycle regiments; there were no tanks. The army's heavy machine guns were the

Water Barriers of the Low Countries

Rivers and canals served as major obstacles for defence in addition to offering ideal defensive lines. Almost every major defensive line was formed by a water barrier in Belgium and the Netherlands because of the nature of the geography of these nations. Large canals

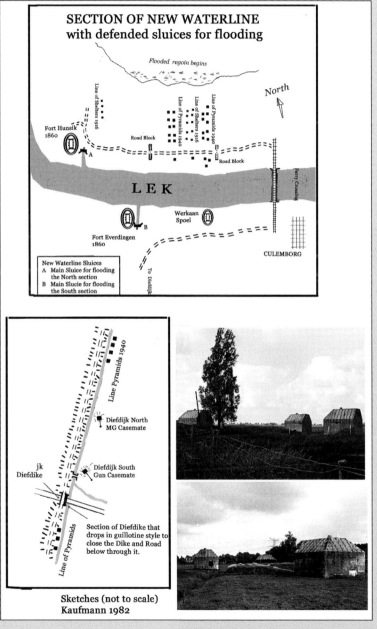

Sketches showing the positions guarding sluices on the Lek and the location of the Diefdijk. (*Authors*).

generally formed a more formidable obstacle than most rivers because they had a constant depth, no fords and often steep embankments the defender could use. The Belgians even built bunkers into the embankments of their newest canal.

The Dutch prepared vast areas for inundations. In Fortress Amsterdam, they created the basins between 1892 and 1895, before most of the forts. The basins could flood in

Barriers

Below - Plofsluis

Waterway Widened

Location of old bank

Silos in the roof over two passages below filled with sand and gravel to block canal

Plof Sluice   Amsterdam - Rhine Canal

AA guns on roof   Canal widened after the war to over twice its width

Above - regular sluis
Left - Road barrier then
and 40 years later, to
seal dike and close road.

Water defence barrier. Photos on the left are of a guillotine-type barrier that closes a new road, but it is also part of a Diefjik and used to seal the dike during flooding. Top right is the incomplete Plofsluis that was to seal a waterway during an attack. Note: the waterway has been widened since it was built and that is why there is open water to the left of it. Bottom right is a regular sluis.

1935 AT GUN CASEMATE of DIEFDIJK ZUID
57mm Mle 1896 replaced by
new 50mm AT gun in 1940

FIRING CHART DRAWN ON WALL

B.P.G. = Armor Piercing Shell

B.G. = High Explosive Shell
   PAAL = Pole or Post
   VIERSPRONG = Crossroads
   VERSPERRING = Barricade
   Boomen LI V/D BOERDERU =
        Trees to left of farm
   Range in metres
   O.H. = Elevation in degrees

W21-28 Standard

   Front Wall 180 cm thick
   Roof 150 cm thick
   Other walls 100 cm thick

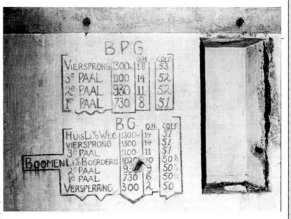

Casemate Diefdijk Nord was for a MG

Diefdijk Zuid gun casemate built in 1935. A 50mm anti-tank gun replaced its 57mm Mle 1896 gun in 1940. The casemate still has its range table marked on the wall. To the north of this bunker was the Diefdijk Nord machine-gun casemate. (*Authors*)

about half a day and reach an effective depth of about 50cm. To achieve this, the sluices had to be carefully controlled because the polders created by draining large parts of the province of Holland ranged from 7.0m to 0.5m below sea level and letting too much water in would allow the enemy to use boats. This meant that the Dutch had to maintain about eighty different inundation sectors or basins. In addition, throughout the First World War, several warships stood ready to intervene if enemy troops tried to cross a flooded basin.

In the provinces with large areas subject to inundation that were part of the defensive plan, the Dutch government built sluices that could quickly block a canal in time of war, but let boats pass easily in time of peace. One of the most impressive sluices built in the 1934 was the Plofsluis (Flop Sluice) a short distance south of Utrecht where the new Amsterdam-Rhine Canal, then under construction, passed through the New Dutch Water Line. All the water for the inundation of the New Dutch Water Line originated in the Lek River at the site of Fort Honswijk, a mid-nineteenth century fort that was modernized in the 1880s and drained through the new canal. The Plofsluis included five containers with 40,000 tons of sand and stone to block the canal and special outlets to direct the water in either direction during wartime.[27] It had thick concrete walls to resist bombardment and was gas-proof. A lock for ships that spanned the remaining width (40m) of the watercourse was under construction, but it was not completed by the time the war began thus making this an ineffective obstacle. Its purpose was to prevent the enemy from draining the water from the basins of the Antwerp Ring.

The major rivers incorporated into the defensive system included the Ijssel, Lower Rhine, Waal, Maas (Meuse) and Scheldt which varied in depth and width. Some of the canals and smaller rivers included:

Major Waterways

Name	Depth	Width	Length	Year Opened
Juliana Canal	3.00m	25m	36km	1935
Zuide-Willemsvaart	3.50m	25m	123km	1826
Dieze River	3.50m	55m	–	–
Wilhelmina Canal	3.50m	25m	68km	1923
Maas–Waal Canal	–	–	13km	1927
Noorder Canal	2.00m	13m	–	1876 (1929)
Wessem-Nederweert Canal	3.50m	27m	17km	1929
Antwerp-Turnhout-Hasselt Canal	2.00m	14m	63km	1875
Maas–Scheldt Canal	2.00m	14m	16km	1846
Nethe River	–	40m	–	–
Rupel River	Seagoing Vessels	300m	28km	1922 (modernized)
Demer River	2.00m	10m	–	–
Albert Canal	3.40m	54m	135km	1935

The Diefdijk or 'Thieves Dike', built in 1809, runs from the stream of Linge near Asperen north to the Lek. Its main sluice, built in the mid-nineteenth century, was located near Fort Everdingen. Opposite Everdingen on the north bank of the Lek is Fort Honswijk. The Diefdijk controlled flooding of the polder between the Lek and Waal Rivers and contributed to the defence of the New Dutch Water Line. Several concrete shelters were built on the glacis of Fort Everdingen during the First World War. Fort Asperen, at the southern end of the Diefdijk, protected inundation sluices, but early in the 1930s, the entire position was split with the construction of the Utrecht-Hertogenbosch highway that went through the dike. A bridge-like structure was built to fill a gap in the dike in case of flooding or to produce inundations. On its tower-like structures, it held two large and two small gates that were lowered to seal the gap and reform the barrier.[28] The gate was protected by several bunkers built on man-made sand hills and later, by Type G armoured positions. Other Type G bunkers were built on the dike and shelters for the crews behind the dike.

The Juliana Canal serves as a bypass for a non-navigable section of the Maas River between Maastricht and Maasbracht providing together with the river – which it parallels at a distance of no more than 3km – a double obstacle. The Zuid–Willemsvaart (South Willem's Canal) runs from Maastricht to S-Hertogenbosch when the Wessem–Nederweert Canal is included. The Wessem–Nederweert Canal connected the Maas River near Roermond to the Zuid–Willemsvaart Canal. The banks of the Zuid–Willemsvaart Canal were dressed with large stones leading to high earth embankments. Most of the road and rail bridges were of the iron swing type, but there were some older wood drawbridges for roads as well.

The Dieze, a small and short tributary of the Maas, flows from Hedel to 'S-Hertogenbosch where it forms a network of canals.

The Wilhelmina Canal runs from the Amer River at Geertruidenberg to Tilburg before flowing north of Eindhoven and on to the Zuid–Willemsvaart Canal. It has sand embankments and, at the time, partially paved roads ran along its sides. The Maas–Waal Canal, which was built mostly as a shortcut, also created a defensive barrier between the two rivers. In 1940, casemates guarded one side of the tree-lined canal at key points and barbed wire, the other.

The Belgian Maas–Scheldt Canal linked the Rivers Meuse (Maas) and Scheldt by connecting with the Zuid–Willemsvaart in the Netherlands. It ran from Bocholt to Herentals and from Bocholt to the Maas northwest of Maastricht and it included a line of bunkers. Its tree-lined embankments were 6m wide. The canal was enlarged in 1928 and bunkers were built along its banks. The economic role of the canal was replaced by the Albert Canal in 1940 and the Belgians decided that they could not use it as a main line of defence thus ending any possibility of a link with the Dutch defensive system. The Albert Canal, built between 1930 and 1939, runs from Antwerp to Liège. A German company handled its construction during the first four years. Although the canal was 54m wide on top, its bottom was only 24m wide, which means that it could handle ships of up to 2,000 tons. In 1940, German intelligence reported that it had six sluices and sixty-six bridges of various types. Some sections of the canal had high embankments with built-in bunkers; other sections were tree lined. In some areas, fields of barbed wire covered the embankments.

The Turnhout Canal, which ran from Antwerp to Turnhout and Hasselt, had steeply sloping banks that made a good obstacle. The paths along its sides were designed for animal transport in the 1800s.

The Demer River begins near Tonger and flows almost parallel to the Dutch border for about 6km before it turns west and parallels the Albert Canal passing through Hasselt before it flows into the Grette River. Both the Demer and Grette include a 1–2km wide network of irrigation canals and wet meadows that often flood when it rains.

The Rupel Canal, one of Belgium's oldest, links Brussels with the Schedlt. Built in the sixteenth century, it was later modernized to take seagoing vessels.

The Dyle River, selected as the main line of defence by the Allies, runs east of Brussels and varies in depth and width after Löwen where it is over 3m deep. At Wavre, the Dyle is 8m wide as it flows south to Löwen where it widens to 15m. As it flows north, it is joined by the Demer whose mouth is 20m wide and moves past Mechelen where it is 40m wide. From there, the Dyle joins the Nethe, which leads to the Rupel and connects to the Scheldt River. Both sides of the Dyle comprise many small irrigation ditches and wet meadows, especially around the mouth of the Demer that includes many hedges and trees.

pre-First World War Austrian water-cooled Schwarzlose M.08/15. Much of its artillery dated from the turn of the century and was mostly German or Swedish. The army's 700 artillery pieces that included 100 obsolete field guns had only fifty-six modern Bofors 105mm howitzers. The main artillery weapon was the 75mm field gun, based on a Krupp design, built before the First World War by Krupp and modernized in the Netherlands in the 1920s. The Dutch owned over 200 of these old guns as well as a number of older, less effective 75mm guns. The Dutch inventory of armoured vehicles consisted of thirty-two armoured cars and a few tankettes. The 125mm and 150mm Krupp artillery pieces dated from the 1880s and were supplemented by the Bofors 105mm howitzers. The anti-aircraft weapons included 75mm Vickers and Skoda guns, a few 40mm Bofors guns and 20mm Oerlikon guns. The air force consisted of a little over 140 aircraft (all of Dutch manufacture except for eleven American Douglas bombers); about ninety of which were modern and over twenty were biplanes. Except for the loss of the key bridge at Gennep, the Dutch advanced lines carried out their mission. The Grebbe Line did not hold out as long as expected and the field army command, before ordering the retreat, was informed that many units were running out of ammunition. Since the Germans were well aware of the situation for the Dutch military before the campaign, they apparently did not expect the type of resistance they ran into, if any at all.

Dutch casualties totalled about 2,500 military personnel dead, about 8,000 wounded and 2,000 to 2,500 civilians dead. The Germans casualties were high for the 22nd Air Landing Division, which lost about 30 per cent of its 10,000 men. Most estimates put German losses at between 2,000 to 2,250 killed, 7,000 to 8,000 wounded and 1,350 taken to Britain as prisoners. The Germans also lost about 250 aircraft or almost double the number in the Dutch Air Force, which was wiped out. Without the German airborne operations against Fortress Holland, the type of resistance put up by the Dutch troops indicates the campaign against the Netherlands would have lasted many days longer with much higher casualties on both sides. The Dutch armed forces were not well enough equipped for an extended campaign although their fortifications appear to have worked as planned, even if they were still incomplete.

Chapter Three

Belgium and the Years of Neutrality

Belgium Defends its Neutrality

Belgium had never been involved in a European war from the time of its creation as a nation in the 1830s until 1914. Like the Netherlands, it had relied on its position of neutrality for protection. A piece of paper signed by the major European powers guaranteeing its position, however, was not enough. In Belgium, unlike Germany and Austria, one man dominated in the construction of fortifications from the beginning until the end of the century: Henri Brialmont (1821–1903), who served as an engineer officer in the army. His first major assignment was to create a defensive system for Antwerp. General Raymond Adolphe Séré de Rivières (1815–95) in France, General Alexis von Biehler in Germany, who replaced the Prussian polygonal fort, and General Daniel Salis-Soglio in Austria can be considered his contemporaries. Unlike them, Brialmont moved from the post-1860s designs to the armoured forts. He left the army in 1892, over ten years after Séré de Rivières, so he had to deal with the genesis of the high-explosive shell and the incorporation of armoured components in his forts.

Although the Belgian revolt of 1830 had begun in Brussels, Antwerp remained the dominant commercial centre of the nation despite the crippling restrictions put on it by the Treaty of Westphalia of 1648, which left the Dutch in control of the islands at the mouth of the Scheldt. When the French under Napoleon occupied the region, they tried to turn the city into a major port once more. When Belgium attained its independence, Antwerp was still cut off from the sea until the government negotiated a toll system with the Dutch in 1864.

The Belgian government realized that the guarantees of neutrality spelled out in Article 5 of the protocol of the London Conference of 20 January 1831 and its confirmation by the treaty of April 1839 was no guarantee that all of the signatories would honour their commitments. Belgium, especially Flanders, had served as a battleground for its neighbours for centuries. Although the Dutch, with whom they shared a 400km border, no longer presented a major threat, that was not the case for those who had guaranteed their independence, except for Great Britain. Even if the British had presented a threat, they would have had to invade by sea. Belgium only had a 65km coastline and Antwerp's access to the sea was through Dutch-controlled waters, which would make an offensive from that quarter rather difficult. In 1839, Prussia did not yet present a serious threat, but that changed with the creation of the Second Reich in 1871 when the 100km-long Belgian-German border became vulnerable. The French presented a more serious and historic threat with their border of 520km. Luxembourg, with whom Belgium shared a 100km frontier, presented no danger unless it was occupied by France or Germany. Most of the Belgian population and economic centres were located to the north of the Meuse in Flanders,[1] the traditional invasion route taken by the French and the Germans.

Belgium still had the remains of the Wellington Barrier, a defensive system created by Dutch and British engineers after the Napoleonic Wars. In 1815, the British government considered it in its own best interests to restore the defences of the southern border of the Netherlands, i.e. the Franco-Belgian border. In August 1814, the Duke of Wellington reached an agreement with the Dutch according to which his army of occupation in France would not withdraw until the defences were restored. Under his direction, about twenty fortresses, including the forts at the ports of Ostend, Nieuport and along the border between Ypres and Boullion, were refurbished. Work was also done along the Meuse and at Namur, Huy and Liège. This second group extended to Maastricht, forming an eastern line. Tournai (Doornik in Flemish), one

The Wellington Barrier

The former Austrian Netherlands (1714–95), taken over by France in 1795, consisted of Flanders and Wallonia. It became part of the new Dutch kingdom of the Netherlands in 1815. Arthur Wellesley, the Duke of Wellington, was in command of the army of occupation after the defeat of Napoleon. When he worked with the Dutch government to secure the borders of the Dutch kingdom from future French invasion, he determined that several old fortifications had to be restored or rebuilt. He delegated authority to Colonel John Jones of the Royal Engineers since his time was mostly consumed with occupation duties. The two worked closely with the chief Dutch engineer, General Krayenhoff. Both countries contributed financially to the creation of this barrier. The project was scheduled for completion in about 1820 before the British occupation forces left France. Wellington conducted inspection tours of the fortifications through the 1820s, even after the occupation was over.

The main sites of the barrier included Ypres, Courtrai, Tournai, Ath, Mons, Charleroi and Dinant. Work was also done further from the border at Ghent, Louvain, Huy, Dendermonde and Antwerp. Along the Meuse were the fortresses of Namur, Liège and Maastricht. On the coast, construction took place at Nieuport and Ostend. Reconstruction of the fortresses of Charleroi, Liège, Ypres, Menin (a classic Vauban fortification on the border south of Ypres) and Grammont (Flemish, Geraardsbergen – located midway between Tournai and Brussels) took longer than most, about four years. In 1820, work was still being done at Courtrai and Mons. Many of these sites, such as Ghent, Oudernaarde, Antwerp, Ypres, Menen, Courtrai (Dutch, Kortrijk), Tournai, Ath, Mons, Charleroi, Philippeville, Mariembourg, Dinant, Namur, Liège and Maastricht were fortresses from the Vauban era. The fortress of Luxembourg was also included. In some cases, the fortress was rebuilt and equipped to resist for up to thirty days with garrisons of from 3,000 to 5,000 men (Antwerp had 8,000 men). Some locations, such as Menen with a garrison of 3,000, were designed to hold out for only one week. The main intent was to give the Dutch army time to mobilize. In some instances, like at Antwerp, Nieuport and Ostend, the Dutch built only forts for city defences.

The Revolution of 1830 brought about British recognition of Belgian independence in early 1831. Later that year, an agreement made in London ordered the razing of the fortresses of Menin, Ath, Mons, Philippeville and Mariembourg (south of Philippeville).[2] These were five of the twenty positions of the barrier established in Belgium. Maastricht and Luxembourg were outside Belgian territory.

of the southern border fortresses, anchored the Scheldt Line, which included fortifications at Ghent and in the vicinity of Antwerp. A fourth line in the north extended from Bergen-op-Zoom to Breda and Venlo – all within the modern Netherlands – and was the last before the major Dutch water barriers of the Maas–Waal–Rhine river systems. By the 1820s, most of the defences were complete. However, the Belgian revolt of 1830 created a conundrum for the allies who had wanted to keep the region neutral in 1815. Thus, the agreements of 1831 and the treaty of 1839 guaranteed Belgian neutrality. The London convention of 1831, which recognized Belgian independence, decreed that five of the fortresses of the Wellington Barrier had to be razed and that the others had to be maintained.

Between the late 1830s and the 1850s, the Belgians had to decide what to do about maintaining their neutrality. In 1847, they abandoned the Wellington Barrier and decided to maintain only the fortifications along the Scheldt and the Meuse (Maas) and create an entrenched camp at Antwerp, which had become a prominent feature in defences of this era. The Belgians followed the example of the Germans and the Austrians who had adopted the polygonal system when they finally began the construction of their new forts. The 1840s produced little more than discussions and plans, but that changed in December 1851 when President Louis Napoleon of France staged a coup and became Emperor Napoleon III. He issued a decree for the annexation of Belgium, spurring the Belgian government into getting something done. Some fortification construction was done around Antwerp in 1854 until the Crimean War reduced the threat from the French. Forts numbered 1 to 7 built south and southeast of the city had bastions and earthen ramparts. Except for Forts 2 and 5, which were bastioned pentagons, they were quadrangular. The decision to turn Antwerp into the National Redoubt was due to its location and economic importance.

The task of creating the fortress of Antwerp fell to Henri Brialmont in 1859. He drew up plans for several almost identical polygonal forts and ordered the removal of the old city walls, which served no purpose at this point. The original earthen forts were redesigned and a girdle of eight forts was formed and completed by 1864. Each had half-caponiers at the corner of the front wall with a double caponier attached to the centre of the front wall. A large three-storey brick redoubt was built in the rear near the entrance and the moats were water-filled. These moats were about 50m wide on the front of the fort and about 48m on the flanks. The artillery was behind earthen ramparts on the front and mounted between traverses on the flanking ramparts. There were defensive positions to the rear. A pair of batteries covered the rear ditch. The artillery used in the Franco-Prussian War showed the need for additional forts placed further out from the city. Thus, after 1878, an outer ring was created for Antwerp with forts at distances of 8–15km from the city centre. There were few forts in the northwest quadrant west of the Scheldt, where the terrain was marshy and prone to flooding. In the south, a major natural obstacle was formed by the confluence of the Rupel and the Scheldt Rivers, where the terrain floods mostly on the south side of the Rupel and between the confluence of the Rupel and the Nethe and the town of Lierre, where both sides of the Nethe are marsh. The newer fortifications, built after 1878, occupied positions south of (in front of) these areas. To the southwest of Antwerp, a bridgehead was added on the Scheldt with work to improve upon the old bastioned fortifications of Termonde (Flemish Dendermonde).[3] In the 1880s, Brialmont calculated that a German army was only four to five days' march from the border and that the fortress of Antwerp needed about two weeks to prepare. This led him to conclude

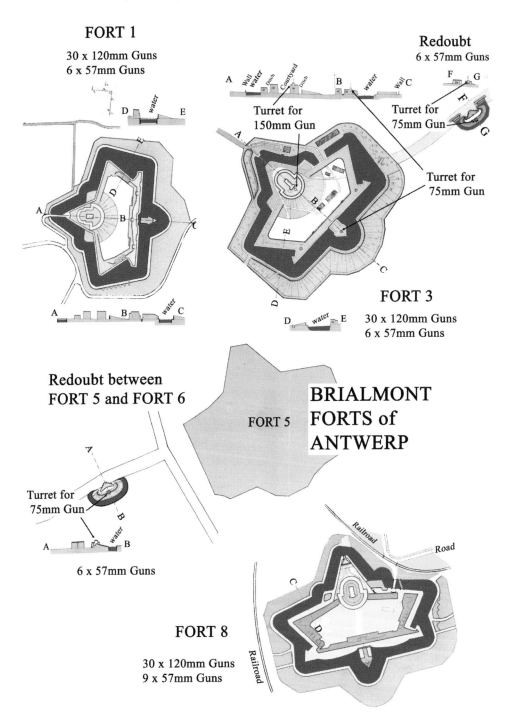

Examples of the Brialmont forts (Fort 1 through 8) and redoubts built in the 1860s and had concrete and 75mm gun turrets (except Fort 1 and 8) added early in the next century. Vertical profiles exaggerated. Fort Merxem was added in the 1870s (Act of 1870) to extend Antwerp's defences beyond the range of German artillery.

in 1882 that the valley of the Meuse needed defences at Liège and Namur. While he was still working on Antwerp and designing the fortress rings of Liège and Namur, he had to take into consideration the development of the high-explosive shell. His work at Antwerp lasted until his death in 1903. The old forts, Fort 1 to Fort 8, were not neglected. In 1870, traverses with brick rooms were added to Forts 1 to Fort 7 and concrete additions were made on some of the forts between 1909 and 1911. As in other countries, the effects of Japanese heavy artillery in the siege of Port Arthur in 1904 spurred efforts to reinforce existing forts to resist weapons of 210mm to 280mm calibre since no-one expected larger artillery pieces to be built for sieges. All the forts were reinforced with concrete except for Fort 8, which served only as a barracks. In some cases, the Belgians replaced old brick traverses with new concrete ones. Armoured turrets were installed on Forts 2 to 7. Some turrets for 75mm guns were added after the construction of a special two-level block. Concrete batteries on the flanks for 75mm guns also appeared. The brick caponiers were also covered with a concrete layer during this period.

By 1914, the forts of Antwerp formed a 95km girdle. Forts 1 to 8 were almost obsolete even though most had been reinforced. Between 1878 and 1882, work had begun on Forts Walem, Lier and Steendorp; Fort Schoten was started in 1885. They had similar shapes to the first eight numbered forts. Between 1883 and 1893, the Belgians added four redoubts, small positions about half the size of the forts, often circular, with wet moats. By 1914, these fortifications were considered antiquated but not yet obsolete since they had been modernized with additional layers of concrete and turrets before the war.

A law of 1906 authorized the construction of new positions, which led to the creation of thirteen additional forts and twelve redoubts. These new fortifications, still largely based on Brialmont's designs, were categorized into two classes, based on the number of turrets for the main armament.[4] The armament of most second-class positions consisted of one turret with two 150mm guns, two turrets with 120mm howitzers and four turrets with 75mm guns. The four first-class forts that were built had an additional turret for 150mm guns and sometimes two additional turrets with 75mm guns. The forts included traditore (flanking) batteries in the rear in a redan-like position with two 120mm and two 75mm guns. Quick-firing 57mm guns were emplaced in turrets in the corners of the fort and in casemates usually for protection of the ditch. The Cockerill Model 1909 turrets were made of steel 22cm thick.[5] The outer walls of the new forts were 2.0m of concrete, the exposed walls 4.0m and the inner walls were 1.4m thick.

At Fort Kessel, a typical second-class fort, the main positions were centrally located, as in most Brialmont forts. It was triangular and had a double caponier with three 57mm quick-firing guns on each side to cover the ditch. Above there were two turrets that mounted a similar weapon. A line of five turrets stood along the centre of the fort. The central one mounted two 150mm guns, the two on each side of it mounted a 120mm howitzer each and those at each end of the line, 75mm guns covering the flanks. On each of the rear corners, there was a turret with a 75mm gun as well. Finally, at the rear a casemated battery of more than one level formed a double traditor with two 120mm and two 75mm guns on each side. At the lower level, two 57mm guns covered the gorge.

Fort Liezele, another second-class position, was begun in 1908 and was still incomplete in 1914. It was pentagonal and had two large caponiers in the front corners of the wet moat that covered part of the front of the moat and a flank. It also included a glacis around the front and sides, a characteristic of most of the forts built after the 1870s. Like most of Brialmont's forts, this one also included firing positions for infantry along the ramparts where its main artillery turrets formed a line. In the rear, like in the other forts, there was a double traditor, which also served as the entrance to the fort. Rolling bridges[6] allowed access to the interior, a feature that later became common in French as well as Belgian fortifications.

The first-class forts included Oelegem, Koningskooikt, Gravenwezel and St. Katelijne-Waver. They were located on the southeastern and eastern front between Mechelen and a point east of Antwerp. Their garrisons were larger, usually numbering about 450 men instead of 300. Fort Oelegem was trapezoidal and similar to some of the second-class forts with the standard moat 40m to 50m wide and 2.5m deep. Like other forts of this class, it had two twin 150mm gun turrets, the standard number of other turrets and a couple of observation cloches. Most forts of both classes included a number of machine guns for close defence like the 57mm guns. The new forts were built east of the Scheldt because the defence of the other side of the river was not critical and the older fortifications sufficed. In August 1914, most of these newer forts had not been fully armed even though they had been completed.

The government approved General Brialmont's request to fortify Liège and Namur and block the main Franco-German invasion route in the mid-1880s. In the early 1880s, the only defences for those key positions in the Meuse valley had consisted of the old citadel at Namur and the citadel of Liège on the left bank and Fort Chartreuse on the right bank. Fort Chartreuse was an old fort with outward-facing bastions. The Dutch had rebuilt it in 1817 and improved the old citadel as part of the Wellington Barrier. The citadel stood at 110m above the Meuse and the fort at about 100m. Both dominated the surrounding countryside, but late in the century, neither was ready for modern warfare.[7]

While Brialmont prepared his plans for the new forts of the Meuse, he also worked with the Romanians on their fortifications of Bucharest and wrote about his views on the development of the high-explosive shell and the direction for modern fortifications. Some of his solutions and recommendations were accepted by many other military engineers possibly because he was the first to build concrete forts. Not everyone accepted his theories, however. At the turn of the century, Sir George Sydenham Clarke pointed out in his book *Fortification* that Brialmont's designs would not hold up under fire. Apparently influenced by Henri Mougin, Clarke favoured the concept of a concrete fort with a large buried concrete block with cupolas. Before the 1880s, Brialmont had designed brick forts with large redoubts as a final point of resistance for Antwerp. The redoubts were the largest masonry structures in his forts, the remainder of which mostly consisted of earthen ramparts and masonry caponiers and shelters. Brialmont modified the designs of the Antwerp forts in the 1870s and 1880s and he appears to have scrapped the idea of the exposed brick redoubt for the Meuse fortresses. Instead, he created a massive concrete subterranean redoubt with gun turrets, which, he thought, was an answer to the high-explosive shell. Although his new system put almost all of the elements of a fort underground, it still had infantry parapets on the surface. Clarke decried the 'Belgian Vauban's' entire arrangement, pointing out that it would fail because the garrison would have to rely on communications and technical equipment that might break down, leaving the men trapped underground without being able to accomplish anything. Although Clarke doubted that the technical problems could be overcome, his most valid criticism was that the infantry would be extremely vulnerable to exploding shells on the surface and that the concentration of the main weapons in turrets in 'the fort's central citadel' would suffer from heavy bombardment. Tragically, he was proved to be all too correct. When the French began arming their own forts with turrets, they dispersed them somewhat better. However, it was the Germans who found a more effective solution to the high-explosive shell and to the vulnerability of close concentration by creating the Feste.[8] Brialmont's 1880s generation of forts at Antwerp had an improved design since the main turrets formed a line instead of being concentrated around a central citadel. However, they were not built as concrete blocks and the concrete protection was added later. Most of his forts of the 1880s and 1890s were better suited for warfare prior to the 1880s.

When the government imposed limitations on Brialmont, he was forced to economize on the forts of the Meuse. The forts he built in 1880s were the first made of concrete. They were armed with the newest weapons and most also had armoured components. However, being the first of a modern generation of forts, they had some design failings. In addition, other nations had time to correct and improve the concrete mixture after these forts were built. Brialmont's large and small concrete forts tended to be either triangular or trapezoidal. The central citadel or massif was essentially a large concrete block. In large forts, the main turrets included one twin 150mm gun turret, two twin 120mm gun turrets and two turrets with a 210mm howitzer each. In small forts, they comprised a 150mm gun turret, two turrets mounting a single 120mm gun and one turret for a 210mm howitzer, all concentrated in this block. The central citadel was triangular in small forts and rectangular in the large ones. The main weapons were concentrated for reasons of economy rather than practicality. None of the turrets, except those for the 57mm guns, could retract. A single one-man retracting searchlight turret was located at the centre, the high point of the central massif, where it could light up the terrain around the fort at night. In the large forts, four 57mm gun turrets were located at the corners for local defence. In the smaller ones, there were three turrets. The triangular forts had a large double counterscarp casemate with 57mm guns and machine guns that covered the right and left flank ditches. The third side of the fort constituted the gorge, which included a caserne and other facilities on the scarp side and the entrance on the counterscarp side. Counterscarp galleries protected the ditches in both triangular and trapezoidal forts. The 57mm gun turrets near the gorge were mounted on the gorge caserne, which, in turn, was linked to the central citadel that was either triangular in small forts or a quadrilateral in large forts. A subterranean gallery led to the 57mm gun turrets at the front of the fort and to the double-counterscarp casemate.[9] The counterscarp was steep and revetted whereas the scarp was earthen.

The Brialmont forts were built between 1887 and 1892.[10] The reason the construction took so long is that it entailed the building of twelve forts at Liège and nine at Namur and required the hiring of specialized personnel who could not work on every site at the same time. The last of the concrete positions were poured in 1890 at the smaller forts like Fort Embourg. The extensive use of concrete was a new procedure and required new types of technicians. Once the excavation of a site was completed and the construction equipment and materials were delivered, production could begin. The concrete could not be poured continuously because the construction crews of the time did not have the equipment needed to work at night. The result was inadequately-bound layers, weaker than continuously-poured layers. The French, who began to build concrete forts later than the Belgians did, were able to pour their concrete continuously, creating a homogenous structure that held up much better to the stress of shelling. According to some authors, the Belgian concrete mix was also inferior to the French

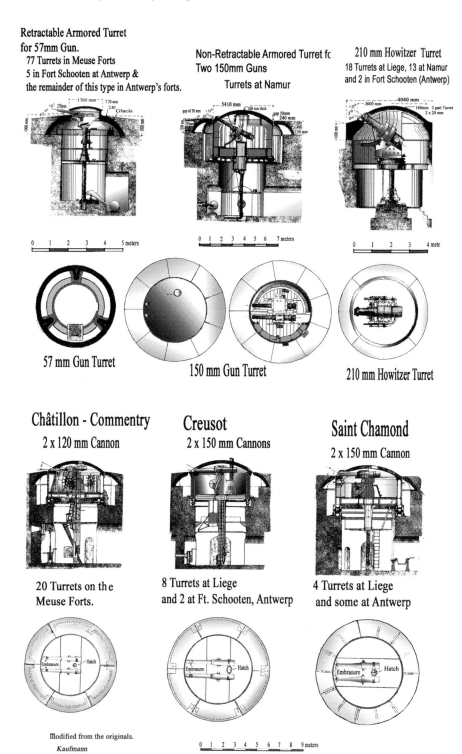

Retractable Armored Turret for 57mm Gun.
77 Turrets in Meuse Forts
5 in Fort Schooten at Antwerp &
the remainder of this type in Antwerp's forts.

Non-Retractable Armored Turret fc Two 150mm Guns
Turrets at Namur

210 mm Howitzer Turret
18 Turrets at Liege, 13 at Namur and 2 in Fort Schooten (Antwerp)

57 mm Gun Turret

150 mm Gun Turret

210 mm Howitzer Turret

Châtillon - Commentry
2 x 120 mm Cannon

Creusot
2 x 150 mm Cannons

Saint Chamond
2 x 150 mm Cannon

20 Turrets on the Meuse Forts.

8 Turrets at Liege and 2 at Ft. Schooten, Antwerp

4 Turrets at Liege and some at Antwerp

Modified from the originals.
Kaufmann

Various types of turrets used in Belgium and The Netherlands.

or German mixes during the First World War.[11] This, however, had been uncharted territory for Brialmont who was the first to have to determine how thick to make the walls and roofs to withstand bombardment. He set the standards based on testing done with 220mm weapons, the largest available to the French and Germans in the 1880s. In 1887, he failed to anticipate larger weapons.[12] Thus, he concluded that the concrete thickness had to be 1.2m for unexposed walls and 2.5m for exposed walls and roofs, which was adequate for the 1880s and the early 1890s. However, improvements in artillery quickly changed the picture. Reinforced concrete, which was part of the answer to the new development, was used in all major structures from the late 1890s on, but it was too late for Brialmont's forts.[13]

Before he selected turrets for his forts, Brialmont ordered the testing of both German and French types at Bucharest, Romania, in the mid-1880s. Although he thought that the French turrets stood up better to the ordnance, he ultimately selected Grüson turrets for the 57mm guns, the 150mm guns and the 210mm howitzers. He did choose the French St. Chamond and Châtillon turrets for the 120mm and some of the 150mm gun turrets. Except for the Swedish-designed 57mm Nordenfeldt gun, all the artillery pieces came from Krupp.

Brialmont's forts were completed in 1891 and 1892. They had almost everything they needed for independent operation including kitchens, latrines, medical facilities, food and ammunition stores and a powerhouse for supplying electricity for the machinery. Unfortunately, some facilities were located in vulnerable areas.[14] The garrisons numbered up to 400 men, comprising 300 artillerymen, over eighty infantrymen and various specialists. The forts also included infantry positions on the surface to repel assaults if the enemy should reach the counterscarp. As Clarke pointed out, these soldiers would be exposed to enemy artillery while taking up positions on the parapets. Even the German Feste had infantry positions with concrete trenches, but these were not concentrated around their fort's artillery. The Belgians had shelters behind the scarp for the troops that manned the ramparts, but no covered walkway to lead to their firing positions. An even more serious problem in the forts of the Meuse was that they did not have observation cloches or observatories. Observation from the forts could only be done through turret embrasures or from a position on the parapets. Observatories were placed up to 3km in front of the forts, but they would be of little value once the enemy reached them.

The ring of Liège had a circumference of about 46km and its forts were up to 9km from the city bridges whereas at Namur, it was 39km with forts no further than 8km from the city limits. That left a gap of over 3.8km between some of the Fortress Liège forts. At Namur, on the other hand, the gap between some forts was greater, leaving large tracts between forts unprotected unless they were covered by troops and field artillery.

After 1905, the Russo–Japanese War gave military leaders much food for thought on the subject of defences. As a result, the Belgians set up networks of barbed wire, using wooden posts, at the base of the fort glacis. In October 1912, Belgian military officials attended artillery testing of turrets at Ochakov, Russia, on the mouth of the Dnieper. A French turret mounted on a position similar to the Brialmont forts was fired upon with various calibre rounds. The 150mm rounds broke up the non-reinforced concrete, jamming the turret. The 280mm rounds inflicted even greater damage to the concrete and popped the turret out of its well. The cast-iron glacis armour was unable to hold up once the concrete was displaced. The Belgian military engineers realized that they would have to add reinforced concrete to the glacis. This work, however, was not done in time for the next war.

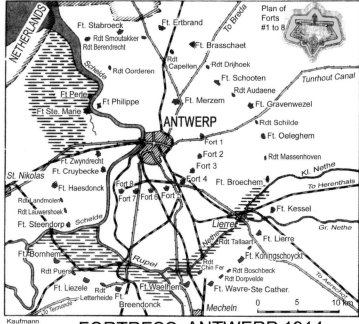

FORTRESS ANTWERP 1914

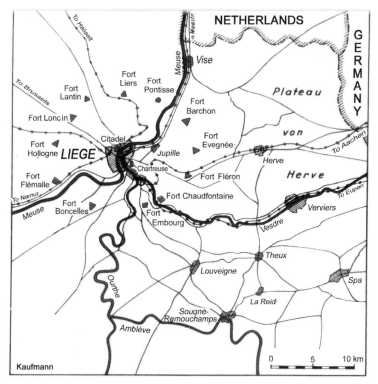

FORTRESS LIEGE 1914

The Great War

When the German army mobilized on its western frontier in August 1914, both the Dutch and Belgians became concerned. Armed neutrality appeared to be the best option, but the Germans had already formulated their plans and Belgium was the main target for the initial phases of the offensive that was intended to sweep through the valley of the Meuse and reach the French border. The Belgian army was poorly equipped and its forts were not designed to resist the new 420mm weapons.

General Gérard Leman commanded the 3rd Division and Fortress Liège with a total of 36,000 men, about 5,000 of which were tied to the defence of the forts. The intervals between the forts were insufficiently protected. General Otto von Emmich, who had the mission to take Liège with an assault force of almost 60,000 troops detached from the Second Army, crossed the border on 4 August, the day after the declaration of war on Belgium. On 4 August, three of Emmich's six infantry brigades and three cavalry brigades approached Fortress Liège with the intention of encircling the fortress. Belgian resistance held up the German cavalry before they reached the fortress perimeter and they were unable to cross the Meuse that day. That evening, German infantry moved against the fortress line as the supporting artillery bombarded Forts Pontisse, Barchon, Evegnée and Fléron. Searchlights from the forts illuminated masses of German infantry tangled in the wire obstacles of the glacis and the trenches of the intervals during the night engagement. When the fighting came down to hand-to-hand combat, the infantry companies that formed part of the fort garrisons proved to be invaluable.[15] According to a possibly exaggerated estimate, the Germans lost 10,000 men that night. On 5 August, German troops concentrated on the interval trenches held by the Belgian 3rd Division and broke through gaps in the fortress ring on both sides of the Meuse. Even though their losses continued to mount, the German troops reached Liège after breaking through additional interval gaps that night. As the Citadel fell on 6 August and the interval defences continued to melt away, General Leman escaped from his command post in the city to Fort Loncin. At that point, he ordered the 3rd Division to join the still-mobilizing army to the west and to leave the Liège forts to their own devices. When the city of Liège surrendered on 7 August, the Germans had suffered almost 42,700 casualties and not a single fort had fallen. On 8 August, the German artillery continued to pound the forts until the 210mm howitzers damaged the turrets and the concrete of the central massif of Fort Barchon, forcing its commander to surrender several hours later. German 280mm weapons bombarded Fort Evegnée on 11 August, badly damaging it and putting all its artillery out of action by the end of the day, which forced its commander to surrender as well.

Meanwhile, on 11 August, a battery of 420mm Krupp Mörsers, Germany's secret weapon, moved into position and opened fire the next day.[16] The guns pounded the already damaged Fort Pontisse until it surrendered on 13 August. On 13 August, Fort Chaudfontaine, under heavy artillery bombardment, drove off one infantry assault with the assistance of Fort Embourg. Resistance lasted until its magazine blew up, killing over 100 men and wounding almost half of the garrison. Its surrender was soon followed by that of Fort Embourg. Fort Fléron began to suffer crippling damage as well and during the night, German combat engineers moved close enough to pummel it with mortars. On 14 August, it lost its power supply, all its turrets were knocked out and, like in other forts, its ventilation system was unable to handle the foul air and poisonous fumes from exploding shells and local fires. Its commander had no option but to

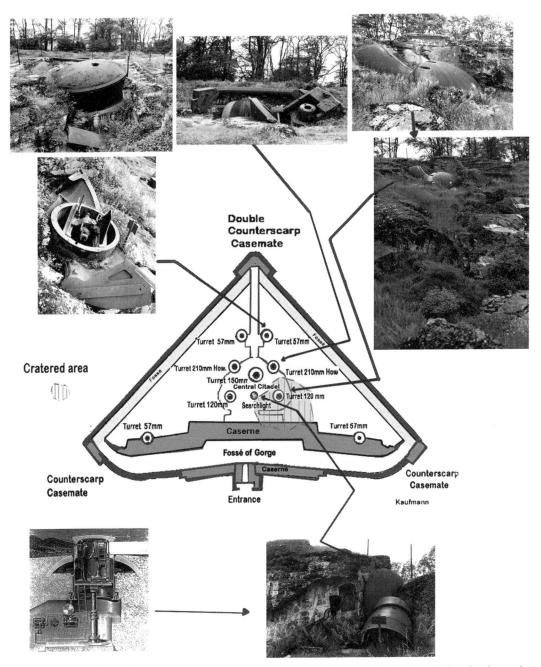

Plan of Fort Loncin at Liège showing damage from explosion of the magazine during the bombardment in 1914. (*Authors*)

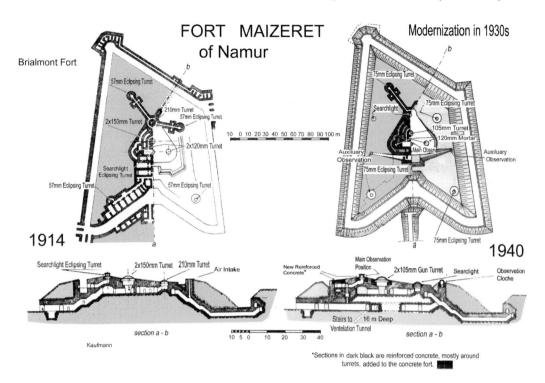

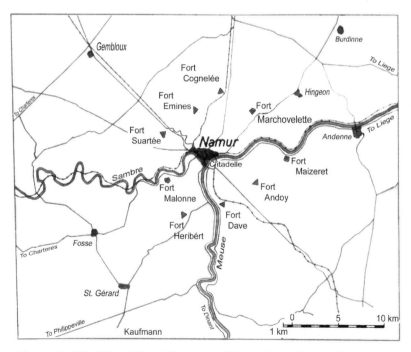

Map of Fortress Namur in 1914. Plan of Fort Maizeret in 1914 and plan showing its modernization in the 1930s.

raise the white flag early in the morning. Fort Boncelles surrendered in the morning and Fort Lantin at about noon on 15 August. Both garrisons were exposed to chocking fumes like the men at Fléron. The Germans moved the 420mm Mörser battery to a new position after the fall of Fort Pontisse and targeted Fort Loncin late that afternoon. One round detonated the fort's magazine, destroying much of the central massif and most of its turrets and killing over half of the garrison. According to legend, General Leman was pulled from the rubble unconscious and taken prisoner. On 16 August, Forts Flémalle and Hollogne yielded at about 7 a.m. after their commanders were convinced that resistance was futile.[17]

The forts were unable to withstand a concentrated bombardment even from the type of guns they were designed to resist. The 'Big Berthas' destroyed their ventilation systems and smashed through their concrete roofs. Without proper ventilation, fumes from sewage and explosions badly fouled the air making it even more difficult for the garrisons to fight. At the same time, the turrets became inoperable or they were destroyed by additional hits. Upon hearing the news of the events at Liège, the French concluded that their own forts would be as vulnerable as the Belgian ones had been. Thus, the order went out to abandon the French forts and use them as support facilities until it was discovered during the Battle of Verdun in 1916 that they were better built than the Brialmont forts had been and that they could actually take quite a beating.

On 18 August, the German troops swept up the Meuse reaching the fortress ring of Namur where two corps of the Second Army carried out the assault. The Belgian 4th Division had been assigned to hold the fortress with 37,000 men. The German super-heavy artillery arrived and on 21 August and joined the bombardment of Fort Maizeret, which had begun on the previous day. The fort was reduced by the next day. Forts in other parts of the ring were also bombarded between 22 and 24 August and they went down one by one. The 3rd Division pulled out on 23 August and Forts Cognolée and Marchovelette succumbed that day as well. Forts Héribert, Emines and Andoy lasted until 24 August and Fort Dave one more day.

The German bombardment of the Meuse forts created havoc in their gorge casernes, preventing the garrison from using the facilities in the counterscarp, which had no protected access. Most of the latrines were also in the counterscarp section of the gorge. The windows of the caserne in the gorge were additional weak points. Brick chimneys did not last long and the primitive ventilation system was unable to handle the requirements of the garrison in combat.

Antwerp lasted longer, not because of its strength, but because the German armies invading Belgium were hastening toward the French frontier intent on turning the French left flank. The Belgian King ordered 65,000 troops of the army located between Antwerp and Liège to join the 80,000 defenders of the National Redoubt after the fall of Liège. Brussels fell on 20 August since it was largely undefended. On 25 and 26 August, the Belgians launched an attack from Fortress Antwerp against the German flank hoping to slow their advance against the French. General Victor Deguise (1855–1925) was appointed commander of Fortress Antwerp on 6 September. Another sortie began on 9 September and ended after five days, attracting the attention of the German First Army. The Germans brought back the heavy artillery consisting of four 420mm howitzers and five 305mm mortars from the French border to begin bombarding the forts of Antwerp on 28 September. On 3 October, the British Royal Naval Division began massing at Antwerp to help the defenders.

Frobenius on the Forts of 1914

The renowned German military historian Herman Frobenius (1841–1916), a retired colonel of the Prussian army, was one of the most respected military historians and theorists at the beginning of the twentieth century.[18] In an article for *Kriegstechnische Zeitschrift* (Jan–Feb 1915 issue) that was summarized and translated in the *International Military Digest Quarterly* of 1915, he wrote that in 1914,

> At Namur the Germans brought up 32 modern siege pieces, which were placed in two groups at about 3 miles from the Belgium lines. These hammered away at a single sector of the defences and were themselves well out of range of the heaviest Belgian ordnance. The garrison clung to the trenches for protection without being able to answer the fire. It is an actual fact that Fort Maizeret only fired 10 rounds. It was struck by 1,200 shells, fired at a rate of 20 a minute. This fort was on the left bank of the Maas. On the right bank and forming the northeastern sector were forts Cognelée and Marchevolette. Against these were directed the fire of the 42 cm. howitzers and the Austrian 12' [305mm] mortars. Fort Suarlée at the northwest front was shelled from Aug 23 in the morning until it capitulated at 5 p.m. Aug 25. Three heavy batteries delivered against the work 3,500 shells.
>
> The siege progresses as follows: On Aug 21 the infantry moved against the outer lines and drove in all outposts. The fire of the forts slackened on Aug 22 when the heavy siege guns began to open up. On Aug 23 the infantry moved forward and the smaller field guns engaged the lines of communication between the forts. The artillery attack reached its height on 24th and Fort Maizeret surrendered. On the 25th the infantry pushed up between the forts and into the city. Five forts were silenced and the city fell on the 26th with the surrender of the last four forts. About 26,000 of the garrison escaped the city, but were captured at Bois-les Villers. This was the first appearance of the 42 cm. howitzers.

German infantry moved against Maubeuge on 27 August and by 3 September advanced to within 2km of the French defences. They waited for the heavy artillery to go into action against the fortifications. After the bombardment began, the artillery reduced three forts on 6 September. On 8 September the city capitulated and 40,000 men became prisoners.

> The principal events of the siege were investment, bringing up heavy artillery, bombardment of the forts, forward movement of the infantry, attack on the intervals and eventual penetration of these points. The rapidity with which each phase followed the other is largely due to the superior range of the German guns.

Frobenius concluded, 'the fortress is and always will be an easy mark for the artillery so long as the garrison permits the enemy's guns to approach within effective range and so long as they continue to offer conspicuous targets'. Apparently, the Germans and French took heed of his warning between World Wars by building more dispersed and less conspicuous fortifications while the Belgians did so to a lesser degree.

[Source: Herman Frobenius, 'Permanent – Experience With Europe's War' ('The Fortress in the Present War') *International Military Digest Quarterly* Volume 1 (1915).].

Meanwhile, the Germans began cracking the line of forts south of the Nethe on the southeast side of the outer fortress ring between Mechelen and Lierre. Hits by a 420mm howitzer caused the evacuation of Fort Wavre-St. Catherine on 29 September. Fort Walhem surrendered on 1 October, after enduring a pounding from heavy artillery. Fort Koningshooikt, one of the first-class forts with 450 men, which had been strengthened to resist 280mm rounds, was targeted with Skoda 305mm mortars beginning 28 September. On 30 September, the 420mm howitzers joined in the bombardment delivering two hits on ammunition magazines on 1 October, which forced the evacuation of the fort the next day. Fort Lierre also fell. On 4 October, 420mm and 305mm guns battered Fort Kessel with over 120 rounds and destroying the 150mm turret. The garrison evacuated the fort before it was destroyed by additional hits. On 5 October, German forces broke through at the town of Lierre, triggering the beginning of the collapse of the defences of Antwerp as the gap widened with the fall of Fort Broechem on 7 October. In the morning of 8 October, the Germans began bombarding Fort 4 and in the afternoon, Forts 3 and 5. Although damage was limited, much of the garrison of Fort 4 fled, leaving 200 British troops behind. Additional British troops joined the defenders of Fort 3 while troops at Fort 5 were in a state of panic. Meanwhile, the Germans redirected their artillery on Antwerp. The next day, only Fort 1 and Fort 6 of the inner line had not been abandoned during the night. Thus, by the dawn of 9 October, the Belgians had abandoned the defences of the right bank of the Scheldt and had blown up several of their forts including Forts Schooten, Brasschaat and Merksem. The bombardment of the city finally ceased and negotiations began. The news caused the garrison of Fort 6 to flee before the official surrender took place on 10 October. About 75,000 troops got away before the capitulation. The army withdrew west of the Scheldt while 33,000 troops, many from the garrisons of the forts, escaped to the Netherlands where they were interned. About 9,000 Belgian soldiers died in the defence of Antwerp, 15,000 were wounded and 40,000 were taken prisoner. The Germans incurred fewer losses because, after their initial assault on the Liège forts, they learned that it was best to first reduce the forts with heavy artillery and let the enemy take the heavy casualties.

The 'Big Bertha' in Action

The 420mm weapon was developed secretly before the war. By August 1914, the Krupp factories had produced several of these weapons. Originally, these guns had been designed for naval coastal defence artillery. The first of this type, the Gamma Gun, required six railway cars to carry its components, which weighed a total of 175 tons and one wagon for the auxiliary equipment. A railway spur, if not already present, had to be built at its firing position. Assembling the gun alone took thirty-six hours. A lighter version, the 'M' model built in 1913 and nicknamed the 'Big Bertha' (Dicke Bertha), had a range of about 9km compared to the Gamma's 14.5km. The effective ranges of these two guns were about 5km and 8km respectively, but the Gamma was more accurate. Since they were naval weapons, they were identified as Kurz Marine Kanone (KMK or Short Naval Cannon). They formed batteries commanded by army captains who were also technicians who had trained with these weapons at the Krupp Meppen range at Kummersdorf. An 'M' battery consisted of two guns with 200 men from the Prussian Foot Artillery and 80 drivers and mechanics. The 'M' guns (Big Berthas) were moved in ten tractor-pulled wagonloads, which made them more mobile than the Gammas were. The Gamma Guns, identified as Eisenbahn or railway guns, formed two-gun batteries and a third piece formed a half battery. By August 1914, three of these batteries were ready: Battery 1 with two Gamma Guns under Captain Ferdinand Eugene Solf (1876–1928), Battery 2 with two Gamma Guns under Captain Heinrich E. Becker (1879–1940),[20] and Battery 3 with two 'M' guns under Captain Erdmann.[21]

In a lecture about his experiences of September 1914, Captain Karl Becker mentioned the effectiveness of his battery, KMK 2, when it first went into action at Antwerp. Solf's more mobile battery of Big Berthas had already been in action at Liège since August while the Gamma Gun batteries had waited for the railway lines to become operational. Becker's battery arrived outside Antwerp's fortress ring in September and went into action on 29 September against Fort Wavre St. Catherine.

> I had fired a few rounds at the fort for adjustment. On the morning of the 29th I fired with the second piece … at the heavy guns in the armored cupolas, while using the first piece against the concrete casemates … [I] directed the telescope upon the air just above the target; with a little practice the shell could be picked up in the air and the impact itself observed. On this day, I saw my eleventh shot strike fair upon the top of the cupola, where the enemy's guns were actively firing. There was a quick flash, which we learned at Kummersdorf to recognize as the impact of steel upon steel. Then an appreciable pause, during which the cupola seemed uninjured; then a great explosion. After a few minutes the smoke began to clear and in the place of the cupola we saw a black hole, from which dense smoke was still pouring. Half the cupola stood upright, 50 metres away the other half had fallen to the ground. The shell, fitted with a delayed action fuse, had exploded inside. When I visited the fort later, I found a clear round hole in the part of the cupola that had been thrown to one side, punched out by the projectile …
>
> A little later, I got another clean hit on the same fort, which exploded the magazine. A cloud of smoke shot up a thousand metres; numerous small explosions followed and the whole fort took fire.

Next, his battery was assigned to fire on Fort Koningshooikt, which had been shelled by four Austrian Skoda 305mm mortars for two days, but whose 'concrete work was not materially injured and the turrets were intact'. Becker's Gammas soon put the fort's two 150mm gun turrets out of action. When he inspected the fort, he noticed that 'both turrets were jammed by injuries to the concrete work.' Later, it took Krupp mechanics several days to restore the turrets. The 420mm batteries also spread their devastation to the forts of Namur and Maubeuge.

[Sources: Becker, 'The 42-cm Mortar: Fact and Fancy', *The Field Artillery Journal* (1922); Ley, 'German Siege Guns of the Two World Wars', *Coast Artillery Journal* (Jan/Feb 1943); and Rottgardt, *German Armies' Establishments 1914/18* (2010).]

During the war, the Germans occupied a number of the Belgian forts of Liège and Namur, added concrete to some of the weaker sections, rebuilt the posterns for better defence and improved the ventilation of the forts. They had no interest in restoring the gun turrets. Later, the Belgians took advantage of these improvements.[19]

Antwerp and the German Defence against Invasion 1916–18

Occupied Belgium was not secure enough for the Kaiser's Army not to fear an Allied masterstroke that could collapse the entire Western Front. Despite the incompetence evidenced by the Allied leaders during the fiasco at Gallipoli, the German High Command considered the possibility an Allied attack directed through Dutch territory against Antwerp.

A little over a hundred years earlier, in July 1809, British forces landed on Walchern Island and South Beveland. The goal was to strike at the defences of Antwerp, which were weak, according to most reports of the period. The campaign bogged down during the month of August. The British forces on Walchern suffered so heavily in the flooded and unhealthy conditions that a quick move on Antwerp had to be cancelled and the invasion force had to withdraw. In 1916, neither the bloody battle of Verdun nor the Allied offensives on the Somme broke the stalemate on the Western Front. The Germans realized that they had no way of breaking the stalemate, but they thought the Allies did because they believed that the Dutch would not resist any Allied landing at the mouth of the Scheldt. They concluded, therefore, that despite the lethargy shown at Gallipoli, the British could quickly assemble their forces and strike at Antwerp thus turning the German flank and causing the Western Front between the sea and the Ardennes to collapse. To prevent this disquieting scenario from taking place, they began the construction of a line of bunkers stretching from the North Sea at Knokke to Turnhout. At the time, their army engineers were working on the Hindenburg Line on the Western Front. In addition to trenches and shelters, both lines were to include concrete bunkers instead of wooden blockhouses and other large forts as key resistance positions not easily overcome.

The position along the Belgian frontier is often called the 'Holland Stellung' and can be divided into sectors, one of which was given the same name. The German army and navy built most of the bunkers in 1917. According to Dutch historian Hans Sakkers, Johan den Hollander and Ruud Murk, authors of *De Hollandstellung* give the following details for the bunkers built by the army:

- Hollandstellung (from Zwin to Antwerp) – 411 bunkers.
- Stellung Antwerp – 830 bunkers.
- Turnhoutkanalstellung (along the Turnhout Canal) – 132 bunkers.

The navy built their bunkers by pouring concrete into a form, while the army preferred using prefabricated concrete blocks. Some bunkers served as troop shelters, others were for machine guns and observation. Their designs were based on a set of standards established by the army engineers, much like in the 1930s and 1940s.

The exposed sections of the bunkers were up to 1m thick, while the other sides were about 0.5m or less. The ceilings were from 0.6–0.8m thick. Rails reinforced the roofs and a sheet metal layer prevented spalling of the concrete. The bunkers had double sets of armoured doors, apparently for gas protection. Some bunkers were specifically designed for an artillery piece; others had embrasures for machine guns and rifles. After the war, the Belgian military gave the bunker types different designations and reused many of them in the 1930s. Those with an armoured plate included the Type IX infantry observation bunker, the Type X command bunker and the Type XIV artillery observation bunker. Type I and II bunkers served as storage units. Type III was a small, simple infantry observation bunker and Type XII was meant for artillery observation, but had no armour. Type IV

The Holland Position. In 1917 the Germans constructed a line of bunkers from Turnhout to the North Sea as protection against a British landing in neutral territory to strike at the German flank. Top photo is a hole large enough for an observer to put his head through. The cover is partially closed. Some of these bunkers were used by the Belgians in the next war. (*Authors*)

and V were machine-gun bunkers. Type VI, a shelter for small weapon crews, was the most common kind of bunker. Type VII, a large crew shelter, was built in small numbers. Type VIII, one of the rarest, mounted 75mm guns taken from the forts. Type XVII was a communications bunker.

The forts of Antwerp – Ste Marie, St Philippe and La Perle, which had been reinforced – on the lower Scheldt had some importance because they had a role in coastal defence. Fort St Philippe included a turret for two 280mm howitzers, two turrets for two 240mm howitzers each and positions for six 150mm cannons. Fort Ste Marie had an armoured battery of six 240mm howitzers. The fort also mounted sixteen 150mm cannons and twenty-four 57mm guns. Fort La Perle had four 240mm howitzers and twelve 150mm cannons. Turrets like those at Fort St Philippe had been in the plans. The Germans stripped many of Antwerp's forts of their turrets and weapons. All the forts of the inner and outer rings included 31 turrets for 150mm guns, 30 for 120mm guns, 112 for 75mm guns and 55 for 57mm guns before the Germans attacked.

[Source: Sakkers, et al. *De Hollandstelling*; *Denkschrift Antwerpen und Reduit National* (15 March 1940; correspondence with Frank Philippart).]

Forts and Redoubts of Antwerp

Forts & Redoubts Turrets & Cloches	280mm Turret	240mm Turrets	210mm Turrets	150mm Turrets	120mm Turrets	75mm Turrets	57mm Turrets	Obsv. Cloche
Ft. Stabroeck				1	2	4	4	4
Rdt. Smoutakker						1		
Ft. Ertbrand				1	2	4	2	4
Ft. Cappellen				1	2	4	4	2
Ft. Braschaet				1	2	4	2	4
Rdt. Dryhoek						1		
Ft. Schooten			2	2			5	3
Rdt. Audaen						1		
Ft. Gravenwezel				2	2	6	4	2
Rdt. Schilde						1		
Ft. Oeleghem				2	2	6	2	2
Rdt Massenhoven						1		
Ft. Broechem				1	2	4	2	4
Ft. Kessel				1	2	4	2	4
Ft. Lierre				3	3		4	2
Rdt. Tallaert						1		
Ft. Koningshoyckt				2	2	6	2	2
Ft. Chemin de Fer				1			2	
Rdt. Boschbeek						1		
Rdt. Dorpvelde						1		
Ft. Wavre-St. Cat.				2	2	6	4	2

Forts & Redoubts Turrets & Cloches	280mm Turret	240mm Turrets	210mm Turrets	150mm Turrets	120mm Turrets	75mm Turrets	57mm Turrets	Obsv. Cloche
Ft. Waelhem				3			4	2
Ft. Breendonck				1	2	4	2	4
Rdt. Letterheide						1		
Ft. Liezele				1	2	4	2	4
Rdt. Puers						1		
Ft. Bornhem				1	1	4	6	4
Ft. Steendorp				1		2		2
Rdt. Lauwershoek						1		
Rdt. Landmolen						1		
Ft. Haesdonck				1	2	4	2	4
Ft. Merxem						2		
Fort 1								
Fort 2						2		
Fort 3				1		2		
Fort 4						2		
Fort 5						2		
Fort 6						2		
Fort 7						2		
Fort 8								
Rdts. 1–18						18		
Battery South						2		
Ft. Cruybeke								
Ft. Zwyndrecht								
Rdt. Berendrecht				1				
Battery 1								
Battery 2								
Battery 3								
Ft. Lillo								
Rdt. Corderen				1				
Ft. St. Philippe	1	2						
Ft. Ste. Marie								
Ft. La Perle								
Ft. Liefkensnoek								

Forts & Redoubts Artillery Pieces	290mm 280mm Howtz.	240mm 210mm Howtz.	210mm Mortar	150mm Guns	120mm Guns	120mm Howtz.	75mm Guns	57mm Guns
Ft. Stabroeck				2	4	2	8	16
Rdt. Smoutakker						4	5	
Ft. Ertbrand				2	4	2	8	14
Ft. Cappellen				2	4	2	8	12
Ft. Brasschaet				2	4	2	8	14
Rdt. Dryhoek						4	5	
Ft. Schooten		2 ****		4	4		4	17
Rdt. Audaen						4	5	
Ft. Gravenwezel				4	4	2	10	16
Rdt. Schilde						4	5	
Ft. Oeleghem				4	4	2	10	14
Rd Massenhoven						4	5	
Ft. Broechem				2	4	2	8	14
Ft. Kessel				2	4	2	8	14
Ft. Lierre				6	4	3	4	16
Rdt. Tallaert						4	5	
Ft.Koningshyckt				4	4	2	10	14
Ft.Chemin de Fer				2	4		4	8
Rdt. Boschbeek						4	5	
Rdt. Dorpvelde						4	5	
Ft.Wavre St. Cat.				4	4	2	10	16
Ft. Waelhem				6	26		4	4
Ft. Breendonck				2	4	2	8	14
Rdt. Letterheide						4	5	
Ft. Liezele				2	4	2	8	14
Rdt. Puers						4	5	
Ft. Bornhem				2	4	1	8	18
Ft. Steendorp				2	16		6	8
Rdt Lauwershoek						4	5	
Rdt. Landmolen						4	5	
Ft. Haesdonck				2	4	2	8	14
Ft. Merxem					22		2	6
Fort 1					30			6
Fort 2					30		2	6
Fort 3				2	30		2	4
Fort 4					30		2	4
Fort 5					23		2	6
Fort 6					30		2	6
Fort 7					23		2	6
Fort 8					30			8
Redoutes 1 – 18							18	108
Battery South					4		2	1

Forts & Redoubts Artillery Pieces	290mm 280mm Howtz.	240mm 210mm Howtz.	210mm Mortar	150mm Guns	120mm Guns	120mm Howtz.	75mm Guns	57mm Guns
Ft. Cruybeke					16			10
Ft. Zwyndrecht					30			6
Rdt. Berendrecht				2	4		4	
Battery 1								
Battery 2	4*							
Battery 3		4***						
Ft. Lillo				4				
Rdt. Corderen			4	2	8			6
Ft. St. Philippe	2**	4***		6				
Ft. Ste. Marie		4***		16				
Ft. La Perle				12				24
Ft. Liefkensnoek					4			

*290mm. ** 280mm. *** 240mm. ****210mm.

Forts Weapons	Range	Barchon	Loncin, Flemalle, & Chfnt*	Hollogne, Fleron
Grüson turret, Krupp 210mm how.	6.9km	X		X
Grüson turret, Krupp 210mm how.	3.25km		X	
Creusot turret, 150mm Gun	5.7km	X	X	
Creusot-Vandekerchove 150mm Gun	8.5km			X
Châtillon turret, Krupp 120mm gun	5–8km	X		
Châtillon turret, Krupp 120mm gun	4.95km		X	
Châtillon turret 120mm gun	8km			X
Grüson turret, 57mm gun	3.37km	X	X	X

* Chaudfontaine

Chapter 4

Belgium Returns to Neutrality

Belgium Prepares, 1920–1940

For centuries, Flanders and much of modern-day Belgium have been a battleground, like Poland in the East in many ways since it has occupied a key position coveted and contested by its neighbours. As a new nation, it survived for a little less than a century without war until, in 1914, it became part of a conflict more devastating than any previous one in the history of the region. When the battle of Liège began, the Germans used the city as the first target for terror bombing by Zeppelins. That was only the beginning of a tragedy that turned Belgium into the Devil's playground. Some of the bloodiest battles fought on its soil, like Ypres, Messines Ridge and Passchendaele, are as infamous as Verdun. In addition, the German occupation was harsh and brutal. When the war ended, the Belgians and King Albert realized that neutrality did not mean security. In theory, the Versailles Treaty crippled Germany and prevented it from becoming a major military power again. However, the French, who helped write the treaty, were seeking retribution and the Belgian military leaders continued to fear a resurgence of German power. The French, convinced that the threat from Germany would resurface, began planning new defences for their borders in the 1920s. The Franco-Belgian Military Accord was signed in 1920, but the British were not interested in entering into a new alliance.[1] The Versailles Treaty awarded Belgium a slice of German territory that included Eupen, Malmédy and St Vith. In 1923, when the Germans were unable to make their reparations payments, the Belgians and the French occupied the Rhineland and the Ruhr.

In the early 1920s, General Henry H. Maglinse, the chief of staff of the army, wanted to cooperate with the French and rebuild Belgium's defences especially to cover the German border. Military and government officials were divided on the issue. In January 1926, General Émile Galet (1870–1940) replaced Maglinse and convinced the new Minister of Defence, Charles Broqueville (1860–1940),[2] to appoint a commission to study the problem of national defence later in the year. Similar events were taking place in France where study commissions had assembled earlier. While the French debates concluded with the resolution that the proposed Maginot Line[3] was the only way to defend France's border, the Belgian leaders argued about the strategy to pursue and the question of whether it was worthwhile to defend their border. General Galet opposed the idea of committing the army to the defence of the frontier from the day he began his tenure as chief of staff to the day he retired. He had concluded as early as 1926 that the best move in the face of overwhelming enemy superiority was for the Belgian army to make a fighting withdrawal toward the coast where it would join with a British contingent. Galet was appointed to the commission for the study of Belgian fortifications in 1930, but he could not favour the idea of static defences if it meant a sacrifice in proper equipment and modernization for the army. He agreed to border fortifications, but only if they were incorporated into a scheme of successive fortified lines that would allow a fighting retreat. The most economical method to achieve this would be to restore some of the old forts of Liège, Antwerp and Namur. The commission decided to build Fort Eben Emael at the same time as construction began on the new Albert Canal, which was not completed until 1939.[4] Actually, initial plans called for the construction of two forts to cover the flank of the Liège defences against a German assault through the Dutch Maastricht appendage. The second fort was to be at Pietersheim (Lanaken), a little less than 10km north of Eben Emael. Both forts were to have casemate artillery that created interlocking fires to cover the Albert Canal crossings sites effectively.

While the French began the construction of the Maginot Line in late 1929, the Belgians continued to study the question until 1931. They finally decided to rebuild the defences of the three major fortress cities and to add a new line. This resolution brought a strong political reaction because Broqueville, the defence minister at the time, was a member of the Flemish Catholic Party whose only opposition was the Liberal Party. Liberal leader Albert Devèze (1881–1959), who had been defence minister in the early 1920s and was still active in politics, got involved on behalf of the Walloon population. The proposed plans called for defending the industrial northern half of the nation, which was largely Flemish and included Liège and Namur that were Walloon. The southern part of Belgium – south and east of the Meuse – with its majority Walloon population would be left to the mercies of the enemy, whereas the Flemish areas would be the best protected. Devèze managed to bring about a compromise that included the creation of strongpoints in the Ardennes at Beho (near St Vith), Bastogne and Arlon. The army would also form several regiments of Chasseurs Ardennais to defend the region. Since this plan added to the expense, the idea of rearming the old forts of Antwerp was abandoned and the creation of bridgehead at Ghent was delayed. These two positions were part of General Galet's successive lines for retreat. At this time, the majority opinion appeared to be that the French would hasten to help the Belgians defend their border, especially since the French Maginot Line had been built only as far as Longuyon by 1932 and it would not cover the Belgian border.[5] Albert Devèze returned as defence minister in December 1932, serving until 1936 and General Galet retired in the same month. This led to a second phase in the development of the Belgian system of fortifications. Galet's deputy, General Prudent Armand Nuyten (1874–1954), took over as chief of staff at the time the construction of the new defences began. Like André Maginot of France, Devèze strongly advocated fortifying and holding the frontier. However, General Nuyten soon concluded that Galet had been right and that it would be impossible to hold the German frontier. Most of the military establishment agreed with him, so in May 1934, the debate with the government and Devèze took on new life. Nuyten insisted that the Belgian army was too small to hold the front and that the French army would not arrive in time. That month, Devèze gave Nuyten an ultimatum: conform to the government's strategy or resign. In October, Nuyten was reassigned as commander of II Corps, but he decided to retire. Ultimately, General Galet's viewpoints were vindicated.

Since General Eugène Cumont (1869–1945), who replaced Nuyten as chief of staff in 1934, shared Devèze's views, relations with the government proceeded more smoothly until 1935. Cumont intended to hold the frontier and even agreed with the defence minister on the necessity to create a mobile force, the Chasseurs Ardennais, to hold the south. He tried to coordinate with the French and even told them that he would need four French infantry divisions by the fourth day of the war to reinforce the troops that would hold the front before

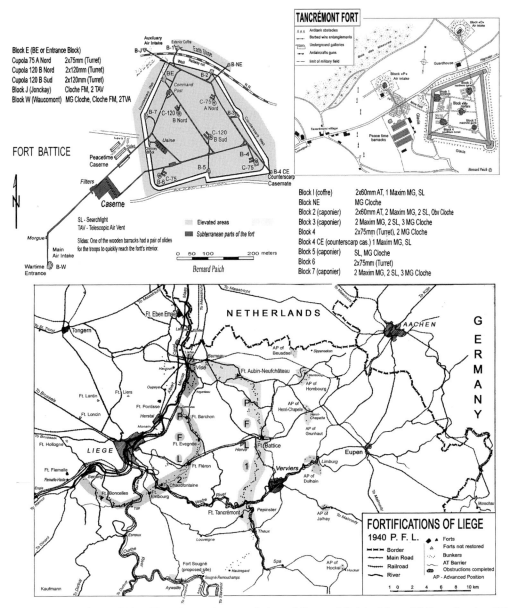

Plan of Fort Battice and Fort Tancrémont by permission of Bernard Paich. Map of Liège showing PFL (Fortified Positions of Liège) 1 and 2 in 1940.

Liège and the line of the Albert Canal. Even though plans on coordination were coming together, the Belgian army establishment remained divided. Early in 1936, after King Leopold ordered Cumont to put an end to the discord within the army, he replaced him with General Edouard van den Bergen who remained as chief of staff until 1940. Van den Bergen and his staff worked closely with the French in planning defensive operations to hold the fortified frontier until the king declared Belgium's return to neutrality in the autumn of 1936.

While the arguments raged during 1933, the Belgian army engineers were making a survey of the best locations for fortifications on the Herve Plateau.[6] The site of Fort Eben Emael had already been picked based on the construction of the Albert Canal in 1929 and planning for it was underway by 1932. In April 1933, as its construction began, work on Forts Battice and Tancrémont also received priority. During the first phase, when Galet led the army, the modernization of eight of the old forts of Liège was already underway. After Galet retired, plans were drawn up for three large and three small forts that would be used to form the core of the Position Fortifiée de Liège (PFL) 1. The construction of a fort at Lanaken was cancelled due to budget restrictions, but Devèze was more interested in creating new forts to extend the Liège bridgehead, which formed PFL 1. He showed no interest in modifying the plans for Eben Emael to make it more resistant to heavy artillery, but he agreed to increase the fort's offensive power by adding gun turrets. Since the memory of the tragic events of 1914 were still fresh in their memories, the Belgians had at first little faith in armoured turrets, but their attitude changed, possibly due to French influence.

Initially, the Belgians had planned to build two additional forts on the Herve Plateau at Mauhin and Les Waides, but in 1934, they decided to move one location from Mauhin to Aubin-Neufchâteau; prior to that, they cancelled plans for a fort at Les Waides. The two cancelled forts were to have two casemates for three 75mm guns each, like Fort Tancrémont. Ultimately, Fort Eben Emael became the only Belgian fort to have artillery casemates for 75mm guns, possibly because its construction had already begun. The planners had also considered building another fort at Sounge-Remouchamps further to the south of Liège to block the Amblève Valley, but Cumont concluded in 1934 that it would greatly increase costs and that the funds were needed to mechanize the forces that were going to cover the southern flank in the Ardennes.

By 1936, the work on the new fortifications and defence lines in Belgium was well under way. The government and military leaders committed themselves to making the eastern border with Germany their main line of defences where four new forts were under construction. The new fortified position of Liège would be backed up by a second line east of the Meuse where the old forts had been modernized. The main position stretched from Eben Emael, facing the Dutch border, across the Herve Plateau to the Amblève Valley. PFL 1 included three additional forts and bunkers built in the intervals. Behind it was a backup position following the old fortress ring on the east bank known as PFL 2. On the outside of PFL 2, a line of bunkers referred to as PFL 3 protected the Meuse bridges. On the west bank of the Meuse, two old forts had been modernized and a number of bunkers were built to form PFL 4, the final line of defence. Often PFL 3 and PFL 4 are considered part of PFL 2 even though PFL 3 is more closely related to PFL 1. Since the Germans were expected to attack through the Maastricht Appendage (the narrow strip of Dutch territory along the Maas River between Germany and Belgium), the small Belgian army needed several French divisions to come to its aid within a few days after the initial attack. The French, labouring under the delusion that the Ardennes was impassable to a modern army, thought that only light forces would be required to back up the Belgians. The Belgian defence of the Ardennes was to rest with two new mobile divisions of Chasseurs Ardennais and a few strongpoints. The Belgians established an advanced position in the Ardennes and in front of PFL 1 to give warning and delay an enemy advance. In 1937, they began the construction of brick buildings at the border that served as outposts for four men who would warn of approaching enemy forces by radio or telephone. In 1939, a concrete wall was added to these weak outposts in order to extend their viability for a little longer. Further behind the border, the advance position included nine strongpoints consisting of small, square machine-gun bunkers built in the mid-1930s. The largest strongpoint consisted of fourteen of these bunkers and the smallest of only two. Only two were built in the Ardennes. Their mission was to cover the southern approaches to the PFL to delay an enemy advance. In 1936, they became part of a plan to obstruct the routes into Belgium by buying time for the Belgian troops to carry out demolitions.

In addition to these positions, the Position Fortifiée de Namur (PFN) was created by reactivating and modernizing several old forts and adding interval bunkers. The same was done at Antwerp (PFA), but the modifications to the old forts were only minor. Some work was done on the fortified bridgehead at Ghent, which was, together with the PFA, a non-priority project and was de-funded with the compromise worked out by Devèze in 1933. After the autumn of 1936, the return to neutrality wrought major changes to the strategic planning and marked the beginning of the third and final phase of fortification development. The PFL could no longer be considered the only main line of defence. The army finally scrapped the project for a fort at Sougné-Remouchamps and used the funds to mechanize the Cavalry Corps. Since neutrality meant that there would be no French troops, the Belgian strategy reverted to Galet's defensive concept but Devèze's plans for strong border defence stayed in place albeit watered downed. Instead of consisting of three large and two small forts, PFL 1 was reduced by one large fort by eliminating the projected fort at Sougné and converting Tancrémont into a small fort.[7]

The Fortifications of Neutral Belgium, 1936–1940

King Leopold III, a young veteran of the Great War who had ascended the throne in February 1934, abruptly announced on 14 October 1936 that Belgium was returning to the status of neutrality and ending its military alliance with France.[8] This decision changed everything. The Belgian army was not large enough to hold the PFL and the Albert Canal Line even if it mobilized quickly. Between 1937 and 1940, unofficial planning continued, but the military realized that the King's neutrality policy would not allow French or British troops to enter the country until after a German invasion had begun, which meant that no Allied divisions would be there in time to hold the PFL and Albert Canal Line. The question was how far into Belgium the Allies could advance to make a difference once the Germans launched their attack. The Ghent Bridgehead and even the defences of Antwerp and Namur took on new importance. Until 1940, the French High Command wrestled with a decision on how to help Belgium. Beginning in 1936, the Maginot Line was extended to Villy, between Montmédy and Sedan. Four small Maginot forts were built onto the older forts of the old Maubeuge fortress ring. After the war broke out in 1939, the British and French built a large number of field fortifications, including bunkers, between Maubeuge and the sea. During 1939 and 1940, the French, who did not want the industrial centre of Lille to end up near the front lines, came up with two plans to occupy Belgium: Plan E and Plan D, which consisted of sending light forces of French mechanized cavalry divisions into the Belgian Ardennes. According to Plan E, which was the more modest of the two, the main Allied forces would move to the Escaut River (Belgian Scheldt River) line. The Belgians would fall back to their National Redoubt of Antwerp and to the Ghent Bridgehead. For this plan to work, the Belgians needed to

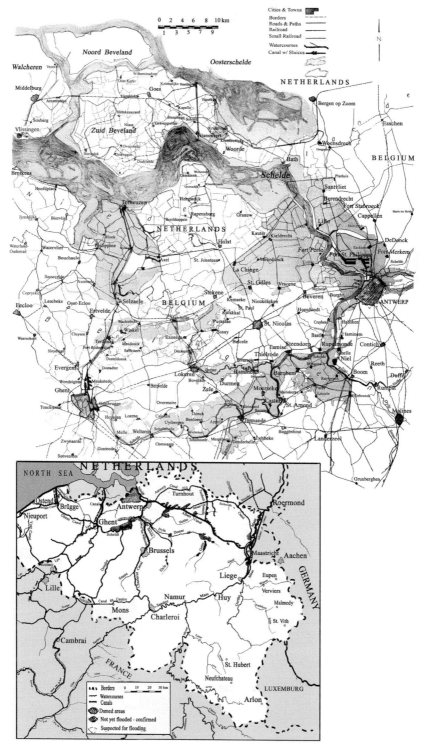

Map showing detailed area of Belgian National Redoubt with emphasis on the Scheldt River and areas believed to be subject to inundation. The National Redoubt was extended from Antwerp to Ghent in the 1930s.

Vise 1 Artillery Casemate

Mi-S Machine Gun Casemate (Germans inspecting)

VERTICAL SCHEMATIC

Artillery Casemate MA 1

MG Block South

MG Block North

Entrance Block

Albert Canal

Intermediate Level 20 Meters Deep
Includes CP and Munitions

Lower Level 40 Meters Deep
Includes Usine and Caserne

B-1 Entrance Block (after the fort fell)

Blocks	Weapons	Blocks	Weapons
B-1	2x60mm AT 3 Maxim MG	M-1	3x75mm GP
B-2	2x60mm AT 2 Maxim MG	M-2	3x75mm GP
		V-1	3x75mm GP
B-4	2x60mm AT 2xMaxim MG	V-2	3x75mm GP
B-5	1x60mm AT 2 Maxim MG	C-Nord	2x75mm Turret
		C-Sud	2x75mm Turret
B-6	2x60mm AT 1 Maxim MG	C-120	2x120mm Turret
Mi-N	3 Maxim MG	Ca-N	1x60mm AT 3 Maxim MG
Mi-S	3 Maxim MG	Ca-S	1x60mm AT 3 Maxim MG
		0-1	1x60mm AT 3x Maxim MG

Area covered by 75mm Casemate guns

Area covered by gun turrets

Areas covered MG

Area covered by MG & AT Gun

Fields of Fire for Close Defence

Fort Eben Emael

AT Obstacles ••••••
Wire Obstacles ×× ×× ××

A. Peace Time Caserne

Flooded Area

Kaufmann

0 20 60 100   200   300 m

Scale

Wartime photos of Fort Eben Emael and plan showing fields of fire.

prepare the old National Redoubt from Antwerp to Ghent. According to Plan D, formulated by General Gamelin early in 1940, the Allies would advance to the Dyle River where no major fortified line existed. However, this option would shorten the front and protect Brussels and a larger part of Belgium.[9] The problem was that the Belgians needed to create defences along the Dyle and in the Gembloux Gap between Wavre and Namur. The PFL and Albert Canal Line, where construction had proceeded unceasingly from 1937 until 1940, would become delaying positions.

The Fortified Position of Liège

The key to the Liège defences was PFL 1 with its four new forts. The Belgian government paid a large sum of money to create these modern forts and make them the centrepiece of their defences, but its policy of neutrality reduced their role to little more than an obstacle for delaying the enemy. Fort Eben Emael, the showpiece of the nation's protection, had the mission of interdicting a German advance through the Dutch Maastricht Appendage and anchoring the main line. Unlike most subterranean forts, Eben Emael had an impassable anti-tank obstacle formed by the steep sides of the Albert Canal where it cut through the limestone Mount Saint Peter.[10] It included two extensive subterranean levels below the combat blocks. The canal flowed 65m below the surface of the fort of the fort's eastern side and was 60m wide and 5m deep. Once the cut was completed, construction of the fort began in April 1932 and largely finished in 1935, but work continued on a wet anti-tank ditch on the northwest side, the installation of a radio, the improvement of the ventilation system and other details until 1940. Eben Emael, the largest of the Belgian forts, was often compared to the forts of the Maginot Line and was thought to be impregnable. However, it was built to resist only 280mm weapons, much less than the blocks of a Maginot fort could withstand. The underground galleries could stand up to more than that, but without combat blocks, the fort was useless.

Seventeen blocks, including two outside the main perimeter, on the surface of the fort served as the fighting element. The fort also had some internal defences. The main defensive weapons used in embrasures included several Maxim 08 machine guns taken from the Germans after the war and modified for the standard Belgian round. A lighter version, the Maxim 08/15 developed by the Germans during the war, was also used. These water-cooled machine guns required a special carriage for mounting in the forts. The Belgians used a reversible mount that held two machine guns mounted one above the other – the top gun in the firing position. It was rotated to switch guns when the barrel got too hot.[11] The weapons were mounted in the embrasures with a ball mount, which included an opening for the sight. The effective rate of fire was only 50 to 100 rounds per minute. The Belgians designed their own automatic rifle, the FM-30 (Fusil Mitrailleur Mle 1930) built by the Fabrique Nationale (FN) at Herstal near Liège. It could fire 600 rounds a minute but was adjusted to fire half that amount and had a range of 2km. The army used Belgian-built 47mm anti-tank gun FRC (Fonderie Royale des Canons) Model 1936 in some of the forts. A more powerful 60mm FRC Model 1936 anti-tank gun was used at Eben Emael and Battice. It had a ball mount that included an opening for the barrel and one for the sight. It fired both armour-piercing and high-explosive rounds.[12] The 75mm GP (Grande Porte – long range) cannon was a modification of a 1905 Krupp 75mm gun similar to that of the French with a rate of fire of about thirteen rounds a minute, but a range of up to 11km. It was used in the casemates of Eben Emael. The new forts had the Belgian 75mm

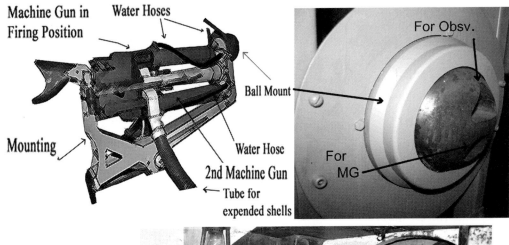

Photos of reversible Maxim machine gun used in many new and old forts. It mounted a pair of machine guns that were rotated with the bottom one coming into position when the top one became too hot. (*Andreas E. Schröder*)

FRC Model 1934 – actually, a Bofors model built under license – in their retracting turrets. In addition to its regular ammunition, it used a shell similar to canister that contained a couple of hundred lead balls, which was intended for close defence of the fort. The Fonderie Royale des Canons also produced the 120mm FRC Model 1931 for both Eben Emael and Battice that had a maximum range of 17km, but a low rate of fire averaging about one round a minute.

Finally, a distinctive weapon used in the forts and some interval positions for defence was the lance grenade.[13] It resembled a weapon used in the Maginot Line, but was simpler in design. It consisted of a tube placed at an angle through a casemate wall that had a cover that

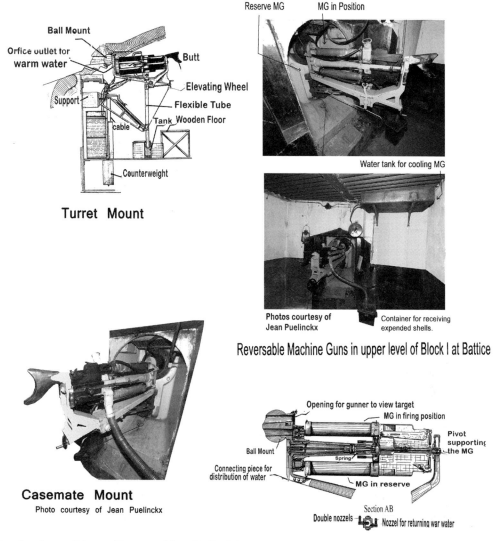

Details of reversible machine gun. (*Jean Puelinckx*)

opened on the inside. A Mills grenade was armed and dropped into the tube to fall to the base of the block and explode.[14]

Eben Emael is shaped like a slice of pie or a cut diamond with the apex at the north end along the canal. From that point, one side extends along the wall of the canal for almost 1km. A combat block, Canal Nord, is located in the wall of the canal, and at the south end there was another block (now gone), Canal Sud. A crew of twenty men manned each of these blocks. Canal Nord consists of two levels. At one time, it was armed with a machine gun on the right flank and a 60mm anti-tank gun on the left flank on the lower level and machine guns with a Cloche FM equipped with a flare gun for illumination on the upper level. Canal Sud was similar, but its anti-tank gun, searchlight and machine-gun positions were on opposite sides. Block 01, located at the top of the cut beyond Canal Sud, is a two-level block with an artillery observation cloche that used to be equipped with a periscope that had a direct view of the locks at Lanaye. Its armament included a 60mm anti-tank gun on its lower level and machine guns on both levels. There was a searchlight on the upper level. The block housed a crew of twenty-five men. At a point about 200m before Canal Sud, an anti-tank ditch with non-reinforced concrete walls extends for about 750m. It was defended by three combat blocks, at each turn and at its end. Block 4, which served as a caponier in the ditch, had a 60mm anti-tank gun on each flank on the lower level and searchlights and machine guns on the upper level covering the flanks and a small observation cloche. At the next turn is Block 5, which includes a 75mm gun turret – designated Cupola Sud – for offensive action. The lower level includes an embrasure on the right flank, meant for a 60mm anti-tank gun. The upper level has an embrasure for a machine gun and a searchlight and gives access to a small observation cloche. Block 6 is located at the end of the ditch and, like Block 5, it covers the left flank, but with two 60mm anti-tank guns on the lower level and a searchlight, a machine gun and a small observation cloche on the upper level.

The wet moat on the northwest side had concrete sides and was 6m deep, filled with water channelled from the Geer River. The river also served to inundate a large area between the moat and the northwest side of the fort. Block 2 covers the moat and the 300m between it and the entrance block with three sets of embrasures on each side for a machine gun, a 60mm anti-tank gun and a searchlight. A small observation cloche stands above an exit with armoured doors that were used to send out patrols.

The entrance block had two machine guns and two electric searchlights on the upper level and two 60mm anti-tank guns on the lower level. It also included a small one-man observation cloche. Like the French Maginot ouvrages and old Belgian forts, a rolling bridge in the entranceway slid into the wall behind the entrance gate for added protection. Further along the entrance tunnel, there are armoured doors and a defensive position with decontamination chambers next to it. The entrance leads directly to the caserne area with complete facilities for the troops, including a medical centre with an operating theatre and a dental surgery. Nearby, the subterranean galleries – up to 40m and 60m below the surface of the fort and on two levels – connected to the command post, engine room, filter rooms and all the blocks of the fort. Only Block 2 and Block 6 have exits for patrols around the sides of the fort; some of the others include emergency exits. The blocks covering the anti-tank ditch used to house twenty to twenty-eight men, except Block 5, which required only seventeen. Near the centre of the fort, the galleries ascend to a higher level reached by a stairway or lifts. This upper gallery, which housed the command post and ammunition magazines, gives access to the artillery and infantry blocks through an 18m to 20m shaft and by means of stairs and lifts in the artillery blocks. There are also internal blockhouses covering the corridors in case the enemy managed to reach the gallery.

Most blocks included latrines to eliminate one of the problems encountered in the Great War when they were situated only in the gorge caserne. The ventilation at Eben Emael was different from the other forts because of its unique location. Above the fort, a large cloche-like structure stood above the chimney block to expel foul air from the engine rooms and the kitchens. The air intakes were located at two points in the vertical wall of the canal cut.

Turret for 2 x 75mm Guns
Cupola Sud, Eben Emael

TURRETS, CLOCHES, and CASEMATES

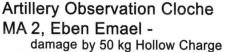

Cloche for Light MG
at Cupola Nord, Battice

Artillery Observation Cloche
MA 2, Eben Emael -
damage by 50 kg Hollow Charge

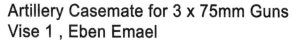

Artillery Casemate for 3 x 75mm Guns
Vise 1 , Eben Emael

Dome shaped Chimney Block

Only Eben Emael had artillery casemates and the dome type chimney block

(Photos by authors)

Photos of Eben Emael and turrets. (*Authors*)

Three of four artillery casemates are grouped on the southwest side of the fort. Block MA (Maastricht) 1 and MA 2 with three 75mm GP guns each with fields of fire covering the bridges on the canal up to Veldwezelt and the eastern approach to Maastricht. Even though the block's façades face toward the front, they are masked from direct view of the enemy by the elevated northern end of the fort. Facing in the opposite direction are blocks Vi (Visé) 2, near this group and Vi 1 near the canal side of the fort firing towards Visé and Fort Aubin-

Neufchâteau. The Germans would have had to penetrate PFL 1 to have a direct line of fire on the façades of these two blocks. Each artillery casemate had a crew of thirty-three men, except MA 2, which had three additional men for its observation cloche (Cloche Eben 3) that had a view towards Maastricht.[15]

Two blocks included a turret mounting two 75mm guns. Block 5, the caponier on the anti-tank ditch, included Cupola Sud. Cupola Nord, which was near the eastern end of the fort, included an exit to the surface of the fort for patrols. Each of these turret blocks had a crew of twenty-five men. Cupola 120 had the fort's heaviest weapons (two 120mm guns) and a crew of twenty-eight men, and was located closer to the centre of the fort. Its guns could fire beyond Fort Aubin–Neufchâteau and even reach the old forts of Barchon and Pontisse. Finally, two blocks for machine guns, located north of the artillery blocks, near the north-centre of the fort, had the mission to defend the surface of the fort with about fifteen men each. Mi (mitrailleuses – machine guns) Nord included two machine guns and two searchlights on the south side covering the area occupied by the artillery blocks, a machine gun on the opposite side covering the north section of the fort, which only included two dummy turrets, an observation cloche and an exit for patrols.[16] A 'V'-shaped earthen rampart from Mi Sud to Mi Nord and Visé 1 obstructed the view from the opposite side of the canal and created an obstacle. It included barbed wire, which was unusual since wire obstacles were absent from the other blocks on the fort's massif. Mi Sud had similar armament, in addition to a searchlight and machine gun on each of its three exposed sides, but it had no exit to the surface. Only one of its machine guns fired toward the artillery casemates; the other two covered the north part of the fort. The surface of the fort also included pits for four anti-aircraft machine guns and a service building manned by twenty-seven men, features not found on the French Maginot Line forts. These weapons could offer only limited protection, but they were in a position to cover much of the southern part of the fort's surface.

Eben Emael included various improvements upon the previous generation of forts. Its latrines were located at various points, including the blocks, instead of being in a single location. Its air circulation and filtration system was improved thanks to a more efficient method of disposing of the gases from expended ammunition. As in the Maginot Line forts, the spent shell cases, still emitting gases after they were fired, were quickly removed from the firing chamber by means of a system that took them to a room below the block to avoid fouling the air in the firing chamber. The shells dropped into that room passed through a flap in the wall that closed to keep the gases confined. The ventilation system forced those gases out of the fort through an opening in the room. For smaller weapons such as machine guns, a flexible tube was attached through which the spent cartridge cases passed into a container holding a mixture of lime and water. When the container was full, it was replaced with a new one.[17]

The engine rooms of the two large forts had three diesel engines and the two smaller forts had two.[18] These generators were too small to meet the needs of the entire fort and operate all systems simultaneously. The army did not try to correct this situation until 1939. The old equipment was replaced with six additional powerful engines in the two large forts and four similar ones in the two small forts.[19] At Eben Emael, four diesel engines handled all the needs of the fort and two were kept in reserve.[20] In contrast, a large French Maginot fort typically had four diesel engines, any two of which were powerful enough to meet the demands of the entire fort in full operation.

The armoured components of Eben Emael and other forts included Belgian-made doors, turrets and cloches. The Fonderie Royale de Canons produced cloches that were quite different from those used by the French or the Germans. Most were made of nickel-chrome steel.[21] The smallest model was the observation cloche whose interior was only 0.8m wide. It had just enough space to allow the observer to climb in and pull up the trapdoor so he had a floor to stand on. It included four small observation crenels with shock-resistant glass and sliding shutters. It was too cramped for the observer to have a weapon, but there was a special position for a flare pistol in the roof. Most of these small cloches were installed at Eben Emael because it was the first fort of its generation. After that, it was determined that these cloches were inadequate. The FRC next produced a better cloche that had a interior 1.2m wide. It was called a Cloche FM and, like many of the French cloches, it could mount an automatic rifle and hold two men. This model came in three types: Type I with four embrasures and a flare gun in the roof for illumination and signalling, Type II – not used at Eben Emael – with a periscope and built to resist 420mm rounds,[22] and Type III with a periscope and six embrasures that could stand up to 520mm rounds designed especially for Battice.[23] Large artillery observation cloches (Eben-2) with six embrasures and a roof periscope were installed at Block 01 at Eben Emael and two blocks at Battice. These were reinforced models. The periscope was the French-built Model N used in the Maginot Line. Other designs of cloches included one for a searchlight and one for a 47mm gun. The only ones actually manufactured and installed are at Aubin-Neufchâteau. They are on Block C-3, which has two cloches built for a 47mm anti-tank gun and a searchlight cloche.

Electric searchlights were commonly used in many fortifications, including in Maginot Line forts and even interval casemates. The problem was protecting them effectively. In the Maginot Line forts and interval casemates, the French generally used an armoured case mounted on the outside of the combat block or casemate and it was remotely operated from the inside. The case cover was opened to activate the searchlight. The Belgians preferred the traditional method, which involved installing the searchlight in an embrasure inside a combat block or an interval bunker. The searchlight occupied a rotating steel cylinder that had an opening on one side for the searchlight. The back part of the cylinder (behind the searchlight) closed the embrasure and formed an armoured shield when the searchlight rotated back facing the inside of the block. In many cases, the forts had two types of searchlights: the WB model with a range of 225m that served as a spotlight at the entrances and the GZ-33 with range of a 700m.

Communications for the forts included a telephone system and radios. An underground system of telephone lines linked forts, observation posts and higher command posts. The radios were for external use and had a range of up to 30km for transmitting and 250km for receiving. One type of radio was for communication with observation aircraft spotting for the fort's artillery. The communications system was not completed at Battice and Eben Emael when the invasion began in 1940 so contact with observation posts was limited. Optical signals or even pigeons could be used if necessary. In addition, klaxons alerted the garrisons to gas attack, air attack, etc.

In the event the enemy breached a block and gained entrance to the fort, the occupants could detonate demolition chambers. Access to the gallery level from the blocks above could be blocked with sandbags and steel beams stored in niches adjacent to doorways. If needed, the steel beams fitted into slots in the walls and the sandbags put behind them formed the barrier.

The main problem for forts like Eben Emael was that, unlike the previous generation of forts, its garrison consisted mostly of artillerymen who had to perform the duties of infantrymen without having the proper training.[21]

Eben Emael may have been known as the impregnable fort, but it had not been designed to stand up to 420mm guns. When the decision was finally made to add gun turrets, the first of these new positions was created for a 120mm gun turret.[25] Devéze ordered the addition of 75mm gun turrets during the second phase. Even though the gun turrets of Eben Emael were similar to those of Battice, the actual thickness of the turret armour (both sides and roof) and the glacis armour was different. Undoubtedly, Devéze could have ordered turret positions for Eben Emael as strong as those of the other forts were and compensated for the expense somewhere else on the PLF, but he chose not to do it. According to the Belgian historian Jean Puelinckx, 'Eben Emael was not able to resist 220mm shells' and, due to the geological makeup of the site, its 60m deep galleries were not really well protected. The concrete of the blocks, Puelinckx points out, was only 2.2m thick and the steel of some of its armoured components only 18cm thick. These weaknesses were due to the fact that the government, having the option of building either a small strong fort or a large weak fort at this site (see table), opted for the second alternative in the belief that the Albert Canal would offer sufficient protection.[26] Turret and glacis armour came in three types: light, medium and heavy. Except for the 120mm gun turrets and the artillery observation cloches, the lightest (i.e. weakest) of the three types were installed at Eben Emael.

At Eben Emael, the galleries were as deep as or deeper than in most of the new forts. The concrete roofs of the blocks were a standard 2.25m thick, with the exception of turret blocks and the canal blocks, which could not resist much more than 220mm and occasional hits from 280mm rounds. Blocks Canal Nord and Sud were up to 3m thick (contrary to the information in the sidebar) since they were exposed to direct enemy fire from across the canal. However, according to some drawings, the concrete roofs of the artillery casemate blocks were up to 3m thick. Wall thickness in most blocks is the same 2.25m and in places like artillery casemates. By French Maginot Line standards, this was enough to resist 240mm rounds for the walls and up to 300mm rounds for the roof although this may not be the case since the concrete mixtures used by the French and Belgians were not necessarily the same.[27]

Only nine 75mm and three 120mm turrets were built for the four forts. Although their design was identical, their armour thickness was not. Why the military and government reduced the passive resistance strength of a fort such as Eben Emael is unfathomable. The standard answer is that Battice was closer to Germany whereas there was Dutch territory between Eben Emael and Germany. In either case, the Germans would have had to move their heavy artillery forward to get within range of the forts and could not hit them from within Germany. Since Eben Emael was built mainly to protect against a German thrust through Dutch territory, it made little sense to design the great fort without the ability to resist the heaviest weapons. The only explanation for this weakness is that the Belgian government wanted to save money. However, it could have just as easily economized on other fortifications. Thus instead of reducing the number of features or changing the design, they opted to build a weaker fort.[28] The nickel chromium steel armour of the 75mm gun turret had a maximum thickness of 380mm. The glacis armour reached a maximum thickness of 360mm and it was designed to resist hits by 280mm rounds. The 120mm turrets consisted of a nickel chromium steel outer layer 210mm

Armour and Concrete of the New Forts

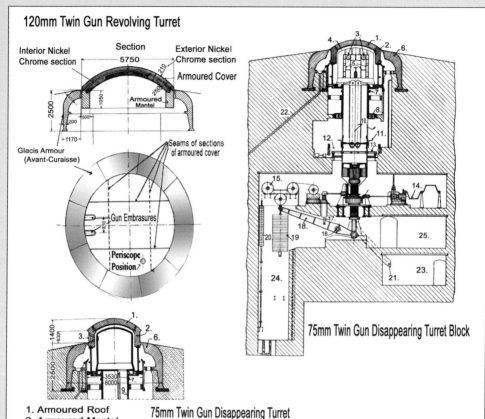

120mm Twin Gun Revolving Turret

Interior Nickel Chrome section
Section
Exterior Nickel Chrome section
Armoured Cover
Armoured Mantel
Glacis Armour (Avant-Curaisse)
Seams of sections of armoured cover
Gun Embrasures
Periscope Position

75mm Twin Gun Disappearing Turret Block

75mm Twin Gun Disappearing Turret

1. Armoured Roof
2. Armoured Mantel
3. Gun Embrasure
4. Interior Mantel
5. Mounting
6. Glacis Armor
7. Worm gear for slow pivoting
8. Worm gear for fast pivoting.
9. Pivot
10. Munitions lifts
11. Hand operation for Munitions Lifts
12. Munitions distribution ring
13. Revolving Floor
14. Main hoist winch
15. Pulley for auxiliary counterweight
16. Rotational axis of balancing lever
17. Connecting rod to auxiliary hoist winch
18. Balancing lever
19. Main counterweight
20. Auxiliary counterweight
21. Shell slide
22. Water drain
23. Room for empty shell casings
24. Well for counterweights.
25. Access to balancing lever

Belgian 120mm and 75mm gun turrets of the 1930s.

Surprisingly, much of the information concerning the Belgian forts remained secret for decades after they were taken out of national service. Based on historian Otmar Rogge's research at the Brussels Archives, information from a German document reveals the strength of the new Belgian forts. At the time of writing, other documents released from the Belgian Archives are still being examined by researchers, so some of the following data may be incorrect.

Rogge discovered that Fort Eben Emael was designed as a 'light' construction capable of resisting 280mm artillery rounds and 350kg bombs, whereas Battice was a 'heavy' type that could withstand 520mm rounds and 1,000kg bombs. Forts Aubin-Neufchâteau and Tancrémont were of 'medium' construction built to withstand 420mm – like the gros ouvrages of the Maginot Line – and 750kg bombs.

In a document identified as 1940 Krupp-Reinmetal Denkschrift, Rogge found the following details:

Blocks		Battice	Eben Emael	Aubin-Neufchâteau and Tancrémont	Notes
Artillery Casemate	Concrete Thickness	None	2.25m	None	
Artillery Turret		4.50m	3.00m	3.50m	
Infantry Blocks		3.50m*	2.75m**	3.20m*	
120mm Cupola		590mm	590mm	None	
75mm Turret		480mm	380mm	430mm	Roof
		(430mm)	(330mm)	(380mm)	(Mantle)
avant cuirasse+		460mm	360mm	400mm	
Artillery Obsv. Cloche	Armour Thickness	300mm	300mm	None	
Heavy MG Cloche		370mm	None	320mm	
Light MG Cloche		335mm	200mm	270mm	Eben Emael Canal Nord & Sud
Searchlight Cloche		None	None	360mm	Coffre 3

* The western side of each structure was weaker, being 2.8m thick.
** The western side of each structure was weaker, being 2.25m thick.
+ Avant-cuirasse is the glacis armour.

thick and an inner layer of 250mm.[29] Plans were made to cover two of the artillery casemates on the southern side of the fort with an added 6m of earth, but they were never realized. The remaining three forts only had turret blocks rather than artillery casemates on their enclosed surface and the two smaller ones a mortar block as well. Medium armour had been used for the turrets of the two small forts and heavy armour for those of Battice.

Dummy Turret

75mm Turret, Cupola N

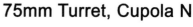

Block 1 (coffre)

Moat

Block J Air Intake

Entrance Block   Glacis

Block 5 (caponier)

FORT BATTICE

(Photos of Fort Battice by authors)

Since Eben Emael was not as strong as it appeared, Fort Battice was the real powerhouse of Belgian forts even though it covered about one-third less space. Battice had no artillery casemates and mounted two 120mm gun turrets compared to one at Eben Emael. It had three 75mm gun turrets, one more than Eben Emael. Battice had thirteen blocks instead of seventeen like Eben Emael and had a garrison of over 900 men instead of 1,200.[30] At Battice, the exposed walls and roofs had 3.5m of concrete and they could resist 520mm rounds. The roofs of all of the Battice blocks were 3.5m thick except for two on the west side of the fort that were 2.5m thick.

Due to the location of Eben Emael on a plateau, its lower galleries were dug much deeper than the 30m at Battice.[31] Fort Battice occupies a key position barring the direct route from Aachen to Liège, only 17km from the frontier. Theoretically, it could come quickly under heavy artillery fire, but in fact the attack could not happen any sooner than at the other forts. The Belgians, especially those who believed that the Ardennes were impassable to a modern mechanized army, thought Fort Battice, with its five artillery turrets, could not be easily bypassed by the Germans. The presence of Battice with a fort on either flank would force the Germans to go through the Maastricht Appendage if they wanted to outflank the PFL 1. The Albert Canal Line and Eben Emael were intended to block such a move. The fortifications commissions created to study the defence of the nation and the construction of positions between the mid-1920s and early 1930s had recommended a greater number of even stronger forts at one point. However, the high cost of construction, the Great Depression and the need to cover the flanks of the PFL, forced the Belgians to scale down these plans. Unfortunately, the cost cutting was applied to the wrong features.

The construction of Fort Battice began in 1934, about a year after Eben Emael. Most of the work was completed by 1937. According to popular lore, German companies built both forts as well as the Albert Canal in its early stages. The facts, however, clearly contradict this view. When the Germans prepared a report on the Belgian fortifications in 1941 (long after the campaign), they included details on concrete thickness for interval positions but not for any of the Belgian forts. In similar reports on the forts of other defeated nations, however, they did include this type of detail.

Battice is located at a site slightly elevated over its surroundings, but not in as prominent a location as Eben Emael. It has an irregular pentagonal shape and a ditch surrounds it on all sides but one. Its concrete counterscarp forms a vertical wall. Its scarp had a slope since it consisted only of earth. The remaining side comes up against a railway cutting. Two blocks and an air intake block are located on the other side of it.

Battice and the two other new forts have peacetime and wartime entrances, unlike Eben Emael, which does not. The subterranean caserne is located outside the area enclosed by the ditch at these three forts and it is linked to the fort by two galleries, except for Tancrémont, which has only one gallery. At Battice the peacetime entrance is Block E (or BE) in the ditch, which is accessed by a road through the railway cut. This access was blocked with anti-tank obstacles like tetrahedrons during wartime. The wartime entrance is Block W (Waucomont), which is located about 1km behind the fort and is connected to the fort by a subterranean gallery. The subterranean caserne is between this entrance and the fort. The entrance block included a Cloche FM, a machine-gun cloche and two telescopic air intakes for the fort. If gas was detected near the ground, the air intakes were raised. If the air was still contaminated at the higher level, it was processed through a special filter system. The entranceway was covered by an FM position. The entryway in the peacetime entrance block was actually better protected than the one in the wartime entrance. A rolling bridge in front of it exposed a pit several metres deep like at Eben Emael. Both entrances included decontamination areas.[32] The engine room was inside the area enclosed by the ditch, near the peacetime entrance. A chimney block for the escaping fumes was located nearby.

The only 60mm anti-tank guns were mounted in Blocks 1 and 2 where they covered the railway cut and the entrance to the ditch surrounding the fort. Three blocks served as caponiers for that moat and a fourth as a counterscarp casemate. All were armed with Maxim 08 machine guns. Some of these blocks included cloches armed with Maxim machine guns that fired over the ditch and covered the glacis on the other side of the counterscarp wall. The peacetime entrance block (BE) in the moat at one time had an embrasure for a machine gun and searchlight, but they were sealed before the war so that the only defence was provided through an embrasure for small arms inside the entranceway. BE also housed a lift for lowering supplies and munitions to the gallery level below. The wartime entrance (Block W) had only a stairway so resupply would have been a bit more difficult. Only one other entrance to the fort existed and it was located in one of the wooden barracks buildings.[33] This unusual entrance consisted of a pair of 20m long slides that ended about 8m below the surface allowing two soldiers with their equipment to slide simultaneously down to a 20m long corridor, which was covered by an interior casemate. The soldiers moved to the end of this corridor and climbed down another 19m to reach the main gallery of the fort. This entrance saved the troops at the peacetime caserne a march of about 200m to the wartime entrance or 300m to the peacetime entrance. However, if several hundred men tried to use this entrance in an emergency, they would pile up inside while waiting for their comrades to descend to the main gallery.

Some of the blocks had an exit for patrols, but there were none on the surface of the fort enclosed by the ditch. This area of the fort had the five artillery blocks, two each with a turret mounting two 120mm guns and three with turrets mounting two 75mm guns each and one – Block 4 – with a cloche. Two cloches actually covered the glacis. There was no defensive protection for this part of the fort because its designers had assumed that the enemy would not be able to reach it. At the gallery level below each of these artillery blocks there were munitions chambers with a monte-charge (a lift usually for ammunition) and other facilities associated with the turret.[34] Block 2 included an artillery observation cloche. The only other subterranean positions were the command post located at a short distance from the peacetime entrance and the engine room near the chimney block. A gallery circled this part of the fort and branched off toward all the blocks, including those on the other side of the railway cut. One gallery cut across the fort to reach the two 120mm artillery blocks.

A few of the blocks have a fossé diamant (diamond fossé)[35] a small angular concrete ditch in front of a weapons embrasure on a casemate. Another feature was positions for six anti-aircraft machine guns inside the enclosed area at Eben Emael. At the other forts, similar emplacements are found near the wartime entrance.

Construction of Aubin-Neufchâteau and Tancrémont, two small forts, began in the late spring of 1935. The 75mm guns of Aubin-Neufchâteau were out of range of Eben Emael, but they did cover Battice. The range of Tancrémont's 75mm guns was less than 1km short of reaching Battice, but artillery from the older forts in PFL 2 was able to cover it. Both of

60mm Antitank Gun

Searchlight and Casing

Photos of damaged Block B1 of Battice showing 60mm anti-tank gun and the searchlight and its casing. (*Jean Puelinckx*)

the two new forts have artillery blocks with 3.5m thick walls and 4.5m thick ceilings like Battice, but their turret armour is of the medium type and it could resist rounds of 420mm. In addition to being smaller, these two forts could accommodate garrisons of over 520 and 400 respectively. Both forts consist of ten blocks of the same types: peacetime entrance block that covered the entrance through the glacis into the surrounding ditch, three coffre[36] blocks (at Aubin-Neufchâteau one is actually on the glacis instead of the counterscarp), two blocks with a turret for 75mm guns and one mortar block. Their wartime entrances are somewhat similar. Their peacetime entrances are similar to the one at Battice, but they were equipped with searchlight and machine-gun embrasures to cover the entryway through the glacis. This block also has machine-gun cloches. The subterranean casernes are outside the surrounding moats. Battice, however, has an additional air intake block near the wartime entrance.

There are, nevertheless, a few differences between Fort Aubin-Neufchâteau and Fort Tancrémont. Aubin-Neufchâteau has two counterscarp casemates that cover the three sides of its triangular, 15m wide and 5m deep moat.[37] Block C-2 is a double casemate, with a 47mm gun on each side, a Maxim machine gun and a searchlight. Block C-3, on the glacis outside of the moat, has three cloches, two of which mounted a 47mm gun and one a searchlight, making it unique. Block-M is of interest since only two of the Belgian forts have these mortar blocks. At one time, it mounted three 81mm breech-loading mortars below ground level firing through a small fossé diamant. Each mortar covered a different direction. The block also has an FM cloche to cover the surface. The 75mm gun turret blocks include two machine gun cloches that cover the glacis. The subterranean facilities are similar to those found at Battice with the filters for gas protection in the caserne area and inside the enclosed fort area a command post, an engine room and chambers for munitions below the artillery blocks. Both forts also have chimney blocks similar to those at Battice.

Fort Tancrémont has a four-sided, 15m wide and 5m deep moat, forming an irregular polygon with three counterscarp casemates (coffre), one of which is a double casemate covering two sides. They were armed like those of Aubin-Neufchâteau. The mortar block, Block-M, only differed from the one at the other fort in that the three mortar positions were 90° from each other. The most unusual feature of Aubin-Neufchâteau was Block 3 with three machine-gun cloches. The Belgian historians Coenen and Vernier note that the reason this strange block exists is that the army originally planned to install a 120mm gun turret in it. Dr. Joost Vaesen has discovered that the turret, which was supposed to be in the centre of the fort, was eventually replaced with the mortar block. The 120mm turret that had been originally built for Aubin-Neufchâteau was installed at Battice instead. Since Aubin-Neufchâteau was originally intended as a large fort, it seems probable that Block 3 had been designed to mount another 75mm gun turret.

Work of one type or another continued on all four new forts through 1940. The old Brialmont forts behind PFL 1 had been modernized and they formed PFL 2. Plans for the renovation of these forts were part of the study made by the fortification commissions in the 1920s. In some cases during the war, the Germans had modified a few of the forts by improving their ventilation system, sealing large openings in the gorge caserne and adding a chicane type of defence to the entrances to replace the rolling bridges. They also had moved the latrines from the counterscarp to the scarp where the troops could access them during combat. The Germans did not use the turrets and removed some during the war. Only Forts Barchon,

Mortar Block Position for 81mm Mortars of Forts Aubin-Neufchateau and Tancrémont.

Firing embrasure of mortar in a diamant fossé.

Photos by Frank Philipart

Profile

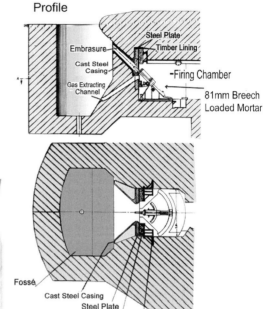

47mm AT Gun

47mm AT Gun in Casemate Protecting Fort's Ditch

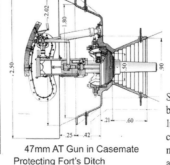

Some blocks of a fort and many bunkers included a grenade launcher. In some of these a cage was used to catch the grenade so the enemy could not try to toss it away and it exploded above ground.

Weapons found in the two small forts of PFL1. They include an 81mm mortar and a 47mm anti-tank gun. (*Frank Philippart*)

Evegnée, Fléron, Chaudfontaine and Flémalle at Liège still had their turrets. Renovation of the six forts on the right bank at Liège began in 1929. Next, the army began to restore some forts at Namur. New weapons were installed in these forts and old turrets were repaired or replaced if they had been destroyed or removed by the Germans. The ordnance specialists

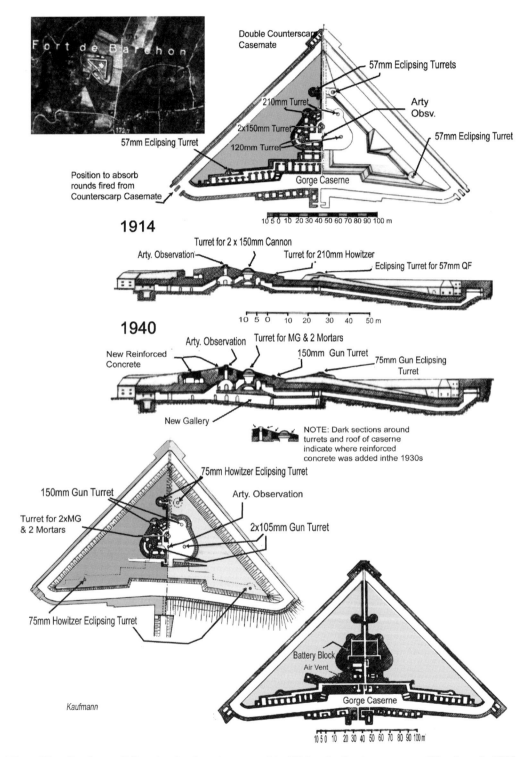

Plan of Fort Barchon at Liège showing how it appeared in 1914 and, after inter-war modifications, in 1940.

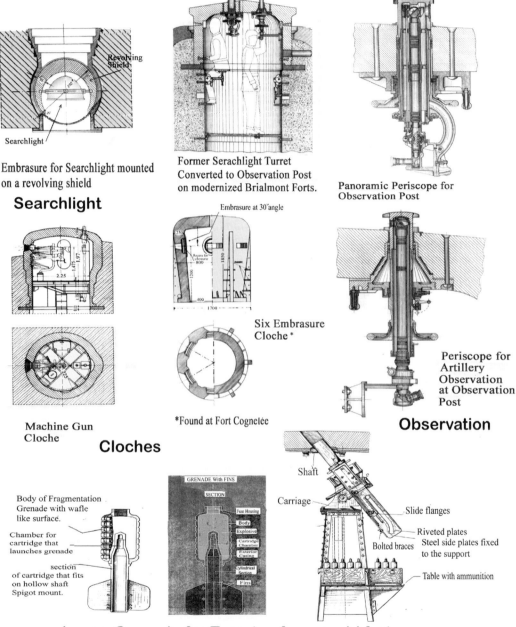

Embrasure for Searchlight mounted
on a revolving shield

Searchlight

Former Serachlight Turret
Converted to Observation Post
on modernized Brialmont Forts.

Panoramic Periscope for
Observation Post

Six Embrasure
Cloche *

Periscope for
Artillery
Observation
at Observation
Post

Machine Gun
Cloche

*Found at Fort Cognelée

Observation

Cloches

Lance Grenade for Turrets of some old forts

Some weapons and equipment used in forts modernized in the 1930s.

replaced old 120mm guns with two 105mm L/35 guns with a range of 12–13km in the turrets of the large forts and with one 105mm gun in the smaller forts. The turret had a crew of five men for two guns or three men for one gun and included a periscope. The 210mm howitzer in the turret was replaced with a 150mm L/40 gun, with a range of 18km. A lance grenade

(grenade launcher) and a reversible pair of light Maxim 08/15 machine guns for close defence were installed in the old, centrally-located 150mm gun turret.[38] The number of machine gun mounts and lance grenades in these turrets varied from two to four and replaced open infantry positions on the surface of the forts.[39] A plug-like device (the Belgians called it a 'Masque') in the roof of this turret could be raised and lowered for observation. It had vision slits and enough space for a man's head. A two-man armoured observation position replaced the searchlight turret position in all the forts. This observation cupola was actually the old searchlight turret modified and rebuilt with positions for two periscopes (one for artillery observation) and with vision slits in the walls for the two observers. The turret was no longer able to rotate or eclipse. The army used 75mm L11 howitzers to replace the antiquated 57mm guns in their eclipsing turrets. Eighteen of these turrets came from Antwerp in 1931 to replace the ones missing at forts Boncelles, Flémalle, Pontisse and three forts of Namur.[40] The 75mm howitzers, old German weapons from war reparations, had a range of only 5.2km.[41] The selected forts did not undergo the same modifications. At Liège, fusils mitrailleurs Mle 1930 were installed in the remaining 57mm gun positions in casemates whereas at Namur, Maxim 08/15 machine guns with searchlights were installed in the coffres to cover the surrounding dry moat and the entrance. In most casemates and cupolas, the weapons, be they 75mm guns, anti-tank guns or machine guns, were installed on ball mounts in the embrasures. In some cases, depending on the type of weapon involved, the ball mount included an opening for a sight.

The old turrets were modified to take new weapons and armoured observation positions were added. The large windows in the gorge casernes, which had proved a vulnerable spot during the previous war, were modified, reduced in size, or sealed altogether with cement. Latrines,[42] medical facilities and water cisterns were added inside the fort and the old steam engines were replaced with modern diesels. Since these forts had not been built of reinforced concrete, it was added to their weak points. Thus, turret positions received 4m wide and 2.5m thick reinforced concrete sections that covered their old cast iron glacis armour. Reinforced concrete was also used to reinforce scarp galleries and posterns and to build the troop quarters inside the fort – usually at the new gallery level, to replace the vulnerable positions in the gorge caserne – and new positions like the guardhouse and the munitions chambers. The army standard for protection was for resistance to 220mm rounds and 500kg aerial bombs in these forts. Concrete poured over corrugated steel sheets was used to reinforce the ceilings. The galleries close to the surface were covered with backfill and a layer of earth. The old staircases to the turret positions were replaced with metal ladders. Coffres of reinforced concrete were built into the old defensive positions in the counterscarp.

Since the galleries[43] were too close to the surface to resist modern heavy artillery, the Belgian Geological Service began surveying and running tests between 1928 and 1930 to build new galleries and air intakes outside the forts. Some of the forts turned out to be located over an aquifer and even coal seams. The only solution, Director of Fortifications General Simonet was informed, was to line the galleries with concrete and that would supposedly stop water seepage. The problem was quite serious at Fléron and Barchon. A coal seam under Fléron, the rights to which had been sold to a Belgian mining company fifty years earlier, further complicated the situation. Nonetheless, the Belgian engineers succeeded in excavating deeper galleries in most forts. The underground facilities included munitions chambers and an area for the troops called a bombardment gallery, safe from bombardment.[44] This was where the troops stayed when they were not manning their posts. Other installations at the level of the new galleries included water pumps, ventilators and command posts. Electric monte-charges had to be added to bring the ammunition from the lower levels to the turrets. Since the aquifer below Barchon precluded these additions, it retained a single gallery level. The spoil from these excavations were used to fill many of the rooms and chambers that were not needed in the renovated forts. Particularly large chambers at the old gallery level of the central massif were filled in or reduced in size.

Corrugated steel sheets were installed in the galleries and rooms for protection from roof flaking or spalling of the concrete during bombardment. Airtight doors were added to the subterranean galleries. Most importantly, the inadequate ventilation system was corrected and the latrines were relocated from the counterscarp of the gorge caserne to the main area of operations inside the forts. New power rooms for two diesel engines, similar to those of the new forts and fuel storage areas were added to provide electric power for the fort. The turrets were motorized to facilitate operations and electrically-operated monte-charges were added. New kitchens with limited facilities were included inside the area enclosed by the ditch, but their main function was to distribute rations during combat. A well was dug inside each fort and a pumping system was installed. Water was stored in galvanized sheet metal reservoirs. Additional facilities included a larger infirmary with an operating room. All these improvements brought these old Belgian forts up to the standards of most modern ones in other countries.

A major improvement to the old forts was a more efficient ventilation system. Labourers excavated special filter rooms. In addition, a concrete air intake tower resembling a water tower was built outside the fort. It was about 19m high and included a sally port for patrols and firing chamber for a light machine gun (FM-30) to cover the men on the surface. At the top of the tower, the air intake telescoped another 5m above the tower. The top of the tower included observation slits and openings much like medieval machicolations for a spotlight and for dropping hand grenades on unwanted visitors below. The tower was located about 400m behind the fort on a reverse slope and connected to the fort by a new gallery, which carried the air ducts and could be used to bring troops into the fort. It served as a second entrance and a point for sending out patrols. This gallery, which was about 15m deep, included munitions storage areas, offices and elevators. This type of air tower was not built in all of the reactivated forts, however. For instance, at Fort Pontisse, on the left bank of the Meuse, an air intake bunker was built instead. The tower and other entrances to the fort were gas proof thanks to hermetically sealed doors. A decontamination area with a shower afforded further protection to the garrison.

During the 1930s, other commissions met to study the remaining problems pertaining to the modernization of the old forts. In 1937, a commission concluded that the power supply was inadequate. This led to the construction of sixteen new 75hp motors built by Ateliers Walschaert in Brussels. They were delivered in 1932 but were eventually replaced with two 130hp Carels diesel engines in each fort. In 1939, another commission determined that the electrical supply, the ventilation and the gas–proofing were still inadequate in many locations. The communications system included underground telephone links to other forts and two types of radio. One radio for communicating with other forts and the army command and the other designed to communicate with aircraft used for recon and artillery spotting for the forts.

Grenade Launcher   **Automatic Rifle Embrasure**   **Position for Telescopic Air Intake**

Metallic Floor
at top   **half way up**

This type of tower-like air intake was used on several of the Brialmont forts at Liège that were modernized in the 1930s. It included fighting positions in the upper level and a defended entrance. (*Clayton Donnel*)

Of the eight forts rearmed at Liège, Barchon and Fléron were the most heavily armed with two turrets mounting a 150mm gun, two twin 105mm gun turrets and four turrets with a 75mm howitzer. These 105mm guns performed well in May 1940, but the 150mm had nothing to absorb the recoil in the turret, which caused problems for the crew. Five of these eight forts kept the same number of turrets as in 1914. In the remaining three forts, the empty turret wells were backfilled and covered over with reinforced concrete. Forts Boncelles and Embourg on the south part of the line were only armed with four 75mm howitzer turrets. Most garrisons remained at 400 to 500 men, except Forts Embourg and Boncelles, which had about 300 men each. About half of these men were housed in a nearby caserne and served as a relief garrison. Much of the work on PFL 2 was completed between 1928 and 1932 before construction began on the new forts of PFL 1. The Germans noted that some of the forts of PFL 2 had problems with observation because of industrialization and urbanization in the area. In 1940, the old 1890 armour of the forts could not withstand even German 37mm guns. German 75mm and 88mm guns smashed many of the turrets during the 1940 campaign.

Modernized Brialmont Forts of Liège and Namur

Fort – size	*75mm How. Turrets*	*105mm Gun (or 75mm GP) Turrets*	*150mm Gun Turrets*	*MG & LG Turrets*	*Air Tower*
Liège					
Pontisse * – LZ	4	1	–	–	–
Barchon – LT	4	2	2	1	X
Evegnée – ST	3	2	1	1	X
Fléron – LT	4	2	2	1	X
Chaudfontaine – SZ	4	2	1	1	X
Embourg – LZ	4	–	–	–	–
Boncelles – LT	4	–	–	–	X
Flémalle* – LZ	4	1	1	1	X
Namur					
Maizeret – SZ	4	1	–	2	X
Andoy – LT	4	(1)	–	2	X
Dave – ST	3	(1)	–	2	–
Héribert – LT	4	(1)	–	2*+	–
Malonne – SZ	4	(1)	–	2	X
Suralée – LT	4	(1)**	–	2*+	X
Emines – ST	–	–	–	(2)***	–
Cognelée – LT	–	–	–	(2)***	–
Marchovelette – ST	3	(1)	–	2	X

MG & LG = Machine gun & Lance Grenade (Mortar)
L = Large, S = Small, T = Triangular shape, Z = Trapezoidal shape, i.e. LZ = Large Trapezoidal shape.
*Located on left bank of the Meuse.
** Suralée had two long-range 75mm guns in its central turret.
*** Emines had a couple of machine-gun bunkers added before the war and Cognelée had two bunkers for machine guns on its central massif.
*+ Suralée and Héribert had only machine guns in its two turrets for close defence.

At Liège, Forts Hollogne, Lantin, Liers and Loncin were not modernized and three of them became munitions depots. Fort Loncin became a memorial and tomb to its 1914 garrison and went out of service. Liège served as a fortified bridgehead and no longer as a fortress ring.

PFL 1 extended in an arc about 60km in length, officially included three new forts, but usually Eben Emael is not included. The bunkers in the intervals between the forts of PFL 1 and PFL 2 were intended to prevent the problem of 1914 when the Germans easily passed between the forts. The various types of bunkers included single, double or multi-embrasured positions for machine guns. In addition, the Belgians built a number of bunkers that mounted a searchlight, a 47mm anti-tank gun and a Maxim machine gun and a few bunkers for observation. Plans for interval casemates similar to large ones the French built were drawn up but the building project never went ahead. Work on the bunkers of PFL 1 and PFL 2 began in 1934 and most structures were completed in 1935. PFL 1 was supposed to have 178 bunkers, but a German count in 1940 showed 162 machine-gun bunkers, six artillery observation bunkers and eight bunkers for 47mm anti-tank guns. The bunkers for both PFLs included enough reinforced concrete (1.3m thick) to resist fire from 150mm guns and a few hits from a 220mm howitzer. Corrugated galvanized steel sheets, like those in the forts, covered the ceilings. Most of the machine-gun bunkers were simple structures consisting of a single firing chamber and a pair of doors for the entrance. The line also included some larger double and multi-embrasure bunkers. The anti-tank bunkers included a firing chamber for a 47mm gun and one for a machine gun. There was also an embrasure for a searchlight. Twenty-five anti-tank bunkers in the PFLs mounted a turret built for the army's armoured vehicles and rearmed with a 47mm anti-tank gun (turret designated APX-2B). In a few bunkers, the entrance was located in a well and two types of armoured doors formed an airlock. The exterior door, identified as Type P1, was a grille that was sealed with a metal sheet during combat.[45] A second door, designated P2, in the entryway was armoured with slats that allowed for ventilation. A similar metal sheet attached with hinges sealed this door when the bunker was under attack. Normally, this second door was located in the wall to the left or right of the P1 forcing a person entering to make a 90° turn. Thus, if the first door were destroyed, the second would not be in the direct line of fire. Most of the large bunkers had a grenade launcher, a toilet and an emergency exit, which was sealed until needed. A few bunkers consisted of two levels and some included a cloche for observation.

Only about sixty interval bunkers were built in PFL 2 and were mostly for machine guns. PFL 3, located between Visé and east of Liège where PFL 2 ended, covered the Meuse crossings with about forty bunkers including some armed with 47mm anti-tank guns. Finally, PFL 4, which included the rearmed old forts of Pontisse and Flémalle, numbered forty to fifty bunkers, some of which were observation positions with cloches. Cloches were also installed the old forts. The bunkers were camouflaged with paint and vegetation. In some cases, they appeared as normal buildings such as petrol stations. In most cases, a wire fence, brambles and plants of the same variety as those growing within the compound surrounded the position. These additions, however, revealed the presence of the bunkers.

In addition to the fortified position of Liège, work on the fortified position of Namur (PFN) got priority. Modernization of the five old forts on the south front and two forts on the Meuse and the Sambre on the northern front began in 1932. The Belgians did not rearm these forts as heavily as the ones of PFL 2. Fort Maizeret had two turrets mounting one 105mm gun each, four turrets with a 75mm howitzer each and two turrets with 120mm grenade launchers for close defence making it the most heavily rearmed fort of the PFN. The other six forts had three to four turrets for 75mm howitzers, a central turret with two long-range 75mm guns and

View of bunkers on the Antwerp anti-tank ditch that remain. Lower Left: remains of one of the outer ring forts used with the anti-tank ditch. The bunkers were located on the enemy side of the ditch and provided flanking fire. Top right: Interior showing MG position and corrugated ceiling. These bunkers had few facilities. Lower right: Example of concrete scales used for camouflaged on many bunkers. (*Authors*)

usually two turrets for close defence with 120mm grenade launchers or machine guns. Forts St Héribert and Suarlée were similarly armed, but had no grenade launchers in their turrets for close defence. Turret positions that had not been restored were, more often than not, filled in and turned into dummy positions.[46] Forts Cognelée and Émines served as munitions dumps. At Fort Cognelée, a few machine-gun positions and brick barracks in the moat were added. The army established two lines of defence in the PFN, which included Forts Maizeret, Andoy and Dave in the first line with about forty interval bunkers of various types and a 4m wide barbed-wire barrier. A second line of seventeen small machine-gun bunkers and two troop shelters were built in 1939. Anti-tank barriers at both Liège and Namur included Belgian Gates,[47] concrete and steel pyramids, or tetrahedron obstacles. Anti-tank ditches came into use where the terrain did not present sufficient natural obstacles.

An unusual weapon in the forts was the 70mm Van Deuren Model 70 mortar (VD 70) developed from trench mortars of the previous war. It had a range of 800m and it was used at Namur and at the sluices of the Albert Canal. The garrison of Battice deployed two of these weapons outside Block-1.

The Albert Canal Line, one of the more important defence lines, was created with the construction of the canal. It only lost significance when the army realized it could not hold the frontier lines without the rapid reinforcement from French divisions, a strategy that became questionable after the declaration of neutrality. According to German estimates, 120 single and multi-embrasure bunkers formed this line and anti-tank bunkers with cloches were located near the bridges. Many of the bunkers were built into the concrete embankment of the canal and some under bridges. The bunkers were spaced up to 1,000m apart. The army held the Ardennes only lightly, to the dismay of the Walloons. The compromise reached between 1936 and 1939 resulted in the construction of about sixty single and six double bunkers, effectively isolating the Walloon regions from the rest of Belgium.

The old Antwerp ring became the Position Fortifiée Antwerp (PFA) and continued to serve as a National Redoubt. Its old forts were not restored to the same degree as those around Liège and Namur were. After 1914, the Germans had taken most of the gun turrets and the government was unable to allot sufficient funds for replacements. Instead, many of the old turret positions were converted into concrete machine-gun bunkers, often with no concrete roof, but a wooden shelter for cover. All the old positions occupied man-made sites that gave them a dominating position over the surrounding low terrain. A water-filled anti-tank ditch was created between the Scheldt River and the Albert Canal, forming Antwerp's major obstacle and defensive line.[48] These bunkers, often of two levels and embedded on the enemy side of the ditch, supported each other with flanking fire. The southern part of the PFA included the Nethe and Rupel Rivers, which flowed into the Scheldt and formed a last line of defence about 5km from the line of forts in front of it. The PFA consisted of twelve old forts, eight redoubts and over 180 bunkers, many of which formed part of another line known as the KW Line. During the mid-1930s, work was also done on the Ghent Bridgehead where over 100 bunkers formed two lines of defence. Three special bunkers for 75mm field guns supported the bridgehead. The Scheldt connected it to Antwerp, but no bunkers were built for this link.

Work began on a new defence line in 1938, the KW Line. It ran from Koningshooikt near Antwerp south to Wavre and it was later extended to the Meuse but not completed. To the Allies it was known as the Dyle Line since it used that river as the main obstacle even though

Machine Gun Casemate with Weir for regulating water flow
on Antitank Ditch of Antwerp

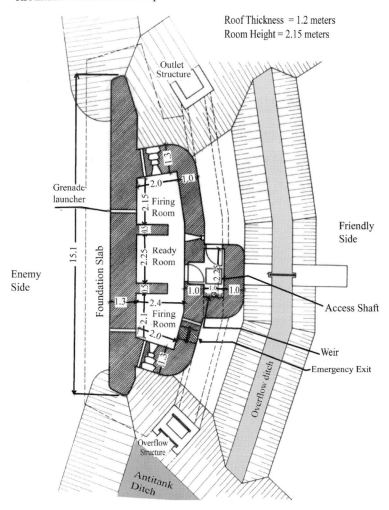

Plan of one of Antwerp's anti-tank ditch bunkers with a photo of a similar bunker. (*Authors*)

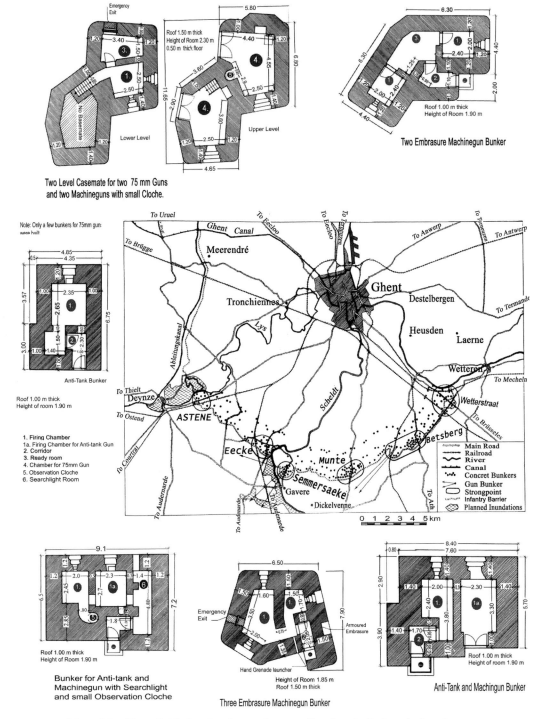

Map of the Ghent Bridgehead and several types of bunkers built there before the war.

the river could be used only near Antwerp. Over 190 bunkers formed three lines of defence. The troops added field fortifications between 1939 and 1940. To close the gap between Wavre and Namur on the Meuse, the army formed a line of Belgian Gates linked to each other, but no bunkers covered this line making it ineffective.

In the late 1930s, the Advanced Position in front of Liège was built to give early warning of invasion and to block key routes. Thirty border alert posts (postes d'alerte or PA) were built in 1937. These small brick buildings for a four-man garrison, incapable of resisting anything beyond small arms, were reinforced in 1939 with the addition of a concrete wall on one or two sides facing the enemy. This addition allowed the occupants to resist a hit or two by light artillery. Further back from the frontier, the army built simple square concrete bunkers (3.2m x 3.2m) with walls 60cm thick facing the enemy and thinner walls on the other sides. The roofs consisted of 50cm of reinforced concrete with the ceilings covered with corrugated galvanized steel allowing this structure to resist a few round from a 75mm gun. These small bunkers had an embrasure for a Maxim machine gun. Situated in groups of three to fourteen, they formed nine strongpoints named for the towns of Beusdael, Hombourg, Henri-Chapelle, Grunahut, Dolhain, Jalhay, Hockai, Malmédy and Stavelot. The mission of the PA positions and strongpoints was to delay the enemy while the army destroyed key bridges and tunnels.

Chapter 5

Neutrality Fails Belgium Again

The Belgian Fortifications in the Second World War

The Netherlands did not last a week after the German attack of 10 May 1940, succumbing to the surprise airborne assault that opened a back door into Fortress Holland. Belgium resisted for eighteen days before King Leopold agreed to an unconditional surrender. The Belgian army had twice as many field divisions as the Dutch. In addition, almost the entire French First Army Group and the British Expeditionary Force advanced deep into Belgium when the Germans attacked whereas the Dutch received only token support from an Allied force that reached Breda. There are several reasons for the rapid fall of Belgium. In the first place, when King Leopold declared neutrality in 1936, he generated an almost impossible situation. The main lines of defence, PFL 1 and the Albert Canal Line, could not hold out without Allied support. Since the Belgian government refused to allow the Allies to enter the country until an actual act of aggression took place, the Allied command could only contemplate an and advance to the Scheldt (Escaut) River – Plan E – or to Central Belgium and the Dyle River Line – Plan D. The first choice offered less risk and the second depended on whether the Belgian army succeeded in delaying the Germans at Liège. In the second place, Hitler had modified the offensive strategy after the Mechelen incident when the Dutch found papers containing the operational plans on a German staff officer when the Me-108 he was flying in strayed into Dutch territory.[1] The new plan called for the main thrust to move through the Ardennes as the Allies rushed into Belgium. Exiting the Ardennes and breaching the Meuse with most of the army's panzer divisions would leave the Allied armies in a trap.[2]

The invasion of the Netherlands and Belgium took place at the same time as the occupation of the small Grand Duchy of Luxembourg with a population of a little over a quarter of a million people. After September 1939, the Luxembourgers had created a line of concrete roadblocks and bridge barriers known as the Schuster Line[3] to delay any invaders. The Luxembourg army of a little over 400 volunteers and about 260 gendarmes could do little beyond creating wire barricades and attempting to destroy a few frontier bridges. In spite of these efforts, most of the country was occupied by 9:00 am on 10 May. The Brandenburgers were in the capital before the invasion even began and German troops quickly overran the country while French forces advanced from the south. Resistance lasted only about two to three hours longer than it had in Denmark a month earlier. The Danes had an army three times larger and even an air force. The royal family of Luxembourg managed to escape.

The Belgians suffered a fate similar to the Dutch, as German air-landed troops targeted several key objectives. In the Ardennes, the Chasseurs were supposed to hold with the help of a few strongpoints until partially-mechanized French cavalry divisions came to the rescue. The Germans, however, flew in small numbers of soldiers in Fieseler Storch aircraft to seize the key points in southern Belgium. Hard on their heels, the bulk of the German panzer divisions

Justification for Violation of Neutrality?

British cartoon from the German propaganda book *Die Wehrmacht* showing the popular view that the war on the West would be one centering around major fortifications on both sides. Map showing what the Germans believed were the fortified areas of Belgium and the Netherlands. It also emphasizes how the Germans claimed the Ruhr was vulnerable to the Allies if they occupied the Low Countries.

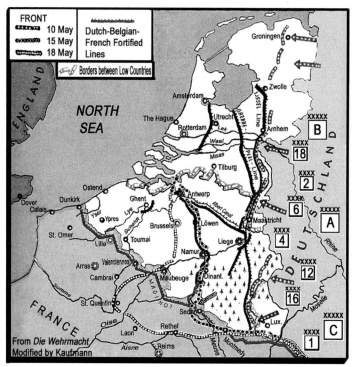

German Offensive of May 1940

Map showing position of German armies before the invasion of the Low Countries (Note: Second Army was actually held in reserve). Bottom map shows the campaign against the Low Countries in May 1940 and includes the locations of German panzer divisions.

German Intelligence about Belgium

What the Germans knew about Belgium is not fully known. German intelligence sources had details on the forts of the Maginot Line and it was believed they had similar details on the Belgian forts, but apparently this was not the case. The Luftwaffe provided aerial photography, but when the special glider assault on Fort Eben Emael was planned, the Germans did not realize that the gun turrets in the northern corner were dummies and assigned teams to destroy them.

US pre-war intelligence reports reveal the extent of the knowledge of American military attachés and one can presume that their German counterparts had similar information. A report dated 11 May 1937 submitted by Lieutenant Colonel Sumner Waite, an infantry officer serving as the assistant military attaché in Paris, reveals the following.

> Liège is protected by three lines of fortifications with pill boxes covering the intervals, tank obstacles barring the lines of approach together with planned destructions.
>
> The first, or outer line, extends from the vicinity of Visé ... through Neufchateau, Battice, Pepinster, Sougne-Remouchamps, to the vicinity of Comblain-au-Pont, on the Ourthe.
>
> The second, or inner line, partially encircles the town but the system of pill box defense is found only to the east of the Meuse and extends from the vicinity of Chératte through Tignée, Fléron, Chaudefontaine, Tilff, Boncelles, to the vicinity of Vals St. Lambert.
>
> The third and final line, covers the eastern approaches of the city itself and consists of pill boxes placed in well sited positions and in some instances camouflaged in a most ingenious manner.

It is doubtful that a German officer would have had an opportunity to inspect some of the positions Waite was allowed to visit. After a visit to Fort Fléron, he reported that it had 'been modernized to some extent, particularly as to living arrangements and gas protection' although no major changes had been made to the trace or design. The fort's main armament, he reported, consisted of two 155mm guns in turrets and a number of 60mm guns and machine guns. He wrote that the 'fort [was] surrounded by heavy barbed wire entanglements ... good for at least ten years'. Anti-tank rails made of railway iron and set in concrete covered all avenues of approach; they were deployed in five rows of alternating height. The commander was a war veteran on the verge of retirement who left his NCOs to handle all instruction. The 'whole layout reflected the spirit of the commander who was content, apparently, to let things rock along'.

Waite next visited Fort Battice, which was still under construction with a completion date of 1938. Its armament, which was in place, consisted of 'four 120mm guns in turrets, six 75mm guns in turrets, four 60mm guns and twenty-seven machine guns'. The fort, he wrote, was

> of reinforced concrete construction and its galleries extend to a depth of 180 feet [54.9m, which is deeper than they actually were] and cover a distance of 5 kilometers.

The fort ... follows the contours of the ground and dominates the surrounding countryside. It has a perimeter of approximately 2000 meters and is surrounded by a sort of moat or fosse, enfiladed by 60mm guns and machine guns with a 60° traverse. The moat or fosse is about 20 feet [6m] deep and 50 feet [15m] wide. Entrance to the fort proper is across a bridge which, when pulled aside, exposes a second moat or pit about 15 feet [4.6m] wide, 15 feet long and 2 feet [7.6m] deep, which prevents entry. The bridge is moved by modern machinery in such a manner as to rest flush with the wall. A machine gun set in a casemate about 30 yards [27 metres] in, cover the entrance. There are absolutely no dead spaces due to arrangement of flanking fires.

The peace strength of the garrison is 50 men, while the wartime garrison will be increased to ... between six hundred and eight hundred.

Diesel powered generators produce the electric current which operates ammunition hoists and provides for other power and lighting arrangements. The machinery is modern. The fort is also wired for electric current from the outside.

Ventilation is by forced draft and in this particular fort there are two air intakes, one nearer the fort and the other 500 meters to the front, both intakes being very ingeniously camouflaged and protected by heavy reinforced concrete.

The intake nearest the work is provided with a collapsible tube which can be pushed to a height of about 45 feet [13.7m] in order to range above any gassed area. All doors are of heavy steel and gas tight.

There are several observation posts within the fort, heavily armored and equipped with eye slits carrying unbreakable glass. One observation post is situated about 700 meters away and is well camouflaged. A nearby pill box constructed inside a lean-to of an adjacent barn provides cross fires in the particular sector and incidentally protection for the O.P.

A railway passes along the northern flank of Fort Battice ... A detached post has been built not the hillside and connected with the main fort by a subterranean passage. This post is armed with machine guns and 60mm guns and enfilades the railway in both directions [?] .

Waite wrote that Fort Neufchâteau was to be completed in 1938. He thought, incorrectly, that it was similar to Fort Battice, but did not specify whether he had, in fact, visited Neufchâteau.

According to Waite, Fort Eben Emael, was 'modern in every particular and is complete except for the moat or fosse, now under construction'. He seemed to think that the wet moat would surround the entire fort rather than protect only the northwest section. He may have been told that it would extend around the fort and that it would be filled with water from the canal. However, the canal was too far below the level of the fort for that to be practical.

Fort Eben Emael's ... galleries penetrate to a depth of about 200 ft [61m] and cover a distance of approximately 4½ kilometres. The armament consists of two 120's in turrets [actually a single turret, so possibly he never saw the combat positions since he makes a similar statement about Battice], twelve 75's in casemates, twelve 60mm guns, six machine guns and five fixed automatic rifles.

The 75's operate through an ingenious ball and socket arrangement. The gun pierces the ball and pivots for both elevation and traverse. The ball rests in a socket in such a manner that the gun port is closed and gas tight. The machine guns and 60mm guns are employed mainly for flanking fire …

Each machine gun is cooled by water taken directly from the water system. Searchlights are available for night firing. The machine guns have a double barrel arrangement, one barrel above the other with a pivot in between … The second barrel may be swung easily and practically instantly into place. The stock is fixed. The ejected cartridge cases enter a flexible tube attached to the gun and are carried through the floor to a container, thus eliminating powder fumes. There is a similar … arrangement for … the 60mm gun. Empty cases are ejected into a hopper which is connected by a tube to a lower level.

Waite's descriptions indicate that he visited machine gun and 60mm gun positions and went into an artillery casemate. Apparently he never saw a turret. He also described the ammunition hoists in the casemates and mentioned that the ammunition was in magazines about 30m below, although he does not seem to have been aware of the ready ammunition. He was told that about 1,000 rounds of 120mm and 3,000 rounds of 75mm ammunition were stored in the magazines. During his visit, there were three diesel generators and he was informed that two were required for full service.[4] The entrance he saw was similar to the one at Battice, but it had a double set of doors for gas protection. Waite also learned that the communications room, which was damp from water seepage, would soon be waterproofed. The troop quarters, he noted, were comfortable and dry and the caserne had modern showers, latrines and mess halls. The kitchens were equipped with electric stoves and boilers and – Waite's guide said – electrical refrigeration was planned. The fort was stocked with rations for a month that consisted of biscuit and preserved foods. Waite was also informed that the garrison of 250 would more than double in wartime, like at Battice.

Waite was impressed with the fort's commander, who, he wrote, was efficient, 'and his command showed it. The entire organization seemed to be "on its toes" and ready for whatever might happen.' It would appear that he was wrong.

Waite's report also mentions the defences of the Albert Canal and the Meuse-Escaut Canals where bunkers were spaced at about 1,200m apart and relied on cross fires.[5] He thought that the bunkers were larger than most with over 2m of concrete thickness. He saw some with two levels and an observation post (a cloche) similar to those on the forts. He also noticed the grenade throwers designed to defend the walls.

In addition to the frontier troops, he met with cyclist battalions and reported that 'all bridges and culverts along roads entering Belgium in this area are mined or prepared for destruction and at the more important points guards live in permanent adjacent quarters'. At all bridges near the frontier, 'Belgian Gates' were ready to be rolled into place where their rollers would be removed and where they would be locked together.

At Namur, Waite came across a series of old forts like those at Liège with bunkers between them, but he saw no anti-tank obstacles. He visited the 2nd Chasseurs Regiment at Bastogne and reported that the sector had over one hundred well-sited bunkers smaller than those he had already seen. 'Inasmuch as the country is wooded and cut up, an invading force would be compelled, more or less, to follow the roads; consequently the defense problem is simplified,' he surmised. In his concluding remarks, he wrote

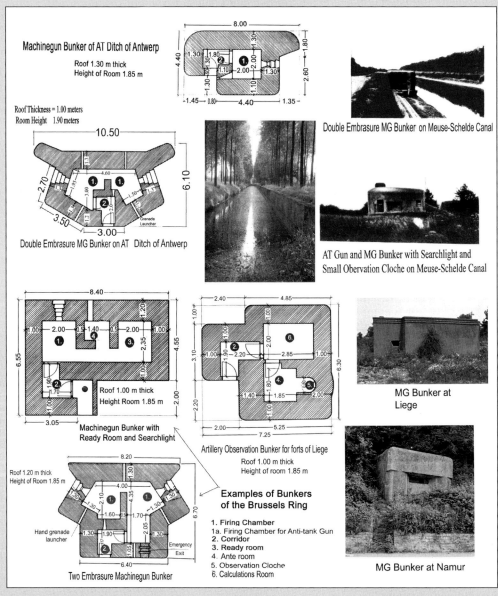

Examples of various types of Belgian bunkers. Centre photo shows part of the Antwerp anti-tank ditch. (*Joseph Hasque*)

Belgium has a much more efficient army than that of 1914 ... Should an attack come from the east, it is believed that rapid progress could be achieved only through treachery within the rank and file of the Belgian army. Belgium today stands as a strongly fortified nation against German ground attack.

Waite's report includes a map of the PFL showing the forts in use, interval positions and frontier positions. He even notes the fort at Sougné-Remouchamps was not built. His map includes the correct shapes of the new forts.

On 14 March 1938, after a visit to the northern positions of Belgium, Lieutenant Colonel Muller, the US Military Attaché to Belgium, prepared a second report in which he related that

> the system of defense in and around Antwerp is probably the least imposing of any inspected. It is certainly the least modernized and the forts and redoubts, which are of somewhat ancient vintage ... in no way compare with the modern fortifications constructed at Liège and elsewhere.
>
> The forts and redoubts ... except those on the inner or second line of defense, are unoccupied and unprepared for defense. No material or any sort whatsoever is installed. Electric lighting system, means of communication and machinery are non-existent. Much labor and considerable money well be required to modernize these works. However, the forts and redoubts are in the main well constructed and the concrete, earthworks and moats are in good condition. Due to the very low flat terrain in which located, all are built up and above the level of the surrounding country, the earth excavated from the moats being used to cover the concrete and form the glacis.
>
> [The forts] are double decked with an overhead thickness of concrete of about ten feet [3m] and a top covering of earth of about the same thickness.
>
> Turrets for 75mm and 105mm guns, as well as observation posts, exist but are in such a state of decay or destruction that it will be necessary to rebuild them completely. The iron and steel work was in almost every instance removed by the Germans [referring to the First World War].
>
> A few of the redoubts were partially destroyed by the Germans ... Where so destroyed, modern pill boxes, usually two, have been constructed on the site ...
>
> The inner circle of forts have been rehabilitated to some extent and a number are now occupied as barracks ...
>
> Much dependence is being placed upon inundating the low areas adjacent to the Escaut and Nethe rivers and their tributaries.
>
> In order to facilitate movement of troops, supplies, etc. as well as for commercial use, a tunnel under the Escaut has been recently built at St. Ann. This tunnel is 1600 meters in length and permits four lanes of traffic.

The fortified position of Antwerp (PFA) actually used twelve of the old forts and eight of the redoubts modified more or less as Muller described them. The Belgians had built about 180 bunkers, including several large ones in the section known as the Antwerp Anti-

"Belgian Gate" used as road block.
Note rollers on front and back for movement.

Belgian tank turret mounted on bunker at Ostend

Belgian Gates linked together to form an AT Obstacle
on the Dyle Line.

Surrender of Fort Boncelles

Abatis created to form a road block in the Ardennes
near St. Vith

Swastika flying over Fort Embourg.

Germany army photos from May 1940.

tank Ditch, which was water-filled. The Belgian Gates that Colonel Waite described were used to block crossing points. The PFA, combined with a water barrier that reached the Ghent Bridgehead, formed the National Redoubt.

Colonel Muller briefly mentioned a few other positions. Most of the remainder of his report included details about the Ghent Bridgehead where, he wrote, there were no forts, only bunkers similar to those in the Ardennes. According to Muller, about 200 bunkers formed two parallel lines: one main line and one reserve line. The area was divided into three divisional sectors further subdivided all the way down to battalion sectors. Each battalion sector formed a centre of resistance. The Belgians planned to add trenches and wire in the event of war and 'each center of resistance will become a veritable fort in itself'. The Belgians, reported Muller, preferred to install these centres of resistance around small villages because the settlements formed an additional obstacle against tank attack. The bunkers were similar to others in Belgium.

> Most were built to accommodate one machine gun and one 47mm gun with the usual projector for night firing. A few were designed to take care of a machine gun and a 75mm field gun. Several have installations for two field guns and one or two machine guns [he identifies the location of three he has seen and there were only three built]. The platforms for the field guns are simple in design and consist of a circular platform that turns thus permitting the gun to be readily traversed. The gun is run onto the platform which has two flanged tracks which guide the wheels into place and prevent any lateral movement of the wheels. The trails rests on a trench built in the concrete floor.

Sand was used in the trench to stabilize the gun. According to Muller, no permanent mounts were installed because of the cost and because a large number of field guns were adapted to this method. There were no personnel shelters, magazines and communication bunkers, which were to be built in time of war. The Belgians had also built some emplacements for 155mm guns.

On the coastline, little to no work had been done and the Belgians planned to use German-built installations from the previous war, which included machine gun and gun emplacements, personnel shelters, magazines, fire-control station and observation positions, all of which were in fair condition and would require little expense to restore. Once again, however, funds for the restoration work were in short supply in 1938. The batteries at Knocke and north of Breedene were to have four 280mm guns that the Germans had turned over to Belgium at the end of the war. Other plans called for two batteries of 155mm guns, two of 75mm guns in and near Nieuport and La Panne, as well as artillery, a machine gun and a 47mm anti-tank gun to cover the beaches and moles.

A position that was not mentioned in either report was the KW Line running from Koningshooikt to Wavre because work did not begin on it until 1938. This line, which rested on the Dyle River – more a stream rather than a river – comprised 190 bunkers in 1940. It consisted mainly of Belgian Gates between Wavre and Namur without bunkers to cover them.

[Source: American military attaché reports from Lieutenant Colonel Waite in May 1937 and Lieutenant Colonel Fuller in March 1938.]

spearheaded the main thrust of the offensive as they sped through the 'impassable' Ardennes. In advance of these operations, however, a special group of paratroopers and glider troops launched a special mission. The glider troops had trained on captured Czech fortifications and their mission, the first action of the entire German offensive in the West, was to land on top of Fort Eben Emael. The 4th Panzer Division and infantry troops were scheduled to rush to their relief across the Maastricht Appendage. The German troops advanced directly against PFL 1, giving the impression that they were launching the main offensive thrust in the West. The success of the operation not only convinced the Allies that this was the main operation, but it made it impossible for them to hold Liège and the line along the Meuse. Liège did not become a repeat of August 1914, but the situation was almost as bad.

Another Invasion – May 1940

Early on the morning of Friday 10 May 1940, German gliders cut their tows just over the Dutch border and soared on silent wings until they reached the Belgian border. The plan was for four teams of paratroopers of Assault Battalion Koch to land almost simultaneously at three bridge sites and on top of Fort Eben Emael. Three of the forty-two gliders aborted their mission, including two of the eleven gliders assigned to Eben Emael. The unmarked craft came under fire over Dutch territory, but provoked no Belgian reaction as they hove into view at Eben Emael. Meanwhile, the three other glider assault teams landed, stormed two of the bridges (Veldwezelt and Vroenhoven) despite resistance and removed the demolition charges, thus saving the bridges. Since there was no adequate landing site for gliders near the Kanne (Canne) bridge, the paratroopers had to jump out of their gliders and run the extra distance fast enough to take it. However, the commander of Eben Emael ordered the demolition of the bridge before they were able to reach it. About forty minutes later, 24-man machine-gun platoons parachuted to join each of the three lightly armed glider-borne assault groups at the bridges and helped them resist counterattacks.[6]

The deployment of paratroopers was not entirely new in this war. German airborne troops had already dropped into Norway. One company had captured Sola airfield in April 1940; Russian experiments with paratroopers in the 1930s had also been widely publicized. However, it was not until after the opening of the offensive in the West that the Allies realized what a threat they could be. The last thing they had been prepared for on 10 May 1940 was paratroopers and especially gliders. The crews of the anti-aircraft guns saw the gliders approaching, but waited for orders to fire since they were unable to identify the nationality of the aircraft.

Eben Emael had experienced a comedy of errors and a series of misfortunes hours before the actual assault. On the day of the attack, the garrison was not at full strength because many of the men were on leave at a nearby town. Major Jean F. Jottrand, the commander, was alerted shortly after midnight, but he delayed for hours the order to fire the 75mm guns as a warning. Before permission to fire came, he ordered his troops to disassemble the two temporary buildings near Block 1. Since the garrison was short of men, some of the crews from the combat blocks were brought over. By the time the order to fire the warning shots was finally issued, the firing pins of the guns were missing in one block and a gun crew was absent from another because it was busy tearing down the buildings outside. It was not until an hour later, at 3:25 am, that the first warning shots could be fired, about ten minutes before Assault Battalion Koch[7] took off from Germany. In addition, Eben Emael had suffered from

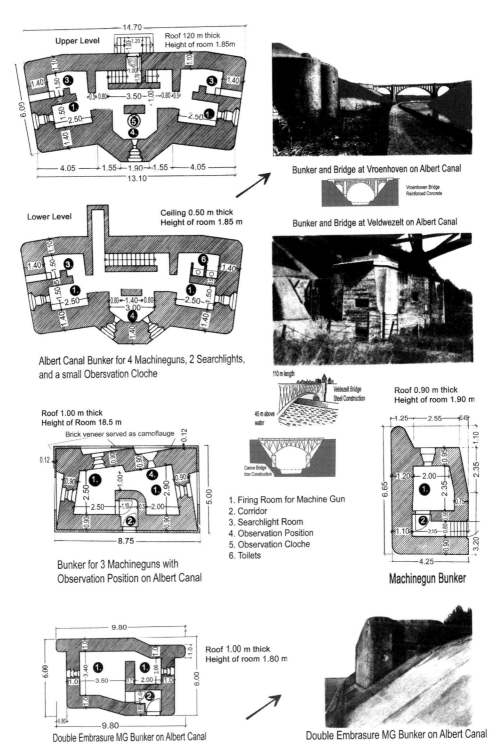

Upper Level

14.70

Roof 120 m thick
Height of room 1.85m

6.00

1.40 ❸ 1.50 0.5 0.80 3.50 0.80 0.5 ❸ 1.40

1.50 ❶ 2.50 ❺ ❹ 2.50 ❶

13.10

4.05 1.55 1.90 1.55 4.05

Lower Level

Ceiling 0.50 m thick
Height of room 1.85 m

1.40 ❸ 1.50 ❻ 1.40

❶ 2.50 0.80 1.40 0.80 ❹ 3.00 2.50 ❶

Albert Canal Bunker for 4 Machineguns, 2 Searchlights,
and a small Obersvation Cloche

Bunker and Bridge at Vroenhoven on Albert Canal

Vroenhoven Bridge
Reinforced Concrete

Bunker and Bridge at Veldwezelt on Albert Canal

Roof 1.00 m thick
Height of Room 18.5 m

Brick veneer served as camoflauge

0.12 0.90 0.90 0.12

0.12 0.90 0.90

❶ 1.00 ❹

2.50 ❶ 2.90 0.90

2.50 1.10 0.5 2.00 ❷ 0.90

5.00

8.75

Bunker for 3 Machineguns with
Observation Position on Albert Canal

110 m length

Veldezelt Bridge
Steel Construction

45 m above
water

Canne Bridge
Iron Construction

1. Firing Room for Machine Gun
2. Corridor
3. Searchlight Room
4. Observation Position
5. Observation Cloche
6. Toilets

Roof 0.90 m thick
Height of room 1.90 m

1.25 2.55 0.45

1.10

6.65 1.20 2.00 2.35

❶ 2.35 0.95

0.75

❷ 1.10 315 0.80 1.5

0.90 0.80 3.20

4.25

Machinegun Bunker

9.80

1.00

6.00

1.0 ❶ 3.40 ❶ 2.00 1.0

1.0 3.50 0.7 2.00 1.10

6.00

❷

0.80 9.80

Double Embrasure MG Bunker on Albert Canal

Double Embrasure MG Bunker on Albert Canal

Albert Canal bunkers and three key bridges attacked to support the assault on Fort Eben Emael.

AT Wall Block V in rear

The Victors

Germans in front of the Entrance Block

Block IV and AT Wall

Entrance Block 1983

AT Gun postion

Eben Emael on 11 May 1940.

mechanical and communication failures. To add insult to injury, some of the blocks were not yet ready for combat. The crew of Cupola 120 worked to repair problems with the gun hoists. The 75mm gun turrets did not have canister rounds to clear the surface of the fort from attackers. Mi-Sud was not manned because its crew had not yet returned from helping tear down the buildings near Block 1. Most of the crew of Mi-Nord was also absent. The boxes of machine gun ammunition remained sealed because the crews had not received permission to open them.[8] The crew of the MA-1 observation cloche had removed the periscope early in the morning because of condensation. Some other positions had missing equipment. A third of the gun crews were not at their anti-aircraft gun positions and their hand grenades had no fuses. After they failed to identify the gliders, they opened fire only when the Germans came crashing down on the roof of the fort. Several gliders were hit, but half the machine guns jammed, allowing the Germans to disembark and race towards their objectives. The occupants of a couple of gliders were pinned in the wire entanglements near the two machine gun blocks, but the Belgians did not fire upon them. The assault teams used special hollow charges, including the heavy 50kg charge divided into two pieces and carried by two men. Two assault teams dashed to the northern part of the fort to destroy two 120mm gun turrets only to discover that they were decoys. Apparently, German intelligence had identified all the positions of the fort, but could not differentiate between dummy positions and real ones.[9] As a result, two of the eleven teams assigned to the fort were isolated for a good deal of the time, while two gliders failed to show up, including the one assigned to eliminate the real 120mm gun turret. The team from the reserve glider took over that assignment, leaving the fort's garrison to deal with seven assault teams scurrying to their targets. Despite the fact that the anti-aircraft guns failed to fire at the gliders when they were most vulnerable, the garrison should have been able to impede the enemy's progress on the fort more effectively. If the Mi blocks had been manned and the ammunition had been ready, the Germans would not have been able to immobilize the artillery blocks as easily as they did. If the canister rounds had been at the gun turrets and crews ready to fire, they might have achieved devastating results. On a proper war footing, the fort might have been able to put up a fight. Even if only one of these conditions had been fulfilled, the German mission might have failed. Despite the 'ifs,' the officers knew that the fort was near the border and should have been prepared for some form of surprise attack at any time.

As it was, the German assault teams succeeded in reaching their objectives. In a few cases, the 50kg hollow charge failed to achieve the desired results, but overall it was effective. The 12.5kg hollow charge also managed to destroy some gun embrasures. Although both charges generally failed to penetrate turrets and cloches, the explosions disabled equipment and inflicted casualties. Within in the first fifteen minutes of landing, the paratroopers achieved most of their objectives. They blasted their way into the Mi blocks and took shelter in them when the Belgians counterattacked with 150mm guns (250 rounds fired) from Fort Barchon, 105mm guns (1,000 rounds fired) from Fort Pontisse and nearby field artillery during the day. The Germans neutralized the MA-1 and MA-2 artillery casemates and the 75mm gun turrets of Cupola Nord and Cupola Sud and eliminated the anti-aircraft positions. Only Cupola 120, which had not been attacked, remained unscathed until the German reserve team detonated 50kg hollow charges after initially disabling the guns by stuffing 1kg charges down the gun barrels. Yet the turret was not put out of action until almost 9:30 am even though it failed to

(Top) View from Block 01 of locks leading to the River Maas. (Bottom Left) Wreckage of stairway leading to Maastricht Artillery Casemate. It was destroyed by the crew after the Germans took the block. (Bottom Right) Latrine in Vise 1 artillery casemate. (*Authors*)

◄--- Staged surrender of a
Belgian position

Section of the Albert Canal
lined with barbed wire obstacles ---►

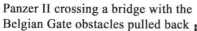

Panzer II crossing a bridge with the
Belgian Gate obstacles pulled back

↑ Column of Panzer I crossing the Albert Canal. A Dutch bunker can be
seen next to the bridge and one below the bridge.

German army photos from May 1940 of crossing of the Albert Canal.

hinder the German operations on the fort or at Kanne because of mechanical problems and orders against firing into Dutch territory. The Germans silenced other blocks, including Block 2 on the anti-tank ditch, while Stukas attacked the entrance block. The crews of the breached combat blocks fled into the bowels of the fort, sealing off access from their blocks by erecting sandbag and steel beam barriers. The garrison, effectively trapped inside the fort, waited in vain for relief from the demoralized Belgian troops stationed nearby. Communications problems did not help the situation. The lightly-armed troops of Assault Group Granite remained on the fort all day waiting for relief from a combat engineer unit from one of the advancing infantry regiments. Since the 4th Panzer Division and infantry divisions had been delayed when the Dutch destroyed the bridges at Maastricht on 10 May, they did not reach the Albert Canal as planned. The engineer battalion crossed the canal in rubber rafts on the morning of 11 May and finally reached the paratroopers at about 5:00 am. Just after noon, Major Jottrand surrendered the fort. His garrison had suffered fewer than one hundred casualties including about twenty dead, while the German assault group lost only six men. Amazingly, the gun crews managed to repair some of the turrets damaged by the German demolitions and get them back in operation until the Germans silenced them for good. The exact manner in which they captured the fort and the details about their hollow charges remained a secret for quite a while and speculation ran rife for many months after the battle. Several years after the war, suspicion lingered that sabotage had crippled some of the gun turrets and other equipment.

Timeline of Events, May 1940

10 May	Netherlands, Belgium and Luxembourg invaded.
	Assault on Eben Emael, Paratroopers land in Fortress Holland.
	Allied troops race into Belgium – Plan D.
	German Army Group A races through Ardennes.
11 May	Albert Canal breached and Eben Emael surrenders.
12 May	German XIX Panzer Corps in Ardennes reaches the Meuse.
	Battle of Hannut begins.
	9th Panzer Division reaches paratroopers at Moerdijk bridge.
13 May	Liège taken.
	XLI Panzer Corps in the Ardennes crosses the Meuse.
	XIX Panzer Corps crosses the Meuse.
14 May	Battle of Gembloux Gap begins.
	The Dutch surrender.
15 May	XIX Panzer Corps breaks through at Sedan.
17 May	Germans enter Brussels, Belgian government moves to Ostend.
18 May	Antwerp taken.
	German panzer division reaches the Somme.
19 May	British Expeditionary Force retreats towards Dunkirk.
20 May	German panzer division reaches the sea.
26 May	British begin Dunkirk evacuation.
28 May	Belgium surrenders.

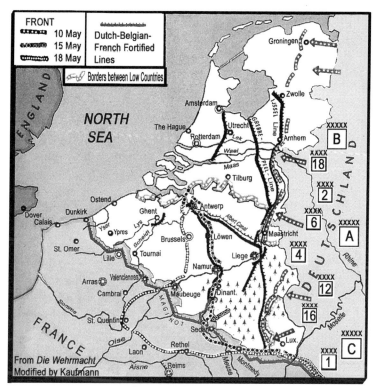

German Offensive of May 1940

1940 Campaign.

However, many years later it was determined that the garrison's lack of action was responsible for the fall of Eben Emael.

After Fort Eben Emael failed in its mission, the Germans flanked the PFL 1 and breached the Albert Canal Line on 11 May. As a result, the defence of Liège became impossible as the Allies advanced to the Dyle Position but came under heavy pressure from the Germans.[10]

Other German units engaged PFL 1 on 10 May and bombarded Fort Aubin-Neufchâteau with heavy artillery the next day. After several infantry attacks, the Luftwaffe joined the artillery and breached the fort's defences on 15 May. Another assault was beaten back on 20 May with support from Fort Battice and Fort Barchon, which had been firing in support for days. A further attack on 21 May finally led to the surrender of the fort and its garrison of over 500 men. All the fort's guns were out of action according to the last message sent from the fort's commander to Battice. In his message, he stated that he would destroy everything and wished the defenders of Battice 'Good Luck'. The white flag went up over Aubin-Neufchâteau at 4:45 pm. During the first days of the war, the Germans had moved up 305mm and 355mm guns to bombard the forts of PFL 1, concentrating on Aubin-Neufchâteau. Eben Emael had already fallen so the big guns were never needed there. Battice, engaged since the first day of the enemy offensive, did not face the heavy artillery brought up to bombard Aubin-Neufchâteau until 13 May when the Germans fired about 200 rounds at it, causing no serious damage. Since the gun turrets of Battice had driven the assault troops from the glacis of Aubin-Neufchâteau more than once, the Germans were anxious to silence them or at least divert them. The German artillery included two 305mm mortars (probably Mörsers M11), a 355mm mortar of Artillery Group 800, railway batteries with two 170mm guns and two 280mm (Kürze Bruno) railway guns. On 21 May, when its neighbouring fort surrendered, Battice became the target of most of the big guns and about seventy Stukas and bombers of the Luftwaffe. The intensity of the attack increased about 5:00 pm, shortly after the fall of Aubin-Neufchâteau. In the space of several hours, the enemy inflicted more damage on the fort than in all previous days since the invasion. The effects were devastating on the garrison of Battice.

One of the Stukas dropped a large bomb that hit an obstacle and ricocheted into the entrance grille of Block 1. The explosion inside the block caused massive damage and detonated one of the anti-tank mines stored inside. The explosion destroyed the access stairs. A second mine, which did not explode, gave off a large amount of carbon monoxide, fouling the air. Rescuers failed to get very far beyond the gallery level and their gas masks failed to protect them. It was not until that night that the defenders were able to make a better assessment and discovered four survivors among the wreckage. About thirty men had died in the explosion. Another bomb struck the entrance to Block 5, destroying the grille, cracking walls and damaging the mount of an FM in its embrasure. One gunner died, the chief of the block was blinded and several men were wounded and taken to the infirmary. The searchlight and weapons embrasures were damaged, only the machine gun cloche remained operational. The enemy artillery and aircraft had inflicted additional damage. When a large bomb cratered the surface of the fort, the resulting debris obstructed the 60mm anti-tank gun on the west side of Block 2 and tore up the railway tracks in front of it. The casemate machine guns and one of the three cloches of Block 3 were knocked out. The 75mm gun turret at Block 6 was still operational, but cracks had formed in the concrete and the lighting was out. In addition, about 20m of the counterscarp wall across from the block had come down, giving easier access to the anti-tank

German troops at captured bunker on the Albert Canal

Surrender of Fort Boncelles on PFL 2

AT Wall & Block 6

Forts of PFL1

Eben Emael surrender on 11 May 1940

Wartime Entrance

Surrender of Aubin-Neufchateau

Surrender of Tancremont on 29 May 1940

Surrender of the Liège forts in May 1940. (*Frank Philippart*)

ditch. At Block 7, the machine-gun casemate on the north side was obstructed by debris from the scarp that filled its fossé diamant and blocked the embrasure.

After the bombardment, the superstructure of the fort was a jumble of mangled reinforcement bars, debris and dust dotted with turrets and cloches. The 75mm gun turrets of Block 4 and Block 6 showed deep gouges left by armour-piercing shells. Block A Nord's 75mm turret had taken similar damage from a heavy artillery round that also smashed the sight used by the turret chief.

The German army group commander, annoyed about his own losses, demanded the surrender of the remaining two forts of PFL 1. At 9:00 pm, a German officer, accompanied by the commander of Aubin-Neufchâteau, drove up to Battice. They negotiated an immediate ceasefire and warned the commander of Battice that he did not surrender on 22 May the bombardment would resume. That night, the commander of Battice ordered his officers to survey the entire fort, including its superstructure and to walk over to Block 1. The devastation at Block 1 and the damage at Block 5 were not encouraging. Considering this was the strongest of all the forts, it appeared to have suffered considerable damage, especially to the blocks along the scarp. The large anti-tank ditch with combat blocks in it turned out to be more of a liability than an asset. The fort's artillery was still functional and it still had a good supply of ammunition. However, the damage to some of the coffre blocks would leave the fort vulnerable to infantry assault in some places. Sometime after midnight, the vast majority of the fort's officers voted to capitulate. Orders went out to destroy weapons and equipment. The white flag went up at 6:00 am on 22 May. The only part of the fort left operational was the section with the medical facilities and one diesel engine that supplied it with power.[11] At this time the BEF, a French army and the Belgian army were cut off from and forming a pocket from Dunkirk to the Belgian coast. The remaining forts at Liège were deep behind enemy lines.

Fort Tancrémont did not surrender until 29 May, the day after the King had capitulated. Its resistance after the other forts succumbed had little significance since the Germans simply bypassed it. Days before the surrender of Battice, German troops that had already advanced upon PFL 2 had already eliminated most of its forts, so that Tancrémont offered no threat to their line of communications after the surrender of Battice.

The forts of PFL 2 went into action on the first day. In an advance towards the Dyle Line, the Germans had to eliminate them to open their line of communications. Forts Barchon and Pontisse, as mentioned, fired in support of Eben Emael on 10 and 11 May. On 12 May, the Belgian army withdrew towards the Dyle Line. The defenders of Liège were unsupported as the Germans penetrated the PFL 1 and advanced toward PFL 2. The German 223rd Infantry Division (Sixth Army) was assigned to reduce the fortress. Early in the afternoon on that day, Fort Barchon's 75mm gun turrets with support from Fort Pontisse drove off German troops trying to penetrate its barbed-wire barrier and two hours later, all turrets went into action to beat off another assault. The fort came under heavy bombardment after midnight and again early in the morning of 13 May. Later that morning, one of the 75mm howitzers exploded, wounding four members of the turret crew. The fort's weapons fired at too high a rate and began overheating, so, to prevent another accident, the commander ordered a break in the firing. The next day, the Germans knocked out a 150mm gun turret and early that evening the fort's guns beat off another assault. The fort remained in almost constant action until the evening of 16 May when a heavy artillery bombardment of several hours heavily damaged the other 150mm gun turret, which went back into action the next day before a heavy artillery bombardment began in the morning. An air attack in the afternoon inflicted additional damage that day, leaving the scarp and counterscarp badly shot up and in a state of imminent collapse while the concrete walls and roofs inside the fort began cracking. On 18 May, Fort Barchon was bombarded with heavy artillery including a Czech 420mm howitzer. A direct hit destroyed a 105mm gun turret that morning and the air intake tower came under attack. At noon, the fort's commandant rejected a demand to surrender. An hour later, the battle resumed with an attack by the German engineer battalion that relieved the paratroopers at Eben Emael, supported by anti-tank guns and 88mm anti-aircraft guns. The engineers' demolitions and flamethrowers eliminated most of the fort's turrets and machine-gun positions, forcing the garrison to surrender, but the crew of the air tower continued to resist. Despite the heavy damage to the fort, only four of the 280-man garrison were killed and twenty-two were wounded between 10 and 16 May. Meanwhile, across the river, Fort Pontisse was bombed and many of its turrets were overturned in the Stuka attack.

On the other side of PFL 2, Fort Boncelles fell on 15 May and that same day Stukas dive-bombed Fort Flémalle, damaging the central turret (machine guns and lance grenade for close defence) and breached the counterscarp. The next day, the Germans launched an infantry assault and the fort surrendered. Earlier, on the evening of 13 May, Fort Embourg was attacked and on 16 and 17 May, it was bombed by aircraft. On 17 May, its neighbour, Fort Chaudfontaine, came under attack and called for supporting fire to drive the Germans from its glacis. Fort Fléron responded with its 75mm guns and once again, enemy aircraft attacked both Embourg and Chaudfontaine. That evening, the three forts underwent another Stuka bombardment. Fort Fléron, bombarded from the first day, lost all electrical power so that the crews had to operate its equipment manually to respond to firing requests in support of Battice, Tancrémont and its neighbouring forts. Fort Chaudfontaine and Fléron fell on 17 May. Fléron did not stand up well to the aerial bombardment that day as part of its scarp wall collapsed, its infantry exit was blocked and the telephone switchboard room and artillery command post were destroyed. The ventilation system shut down and the fort's concrete structures were starting to breakup. One of the 75mm gun turrets and the 150mm gun turret were either jammed or damaged and the ammunition supply for the 105mm guns was exhausted. Before the Fort Fléron fell, a number of men from the garrison of over 280 men escaped through the entrance of the air intake tower.[12] Fort Embourg surrendered on the evening of 18 May followed the next day by Fort Evegnée, after three days of infantry attacks. On 21 and 22 May, as Forts Neufchâteau and Battice fell, the route through Liège was open.[13]

The bulk of the German panzer divisions broke through the Ardennes, crossed the Meuse and drove to the Channel to cut off the Allied forces in Belgium on 15 May. On 16 May, while the defenders of Liège continued to resist, the Allies were already withdrawing from the Dyle Line leaving the forts of PFN, like those at Liège, to fend for themselves.

Stukas dive-bombed Fort Suarlée at Namur on the first day. The fort's telephone lines to its observation posts were cut on 14 May. German troops appeared on 15 May as the French forces defending the area withdrew. On that day, the fort's air intake tower was hit with rounds from a German 37mm anti-tank gun and the fort was bombed from the air once again. The Germans launched an attack on the air intake tower the next night and made an infantry assault on 17 May. During the night of 17–18 May, German troops reached the fort's fossé,

"Belgian Gate" used as road block.
Note rollers on front and back for movement.

Belgian tank turret mounted on bunker at Ostend

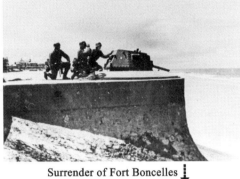

Belgian Gates linked together to form an AT Obstacle
on the Dyle Line.

Surrender of Fort Boncelles

Abatis created to form a road block in the Ardennes
near St. Vith

Swastika flying over Fort Embourg.

Detail of Belgian Gate, Belgian Gates lined as a barrier, an abates obstacle in Ardennes, a coastal bunker, and surrender of Fort Boncelles and Embourg.

only to be driven back. During the day, an artillery bombardment temporarily knocked out the power and ventilation systems, destroyed two of the four 75mm howitzer turrets and jammed the central turret (mounting two 75mm GP guns) and both machine-gun turrets.[14] The next day, another bombardment forced the surrender of the fort.

Fort St. Héribert on the south side of the front began firing its two 75mm GP turret guns at German troops on the other side of the Meuse on 15 May. The fort's armament was similar

The Official Account of the Battle for Aubin-Neufchâteau

According to the official history of Fort Aubin-Neufchâteau, the fort formed the first line of defence together with Eben Emael, Battice and Tancrémont. Captain-Commander Oscar d'Ardenne commanded a garrison of 14 officers and 542 men. The fort's armament included four twin 75mm turrets, three 81mm mortars and five 47mm anti-tank guns. The fort had a reserve of 15,000 shells of all types and fired off 14,827 rounds during the siege. It also had six anti-aircraft machine guns, eleven machine guns, sixteen automatic rifles and trench mortars. The account, summarized below, describes the battle.

As soon as the invasion began on 10 May, the fort went into action. Informed by its outposts and outer observation posts, it proceeded without respite to harass and destroy advancing enemy troops. At nightfall, the fort having fired off 169 rounds and is encircled.

Next day, the battle is going to take a new turn. At dawn the fort is submitted to the unceasing fire from a heavy battery. It defends itself and repels more than 20 attacks of the enemy infantry.

Day after day, the struggle becomes more difficult. The outer observation posts are destroyed, one by one. Fully aware of the fort's strength, the invaders send troops with modern equipment that the defenders unceasingly continue to destroy. The bombers and heavy artillery alternate their assault maintaining a continuous bombardment of the superstructures, opening breaches that the garrison tries to fill during the rare lulls.

On 16 May, a request for surrender is presented and rejected. The battle resumes becoming even more intense. During breaks in the action, both sides tend their wounded and bury their dead.

On Monday 20 May at dawn, a third request for surrender is rejected like the preceding ones. This time, the enemy has decided to finish the battle and the inferno breaks out again. A deluge of fire sweeps down upon Neufchâteau, which defends itself with all its arms. The enemy is everywhere; they shoot at the cupolas and embrasures. Battice, also under violent attack, was called upon to help drive off enemy infantry investing Neufchâteau. The day was very hard for the defenders and the fort badly damaged with several structures seriously damaged or destroyed. In spite of that, the fort continues its desperate resistance and by nightfall, Aubin-Neufchâteau is still holding out, although completely isolated on its hill.

The next morning, the sun rises over a horrible landscape. The hill offers a gloomy scene, ploughed up as it was by thousands of projectiles. Soon, the inferno breaks out again. Feeling that the end is near, the enemy concentrates all their firepower on Neufchâteau and then, the shock troops storm the fort, which is in its last gasp.

Attacked on all sides, the besieged expend most of their remaining ammunition and fight on. The battle is unequal; the end is near. Soldiers are already fighting with grenades and Aubin-Neufchâteau finally falls. It is 5:00 pm on Tuesday 21 May 1940.

The garrison left the fort bearing arms, which they have defended so courageously. Before their departure for a long and painful captivity, they pass a company of the German 46th Infantry Regiment that presents arms.

Belgian Forts of the Great War

Fort	1914 # days Resisting*	1914 # of casualties	1940 # days resisting*	1940 # of casualties
LIÈGE				
Barchon	4 (4–8 Aug)	22 (dead)	8 (10–18 May)	26 (4 dead)
Boncelles	10 (5–15 Aug)	50 (dead)	5 (10–15 May)	13 (dead)
Chaudfontaine	8 (5–13 Aug)	130 (dead)	7 (10–17 May)	13 (dead)
Embourg	8 (5–13 Aug)	?	8 (10–18 May)	?
Evegnée	7 (4–11 Aug)	?	9 (10–19 May)	?
Flémalle	6 (10–16 Aug)	1 (dead)	6 (10–16 May)	?
Fléron	10 (4–14 Aug)	5 (dead)	7 (10–17 May)	10 (4 dead)
Hollogne	11 (5–16 Aug)	?	18 (10–28 May)	?
Lantin	5 (10–15 Aug)	?	–	–
Liers	10 (4–14 Aug)	?	–	–
Loncin	1 (14–15 Aug)	250	–	–
Pontisse	9 (4–13 Aug)	?	8 (10–18 May)	
NAMUR				
Andoy	3 (21–24 Aug)	17 (dead)	? (?–23 May)	5 (dead)
Cognelée	2 (21–23 Aug)	?	–	–
Dave	4 (21–25 Aug)	?	8 (15–23 May)	1 (dead)
Emines	3 (21–24 Aug)	?	–	–
Maizeret	1 (21–22 Aug)	?	? (?–23 May)	?
Malone	3 (21–24 Aug)	?	? (?–21 May)	?
Marchovelette	2 (21–23 Aug)	20 (dead)*	3 (15–18 May)	3 (dead)
St. Héribert	3 (21–24 Aug)	?	3 (18–21 May)	1 (dead)
Suarlée	2 (23–25 Aug)	1 (dead)	4 (15–19 May)	No deaths

*Not including the day of surrender.
**According to the 1922 *Encyclopaedia Britannica*, 2/3 dead

to Fort Suarlée with seven turrets. The German 211th Infantry Division with the mission of clearing the south and southwestern fronts at Namur began the assault on 19 and 20 May. Fort St. Héribert came under heavy bombardment on 18 May and much of its concrete began to break up by the next day, but its turrets remained in action in spite of the fact that two of them sustained a hit. The damage from the bombardment of 20 May was more serious and the situation continued to deteriorate. On 21 May, the machine-gun turret went into action against enemy troops on the glacis. The fort continued to fire upon the Germans who responded with increasing violence. In the morning, Forts Malone and Dave fired in support as the Germans launched a second ground attack that also failed. By late morning, as more concrete crumbled, the turrets were taken out of action, forcing the commander to surrender the fort. In the German regiment involved, 129 men died and over 600 were wounded while the Belgian garrison lost only one man.

On the south front of the PFN, Fort Dave came under attack on 15 May and it was surrounded by 21 May, like forts Andoy and Maizeret. Unable to respond to enemy fire, Forts Dave, Andoy and Maizeret surrendered on 23 May. The garrison of Andoy lost five men, but inflicted 280 casualties on the enemy. On the previous day, German 88mm and 20mm Flak guns had smashed the gun turrets and observation turret of Fort Maizeret. On 23 May, a 37mm anti-tank gun took out the close defence turret mounting grenade launchers and assault troops (including engineers) breached the moat in the morning. Since the exhaust system for ventilation was destroyed, further resistance was futile.

The defences of Antwerp did not last very long and after a key fort at Lierre fell, the PFA was abandoned on 18 May. German troops occupied Antwerp on 19 May after the Belgian army withdrew to the Ghent Bridgehead, which was broken on 26 May. King Leopold III surrendered two days later.

Chapter 6

Fortress Switzerland

The Swiss maintained their independence for centuries by creating an effective military force that eviscerated invading armies in their mountainous strongholds. But the French Revolution and the Napoleonic Era brought a change in warfare with which not even the Swiss soldier using old methods could cope. The forces of the French Revolution dissolved the cantons and established the despised Helvetic Republic in 1798. Napoleon ended that Republic in 1803 and created a more tolerable situation for the Swiss. The Congress of Vienna fully restored Swiss independence and mandated its permanent neutrality in 1815. The Swiss, lacking confidence in paper promises, initiated a system of modern fortifications to stop any future invader or force him to reconsider such an operation.

Switzerland's complex history began with the creation of the cantons of Uri, Schwyz and Unterwalden in 1291 when they rose against the Holy Roman Empire. Located in the central Alpine region of modern-day Switzerland, the Swiss Alps were effective in helping repel invading Habsburg armies. Before long, a confederation with a policy of isolation and independence emerged. However, this did not prevent expansion as the boundaries were pushed out to Lucerne (Luzern), Berne and Zurich by the next century. The Swiss continued to extend their domination into Solothrun, Fribourg, Grisons in the east, Valais in the south and Geneva in the southwest by the seventeenth century. Finally, in 1648, the Treaty of Westphalia ended the bloody Thirty Years War and formally recognized the independence of the Swiss Confederation. Against all odds, this nation of German, French, Italian and Romansh speaking Protestant as well as Catholic cantons faced potentially divisive forces of language and religion. The Congress of Vienna not only restored the independence of the nation, but also allowed it to expand. In 1815, the Swiss brought Valais back into the Confederation. The twenty-six Swiss cantons were united by the common goal of preventing their powerful neighbours from absorbing them.

The return of Valais to the new Confederation was important since it included the Upper Rhône Valley, the back door into the Swiss nation that led into the Alpine barrier in 1815. The construction of the Simplon road between 1803 and 1805 opened a route from Valais into modern-day Italy that interested both the French and Italians. It gave access to a road around Lake Leman (Lake Geneva) into western Switzerland. The Simplon road increased the importance of the town of Brig, while the defile created by the Rhône near St-Maurice formed an easily-defended position. For much of the century, the Swiss military planned and built a series of defensive positions concentrating much of their efforts in the south where the newly-formed Italian nation and a second Napoleonic French empire presented the greatest threat. The Italian wars of unification in the 1850s not only strengthened Piedmont-Sardinia – the emerging Italian nation of the 1860s – but also rewarded Napoleon III of France with Savoy, which bordered with the cantons of Valais and Geneva.[1]

A British War Office report of 1889 best summed up the Swiss situation:

Placed in the centre of Europe, between France, Germany, Austria and Italy, the military importance of Switzerland is very great and out of all proportion to the extent of its territory, the number of its inhabitants, or the strength of its army. A power which should be master of Switzerland could debouch on the theatres of operations of the Rhône, Saône, Po, or Danube. Thus, from Geneva an army can march on Lyon; from Basle it can gain the valley of the Saône by the trouée of Belfort; from Constance and Schaffhausen the valley of the Danube could be reached and the line of the Rhine turned, while Italy can be invaded by the Alps and the lines of defence of that country against France and Austria can be turned.[2]

General Johann Conrad Finsler (1765–1838), who dominated the period following the Napoleonic Wars, was often in conflict with his subordinate, Guillaume Henri Dufour (1787–1875) who had wanted to turn St-Maurice into a fortress in the 1820s. Born in Geneva, Dufour was educated in France and had served in Napoleon's army before returning to his homeland to serve as an engineer officer and cartographer. In 1822, he urged the fortification of Geneva. When he replaced Finsler in the 1830s, he gained control of the situation. He oversaw the construction of new fortifications to the north and south of the town of St-Maurice to defend the Rhône valley in both directions and designed Vauban-type fortifications with bastions. His planning became the foundation of Switzerland's modern defensive system, which began take shape after his death late in the century.

   In addition to being the founder of the modern Swiss defences, General Dufour is famous for his role in the Sonderbund War of 1845. Several cantons, including Valais and the three original cantons created in 1291, formed a Catholic alliance and revolted against anti-Catholic measures.[3] General Dufour led the campaign with almost 100,000 troops against fewer than 80,000 rebels. The war began on 3 November and ended on 27 November 1845 after several engagements. Casualties amounted to a combined total of a little under 100 dead and about 500 wounded and Dufour inaugurated a policy for the injured that led to the creation of the Red Cross. The constitution of the nation was changed creating a federal state with the cantons denied their former semi-independent status.[4]

   During his long tenure in the Swiss army, General Dufour established a National Redoubt beginning with the construction of Fortress St-Maurice. Two other major fortress complexes at Gotthard and Sargans were developed after Dufour's time when major railway tunnels were built in those locations.[5] His designs did not represent the most modern of the era, but the forts occupied formidable positions. The passage of time and the Industrial Revolution affected Switzerland more than most countries, because it opened the country to invasion. Until then, the Jura Mountains had presented the main obstacle against a French invasion and only Basel and the Rhine Valley had been vulnerable. Between the Jura and the Swiss Alps, lay the Swiss Plateau or Mittelland (Central Plateau) occupying about 30 per cent of the country with almost every major population centre except Basel and Lugano. It also encompassed most of its agricultural land, major forests and industry. The Jura extends along most of the French border and forms a barrier between Basel and the Plateau, which, for most of their history, gave the Swiss the ability to take advantage of interior lines. The surrounding mountains confined

Dufour Tower at St. Maurice

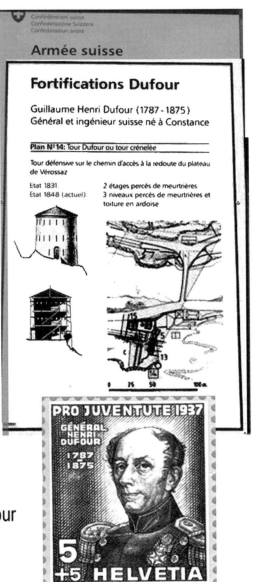

Defensive Tower on the access road to the redoubt of the plateau of Vérossaz.
   2 levels with loopholes in 1831
   3 levels with loopholes in 1848 and a slate roof.
Designed by Guillaume Henri Dufour

A Dufour defensive tower. (*J.C. Moret*). Photo of sign put up by military.

invaders to this plateau. However, improvements in transportation changed the situation. In the past, the road system in Switzerland had been little better than in other nations and had often been primitive in the mountains. Trade increased with industrialization, which led to improved roads on the plateau and to the border towns that linked with major French, German and Italian cities. The development of the steam engine and railways did not bypass the Swiss. In 1848, a railway connected Basel with Zurich. In 1848, Robert Stephenson, son of the man who built the first steam locomotive and railway, proposed a route for a national railway across the plateau connecting Zurich to Lausanne and Geneva. Soon, the socio-economic heart of the nation, located on the plateau, was open to large-scale trade with its French and German neighbours. Extensions of the railway system included the Jura-Simplon line that ran from the plateau to the Simplon Pass. However, they did not offer a rail link to Italy because of the Alpine barrier. The French and Italians first pierced the Alpine barrier in 1871 with the Mount Cenis Tunnel. The 13.59km-long tunnel opened a major route for rail traffic between Italy and France.[6] The Swiss began the construction of the almost 15km-long Gotthard Tunnel in 1871 and completed it in 1881. It opened to rail traffic in 1882, creating a new reason for a fortress complex at Gotthard since a major route had been opened between Italy and Germany. During his tenure, Dufour built some fortifications at Bellinzona (Ticino) to close the southern entrance to the Leventina Valley that leads to the Gotthard Pass. To the east, near Sargans, Dufour found it necessary to block the Rhine valley at Luzigsteig[7] to deny the Germans, Austrians and Italians passage through the Graubünden Alps, but no significant work began there until the 1930s.

Work on the Simplon Tunnel began in 1898 with Italian and Swiss teams working towards each other. The 19.8km-long tunnel, the longest in the world until the 1980s, opened in 1906 offering a more direct route between France and Italy. The Grechenberg and Hauenstein rail tunnels opened in 1915 and 1916 respectively, opening two routes through the Jura to the Mittelland. In 1913, the Lötschberg rail tunnel opened a shorter route from Berne on the plateau to the Simplon Tunnel. Thus, by the end of the Great War, the formerly isolated Swiss nation had established important transportation routes that turned its impenetrable Alpine regions into a veritable Swiss cheese, offering potential invaders access from Germany and Italy and France and Italy. Fortunately, the rugged terrain made it possible to block these routes and destroy the great tunnels and associated bridges. The National Redoubt was developed to block all these new routes.

By the 1870s, the Swiss fortification system had become antiquated since technology had not only created new types of transportation, but also more advanced weapons. Although his planning and construction laid the groundwork for the future, at the end of his tenure Dufour left the nation with obsolete defences needing modifications and new weapons.

The cantons that had originally broken away from the Holy Roman Empire had the advantage of the protection of various ranges of the Swiss Alps, but in the nineteenth century, the main population centres located on the Mittelland became vulnerable. During the Napoleonic Era, foreign armies marched from Zurich to Berne and Geneva. Later in the century, the new transportation routes opened the country to invasion. As a result, the National Redoubt evolved into the main and final line of resistance. The fortress complexes of St-Maurice, Gotthard and later Sargans served to block the main passages needed by French, Italian, German and Austrian invaders. At St-Maurice, a dual threat required a complex that could stop a French advance from Savoy or around Lake Leman via Geneva as well as an Italian assault from the opposite direction. St-Maurice overlooks the point where the Rhône creates a narrow defile defended since Roman times. The remnants of the late fifteenth-century castle occupy the left bank of the Rhône at the valley's narrowest point in front of an old bridge that spanned the Rhône where the river is less than 50m wide. The river's source is the Rhône Glacier near the Furka Pass. From there the river flows through a glacial valley where the Bernese Alps rise to over 4,000m (13,000ft) to the north and other Alpine ranges of about 3,000m (10,000ft) tower on the south side. The steep valley walls form a barrier from which defenders can easily cover the valley below that only averages a width of about 1.5km and only about 100m in the defile near St-Maurice. The St-Maurice complex began to take shape under the direction of Dufour in the 1830s.

Fortifications went up around Château St-Maurice and across from it on the right bank taking advantage of the elevated terrain on both sides. In 1831, Battery Rhône on the right bank, along the road, faced down river. Behind it on higher terrain above the road was Battery Capucins. Battery Arzillier, which was at a higher elevation opposite the old twelfth-century bridge, mounted two guns covering the route to St-Maurice. In 1834, it was reinforced with a crenelated wall for musketry and in 1848, with a caponier covering the fossé. New artillery emplacements added in 1859 at this higher elevation included wooden palisades, walls and ditches of the Grande and Petite Tenailles. The walls of the Grande Tenaille were enlarged in 1859. Just to the north of the Petite Tenaille, the army added Battery Gautier, which covered the road from Bex. On the left bank, adjacent to the castle, were the Château batteries. Behind the castle, at a higher elevation, Tower Dufour and a redoubt above it on the plateau dominated the crossing. Identified by some authors as a Martello or Maximillian tower, Tower Dufour, built in the 1830s, had only infantry positions.[8] Further to the south stood Battery Wielandy and nearby Battery Clocher added in 1848. By the 1860s, Dufour's formidable positions once dominating the defile became vulnerable and obsolete when new types of artillery with greater range were developed.

After 1830, besides St-Maurice, the construction of fortifications was mainly limited to Luzisteig (east of the Sargans and the Rhine), Aarberg (northwest of Berne) and Basel to blocking the main routes of the era until 1871. Commissions studied the problem of defence for many years and drew up plans, but little of a concrete nature happened. The opening of the St. Gotthard rail tunnel in 1881 spurred additional studies and some action. The development of the high-explosive shell of the mid-1880s forced the Swiss to consider new types of fortifications; especially since their nation was surrounded by four major powers engaged in an arms race. Neutral Liechtenstein presented no barrier to Austrian aggression, but rather offered an opening into eastern Switzerland.[9]

The New Era

Hans Herzog (1819–94) dominated the period that followed the Dufour era.[10] After 1866, Colonel Herzog served on the commission for strategy and defence of Switzerland. From 1873 until 1894, he presided over the Commission for Fortifications that included six colonels and a lieutenant colonel. General Herzog died in 1894 while still in service and after making key decisions including the creation of Fort Airolo, other defences of the Gotthard Fortress and the Savatan/Dailly complex for Fortress St-Maurice.

Soon after the planning for the fortifications of the Gotthard Pass began, improvements in transportation routes and new tunnels made it essential to build heavy fortifications for the southern and eastern approaches to the National Redoubt. After the completion of the Gotthard tunnel in 1882, the army and government finally began implementing their construction plans. The tunnel not only opened a corridor through Switzerland which was no longer affected by winter closure, but it also allowed the Swiss to move troops from one front to another, taking full advantage of interior lines. Unfortunately, 1882 was also the year Bismarck created the

Caponier

Roof of Fort from rear

Spherical
Mortar

General Hans Herzog

PRO JUVENTUTE 1939
GENERAL
HANS
HERZOG
1819
1894
5+5 HELVETIA

Defenders of the St. Gothard (World War I)

From St. Gothard Pass

Observation
Cupola

Foppa

2 53mm
Mobile
Turrets

Passageway to
Gothard Tunnel

FORT AIROLO

Fort
AIROLO

C = Caponier
C-84 =
    Casemate 84mm gun
T-53 =
    Turret 53mm gun
T-120 =
    Turret 2x120mm guns
T-120H =
    Turret 120mm Howitzer

Triple Alliance,[11] leaving the Swiss with three possibly hostile major powers on their borders. The defence of the tunnel was mandatory to discourage attempts to seize this highly-prized transportation corridor linking Italy and Germany.[12] The Swiss consulted one of their own, Daniel Salis-Soglio, a fortress engineer serving in the Austrian Army, to design the fort at Airolo. The site, located above the Gotthard Pass at 1,142m (3,800ft), was intended to guard the southern portal of the rail tunnel. Construction on Fort Airolo (also known as Fort Fondo del Bosco) began in 1887 and ended in 1890 although additional work continued for a few more years. The fort forms an irregular quadrilateral excavated into the terrain and has a deep moat and three caponiers for close defence. The only windows and the entrance are in the moat on the north side. The turrets were installed in 1895. Near the centre of the fort, a Grüson armoured turret mounting the main armament of two Krupp 120mm Mle 1882 guns with a range of 10km commanded the valley below.[13] Five Krupp 84mm Mle 1880 cannons with a range of about 5km in two casemates covered the flanks and assured close defence. The fort also had four Grüson 53mm QF Mle 1887 guns in disappearing turrets with a range of 3km. The fort's three caponiers mounted twelve bronze 84mm Mle 1871 cannons. Two Grüson 120mm Mle 1888 spherical mortars, with a range of 3km, occupied armoured positions in the rear centre of the fort to cover the southern entrance of the railway tunnel and gaps outside the trajectory of the fort's guns with indirect fire. In 1902, a single 120mm Mle 1891 howitzer with a range of 5.9km replaced these mortars.[14] Three armoured observation cloches completed the position. Large granite blocks were added to the fort's superstructure giving an additional 1.2m of protection from the newly developed high-explosive shells, since reinforced concrete was not yet in use at that time.[15] Moving the granite from the quarry at Lavorgo – located about 20km to the southeast – was no simple task. The blocks were brought by train to the railway station at Airolo; from there, they were hauled to the fort by oxen. The fort, which dominated the valley below, was invisible from the valley floor. Although Airolo was modern by the standards of 1890s, it was lacking when compared to the German Feste of the same era.

In 1889, a passage was excavated from a position near the entrance of the fort to the railway tunnel for a distance of about 1,050m and was completed by 1892. An additional passage connected the fort to the tunnel in 1909. A large bunker at its entrance (now gone) and another above it covered the entrance to the railway tunnel. Positions for machine guns and later flamethrowers and demolition chambers were created inside the tunnel.

The Gotthard tunnel ran northward for 15km and reached its northern portal at Göschenen at 1,106m (3,650ft) creating the need for additional forts at Andermatt. The Gotthard Pass itself is at an elevation of 2,108m (6,916ft) and runs for 26km across the Lepontine Alps. Andermatt is at the end of the Furka Pass (2,431m or 7,976ft) through which a road was built between Andermatt and Gletsch in the mid-1860s mainly for military purposes. A railway constructed between 1910 and 1927 to the Furka Tunnel[16] linked eastern to western Switzerland.

As work began on Fort Airolo followed by more construction, a British military report summarized the Swiss situation in 1889. Based on earlier publications, the British concluded during the 1880s that the Swiss would develop three defensive systems: a peripheral defence with many frontier forts covering the most important defiles, a central fortified position and a radial defence consisting of a few central fortified lines. At the time of this intelligence report, the Swiss fortifications consisted of a large redoubt at Aarberg,[17] three lunettes (field fortifications) and several other positions incapable of resisting modern artillery. Only the

Beginning of the New Era in the 1880s

According to Swiss historian Günther Reiss, the new era began in 1880 when the Federal Council appointed a new commission, which failed to resolve the problem of defence and ended with a split opinion. In 1882, another commission established two defensive zones that set the policy for future defensive strategy. The first zone was the outer sector that followed the lakes of the Jura region, the Aar River and the Limmat River to the Alps. It defended the Swiss plateau region from the north. The second sector was the Alpine region, which became the National Redoubt. The Swiss intended the Urseren Valley to be the base of operations for this last line of defence.[18] Older Swiss defence plans had relied on controlling the Alpine passes between Italy and Switzerland, but the opening of the Gotthard railway tunnel in 1883 giving access to the Urseren Valley[19] and Andermatt in Canton Uri, offered the Italians a new avenue of attack. Thus, the Swiss government assigned priority to and appropriated funds for the defence of the Gotthard in 1886. Since they lacked experience in fortress building, the Swiss immediately turned to the three nations pioneering new techniques in this field. They dispatched a team of officers to meet with Henri Brialmont of Belgium, Maximilian Schumann of Germany and Daniel von Salis-Soglio. Despite the fact the Swiss had seceded from the Habsburgs centuries earlier, their sympathies still lay with them. Thus, the Austrians heavily influenced the new generation of Swiss fortifications, many of which remained in service well past the Second World War. The Swiss adopted Schumann's Grüson turrets and later mixed French carriages with German guns in mountain positions.[20]

From the end of the 1880s until early in the next century, this phase of fortress-building brought major fortifications to the Gotthard and Furka passes. During this period, with the construction of Forts Dailly, Savatan and Scex, the St-Maurice fortress was converted for defence against modern artillery. The valley walls were laced with various types of fortifications and tunnel systems. In the 1890s, they began installing gun turrets on some of the forts of the Gotthard Fortress including Forts Airolo, Bühl and Bäzberg – the last situated above the town of Andermatt.

At about the same time as the construction of Fort Airolo was set in motion, work started on the 84mm gun battery of Motto Bartola (1888–90) and its extensive gallery system. Motto Bartola was located on the same winding mountain road that passed by Fort Airolo, but 1,000m higher in elevation. Fort Hospiz (or Ospizio), built in 1894, had an observation cloche and two turrets, each armed with a 120mm gun. For close defence, it mounted 53mm Mle 1887 QF guns and old Maxim machine guns in casemates. Maxim Mle 1911 machine guns replaced the older weapons during the First World War at which time 105mm Mle 1917 mortars were added. The plans for Fort Stuei were drawn up in 1891 and the fort was completed in 1894. It occupies the steep slope of a cliff below the hamlet of Stuei. Its casemate for two 84mm guns covered blind spots in the defence of Airolo. The fort's caserne was enlarged in 1910 to allow space for an engine room and munitions storage. A tunnel was excavated to accommodate a 60cm searchlight.

The construction of Fort Galenhütten, which was to cover the Furka Pass, began in 1890. This rectangular fort, covered with granite blocks for added protection, comprised

84mm Mle 1881 cannons in two caponiers. Casemates mounting two Schneider 120mm Mle 1882 guns and a turret with a 120mm Mle 1891 howitzer provided the offensive power. A cloche outside and just above the fort provided a point of observation. On the northern side of the Urseren Valley, Forts Bühl and Bäzberg were completed in 1892. The armament at Fort Bühl consisted of two 120mm gun turrets, two 120mm howitzer turrets and three 53mm retracting gun turrets, supported by an observation turret. Fort Bäzberg, higher up the valley wall, had three 120mm gun turrets, four 53mm retracting gun turrets and two observation cloches. The two forts were, in fact, the first Swiss forts to have armoured turrets. According to Günther Reiss, the two forts' irregularly scattered gun positions and armoured gun turrets built directly into the rock were designed to present the enemy with a minimal target. Reiss also points out that the Austrians had removed turrets from their older forts to create similar positions in 1914. These new fortifications built for the era of breech-loading artillery and the high-explosive shell were also equipped with the newest technology, including telephone lines for communications. Thus, in 1892, Fort Airolo was linked to the two forts at the north end of the Gotthard Tunnel with a cable running through the passageway. In some cases, these new positions included 53mm guns in mobile Grüson turrets that were stored in a tunnel or rock shelter in the mountain and rolled out on a 60cm gauge rails to their firing positions.

According to an article published in the *Journal of the United States Artillery* in 1896, the Gotthard Fortress consisted of five groups: the Airolo Group, the central St. Gotthard Group and the Andermatt Group with the Furka and the Oberalp Groups on the flanks. The Furka Group comprised the Galenhütten Battery and the small fort of Furka dominating the Rhône valley at Furka. The main group, which was at Airolo, included Fort Airolo (Fondo del Bosco) dominating the Ticino Valley and the entrance to the Gotthard Tunnel. This group also included the Motto Bartolo Battery, 'a gallery at Stucci' (Fort Stuei) and two blockhouses to the east. The Central Group, located 4km behind this group, consisted of Fort St. Gotthard flanked by the trenches of Bianchi, the blockhouses of Cavanna and the blockhouse of Pusmeda. However, the entire complex had only one cannon.[21]

The Andermatt Group, 10km to the north of the Central Group, included Fort Bühl and Bäzberg, the flanking gallery of Altkirch, the 'position of Rossmetten', and the blockhouse of Brückenwaldboden.[22] Finally, the Oberalp Group consisted of the Redoubt of Calmot and the 'position of Grossboden'. The article pointed out that 'even without fortifications, it would be difficult for an army to force the 'position of Saint Gotthard' since the sites chosen are tactically inaccessible.' This, claimed the author, was the key to Switzerland, probably because they were the newest fortifications. However, he did not downplay importance of the fortifications of Savatan and Dailly at St-Maurice and the projected work for Luziensteig.

remains of former positions could be found at Schaffhausen. The main fortifications at the time appeared to be at Luziensteig where they included 'a simple curtain flanked by two bastions, with barracks and magazines, some casemated towers and several blockhouses'. At Bellinzona, there was a central lunette with several flanking lesser works and at St-Maurice there were three. Other defences often mentioned at Basel, Berne and Baden had 'entirely disappeared'.

The construction of the Fort Dailly/Savatan complex began in 1892 at positions on the east side of the valley wall where their artillery could control the defile at St-Maurice. The forts were ready for occupation in 1894. Dailly occupies a spur and plateau of the same name that sharply rises about 1,400m above Savatan. Access to Dailly is by a road with over two dozen switchbacks. In 1894, the first heavy artillery at Dailly consisted of four French St-Chamond 120mm Mle 1882 eclipsing guns with a range of 9km (later increased to 10.5km) that formed batteries E1, E2 and E3. The mount of the slow-firing disappearing gun included a horizontal shield through which the gun rose into the firing position. The recoil from firing brought the weapon back below the opening in the rectangular armoured shield for reloading.[23] The mount was mounted on a rolling carriage that moved along a rail placed in a trench and rose over the lip of the trench when it was in the firing position. At the end of the trenches, excavated shelters served as a safe parking area for the guns.[24] Below at Fort Savatan, four Schumann 120mm Mle 1891 howitzers mounted in Grüson armoured turrets controlled the northern access to the valley.

During a period of expansion that began in 1895, batteries C10 North and C10 South were added at Dailly. Each had a pair of 105mm Mle 1881 guns with a range of 10km.[25] Much later, two 120mm guns from the E-batteries were placed in fixed positions to replace Battery C10 South. Battery Rossignol received two 120mm guns to the north and two to the south. One old 150mm Mle 1877, nicknamed 'Gros Fritz', with a range of 8.5km formed Battery C15. M15 battery was located between the C10 batteries on Aiguille ridge. It had a pair of 150mm Mle 1881 breech-loading mortars that covered the fort's blind spots and occupied circular concrete pits covered with a light cylindrical shield. They remained in service from 1894 until about 1925. Battery 06 on the same ridge was a single Schumann 120mm Mle 1891 howitzer with a shield located on the opposite side of the summit from the Battery M-15 mortars. This weapon remained in service after 1937 because new ammunition in 1937 increased its range from 5.9km to 7km.

Close defence was provided by a two–gun battery of 84mm Mle 1880 guns that occupied a concrete coffre in the Morcles gallery on the south front above the village of the same name. Across the fort's surface, mobile 53mm gun turrets for close defence moved on tracks like the 120mm guns of the E-batteries. The two forts had entrenchments. They covered the north, west and south fronts of Savatan. During the 1890s, underground telephone lines were installed linking all the positions. The construction of water reservoirs, barracks, magazines and subterranean casernes was completed. At Dailly as well as Savatan, observation and command posts for artillery fire control and additional close defence positions were added and Savatan received an additional 120mm howitzer.

In the early 1900s, the forts underwent important renovations. The forts were linked to the civilian power grid and power-generation facilities were added. The generators, which ran on alcohol, were to provide the forts with electrical power in case they were cut off from outside access during wartime. The facilities for the troops and defences of the forts were expanded. In 1907, two casemates were built for 75mm Mle 1903 guns. This new Battery Aiguille (not to be confused with C10 North located further to the north of it) covered the northern end of the fort in the direction of Javerne, to the northwest. In 1909, Battery Golèze with two 75mm in open positions was built to cover the northern side of the fort, in the direction of Demècre to the east and rear of the fort.

Fort Dailly / Savantan Complex 1913

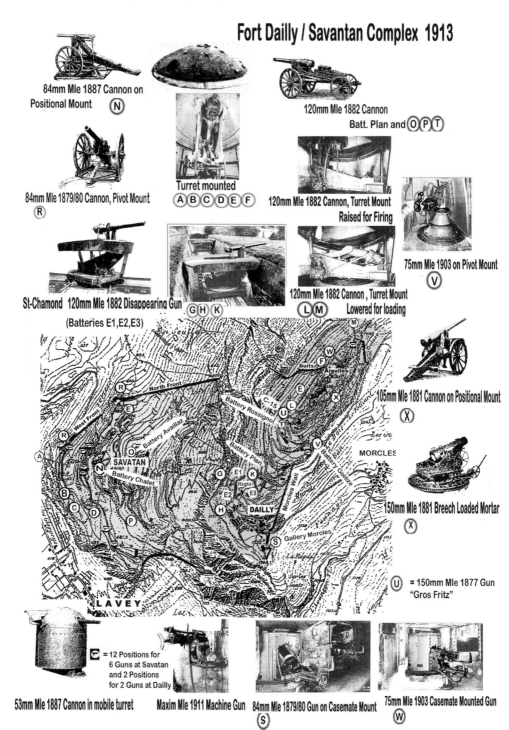

84mm Mle 1887 Cannon on Positional Mount (N)

84mm Mle 1879/80 Cannon, Pivot Mount (R)

Turret mounted (A)(B)(C)(D)(E)(F)

120mm Mle 1882 Cannon Batt. Plan and (O)(P)(T)

120mm Mle 1882 Cannon, Turret Mount Raised for Firing

75mm Mle 1903 on Pivot Mount (V)

St-Chamond 120mm Mle 1882 Disappearing Gun (G)(H)(K)
(Batteries E1,E2,E3)

120mm Mle 1882 Cannon, Turret Mount Lowered for loading (L)(M)

105mm Mle 1881 Cannon on Positional Mount (X)

150mm Mle 1881 Breech Loaded Mortar (X)

(U) = 150mm Mle 1877 Gun "Gros Fritz"

(E) = 12 Positions for 6 Guns at Savatan and 2 Positions for 2 Guns at Dailly

53mm Mle 1887 Cannon in mobile turret

Maxim Mle 1911 Machine Gun

84mm Mle 1879/80 Gun on Casemate Mount (S)

75mm Mle 1903 Casemate Mounted Gun (W)

Extracted & Modified from Report:
"Àrmement de Savatan et Dailly a la fin de la 3 ème période de consruction (1910)"
from Cdt ar Fort 13.   6.2.90   Bibliothèque Nationale Suisse, Bern

The remaining batteries of Dailly included Observatory Battery with four weapons, Battery Plan 2 and Battery Righi, each with two 120mm Mle 1881 guns.[26] In 1930, a fortifications commission concluded that all the open positions on the forts were vulnerable to new artillery weapons and aircraft. Thus, protected gun emplacements replaced some of the exposed positions, which in some cases were left abandoned or served as decoys.

Early in the twentieth century, the Swiss wove their terrain and fortifications into an impressive network apparently unassailable by modern armies. Many of the Swiss forts had been more easily accessible until the mid-nineteenth century because their artillery had a limited range. However, this changed after the 1870s when increased gun ranges allowed the Swiss to locate their new forts in remote locations, which required mountain troops to maintain the gaps. In 1902, W.G. Fitzgerald, after a stopover at Goeschenen at the northern portal to the Gotthard tunnel where he climbed up to the village, described the high alpine regions of southern Switzerland in an article for *Pearson's Magazine*.

Part of the way is up an iron ladder. When you get near the Schollenen Gorge and the Devil's Bridge,[27] where the awful Reuss roars and thunders and makes you gasp with spray-showers, you may look down and up; but if anyone told you that soldiers could manoeuvre in such a country you would not believe him.

Presently you see suspicious doors in precipices and narrow roads where entrance is forbidden. Next you see a string of goats crawling, or rather, jerk up a wall. The goats are troops hauling up a gun. You are in Andermatt among the forts and barracks and although it is a roasting hot day the men are in Arctic rig. For an hour they may be slithering across the blue and green ice of the glaciers, or up to their waists in snow … There are forts here in places only fitted for eagles' nests … Switzerland's only 'standing army' is here – a few hundred men permanently employed in looking after the forts and guns, the gun-moving machinery, with the electric batteries and wires that connect the forts and barracks and conning towers.

You might think these appalling mountains were defences enough in themselves as you gaze idly at the masses of cloud floating below the village of Andermatt, which itself is nearly as high as the topmost crest of the Rigi … During the winter and early spring the permanent garrison of Andermatt consists of gunners and look-out men, a Maxim gun company and sappers and miners. There are special companies told off for the forts near Airolo, Stuei and the southern gates of the Gothard. Other special companies man the forts on the Furka, at Buhl, at Altkirch and on the Bäzberg, above Andermatt; also on the Stockli (Oberalp Road).

Then are special infantry regiments attached to each set of forts; and these have to do their annual or bi-annual service up there under surprising conditions, with all the fatigues of ordinary soldiering plus the labors of a pack mule and the dangerous work of an Alpine guide. There are every summer some 3,000 men in service in the different fortifications on the south frontier of Switzerland.

Many years ago mountain torrent destroyed huge lengths of the St. Gothard road below Airolo. The Swiss government immediately called out four companies of these mountain sappers, who in a few weeks repaired the damage by building a huge wall 6,000 feet long, to support the road along a steep slope.[28]

According to Fitzgerald, the Swiss Alpine troops trained not only at the Gotthard and nearby forts, but also at the forts near St-Maurice. Few countries had trained mountain troops of this quality at the time. Unfortunately for the Swiss, every bordering nation except Lichtenstein formed such units by 1915.[29]

All the renovated forts and the ones built during the twentieth century included well-concealed artillery casemates built into valley or canyon walls and/or turreted artillery. The Swiss Fortifications Commission selected the turrets before the end of the nineteenth century. It chose the French St. Chamond turrets and French carriages to mount some German Krupp cannons. They also picked the German 120mm Kügelmorser (spherical mortar), the 53mm cannon and the observation cloche from the Grüson Werkes. However, the most important changes involving turrets took place after 1939.

Switzerland from the First World War to 1939

From 1866, Swiss soldiers, armed with one of the first repeating rifles, were among the best marksmen in the world. In 1874, the government took charge of equipping and training all soldiers in order to create a uniform military force. In August 1914, the Swiss army mobilized 450,000 men, a number that did not change much until 1939. The government appointed Conrad Ulrich Sigmund Wille (1848–1925) to the rank of general for this crisis. Like many Swiss early in the war, Wille favoured Germany and even tried to impose Prussian methods on the army. In the summer of 1915, he proposed joining the war with the Germans to the consternation of most of his countrymen. Not surprisingly, the French responded by preparing plans to invade Switzerland in December 1915. The French Plan H (Helvétie) called for thirty divisions, two-thirds of which would form two armies that would advance southward through Basel and up the Rhine. A third army was to cross the Jura north of Lake Leman and move across the Mittelland and around the lake to St-Maurice.

The Swiss concentrated six divisions along the northwestern section of the country, mainly covering French and Germany territory where the war might spill over their borders. They built field positions as a first line of defence, which they backed with another line that included concrete positions, some dug into the mountains to form strongpoints to block a potential French or German advance. Four Swiss brigades protected the National Redoubt in the south. As the war progressed, the French came up with variants of Plan H as the possibility of the Swiss becoming their ally increased. When the collapse of Russia became imminent in 1917, Franco-Swiss negotiations began in earnest, as the possibility of a German invasion of Switzerland became ever more real.[30] At that point, Swiss forces concentrated along their border with Germany.

During the war, the Swiss began replacing the old 120mm and 84mm artillery pieces, but the 120mm Mle 1882 remained in their inventory past 1939. After the appearance of automatic weapons like the light and heavy machine gun that dominated the battlefield, having excellent riflemen no longer mattered. The Swiss soldier may have been a better marksman than the German, but, by the 1930s, German infantry squads were built around light, air-cooled machine guns rather than the expertise of their riflemen. The Swiss needed more than riflemen to hold their borders. Their strategy revolved around fortifications to render an invasion a costly option.

Between 1911 and 1920, work continued on the southern defences of the National Redoubt. Additional barbed wire was placed on exposed areas of the mountain fortifications and searchlights were installed in some of the forts. The Gotthard fortress, consisting of the Airolo Group backed by the central group in the pass and the Andermatt Group at north end of the tunnel area, was a formidable position. To the east and west were the Furka and Oberalp Groups. The St-Maurice Fortress was augmented with new positions, including Forts Cindey and Scex.

The journalist Eric Margolis, who visited the massive St-Maurice complex covering the approach to the St. Bernard Pass between Montreux and Martigny in 2001,[31] writes that Fort Dailly is on 'a steep sided mountain spur, the Dailly Massif, jutting into the valley creating a defile less than 2km wide' and dominates the Valais Valley of the Rhône River with neighbouring forts. According to Margolis, Fort Dailly has 60km of galleries excavated in the last hundred years, making it the 'Swiss Gibraltar'. Below and across from Dailly are Forts Savatan, Scex, Cindey (mixed infantry/artillery fort) and Follatères. In addition, the infantry forts of Petit-Mont, Vernayaz Evionnaz and Toveires, which used to provide close defence, give a combined total of over 350km of galleries. After the First World War, new weapons, including well-concealed artillery turrets and gun casemates in the steep valley walls, dominated the entire area with interlocking fires. In 1939 and later, weapons with greater range and firepower came into service.

'Europe's Largest Fortress'[32]

Between 1938 and 1945, the Swiss defensive system was much like an onion. Once you peeled away one layer, there was another. This was especially true within the National Redoubt where beyond the major fortresses; other defences existed to make every route through the mountainous terrain an invader's nightmare.

After the Great War, the government authorized little additional construction at the St-Maurice complex and elsewhere until the 1930s because no threat justified the great expense. The only exception was the excavation of the large subterranean Caserne XIV of Fort Dailly in the Aiguille ridge. After the war, Fort Dailly's old 105mm guns of Battery C10 and the 150mm mortars on Aiguilles ridge were removed. In 1923, 120mm field howitzers with a range of 6km replaced several batteries of old 120mm guns in open positions. In 1938, as fear of fascism rose, major improvements took place. Between 1939 and 1940, special 105mm Mle 1939 turret guns with a range of over 22km developed in the 1930s replaced some of the older batteries at Fort Dailly. The long barrels of these guns, which projected from the turrets, required protection. The turrets were small and all their equipment was located below ground in the concrete shaft pierced in the rock. The armour of the turret was sufficient to resist most field artillery. The gun crew consisted of a gunner, an aimer and a loader in the turret and of a turret chief and other personnel in the two levels of the concrete block below. Electrically operated monte-charges delivered the ammunition to the turret. Two of these turrets were installed on high ground above the fort, about 1km from Aiguille. The turrets, about 300m apart, formed Battery Panaux in 1940.[33] Munitions magazines excavated about 50m into the rock did not require thick concrete walls. This was the case with the rock protection in most Swiss forts.

At Fort Dailly, a second 120mm howitzer added to Aiguille ridge formed Battery 05, replacing the mortars of Battery M-15 in 1930. These two old howitzers remained in service

Switzerland Defences & Terrain 1939 - 1945

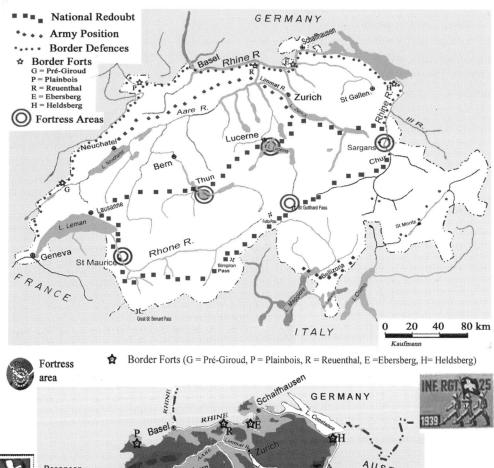

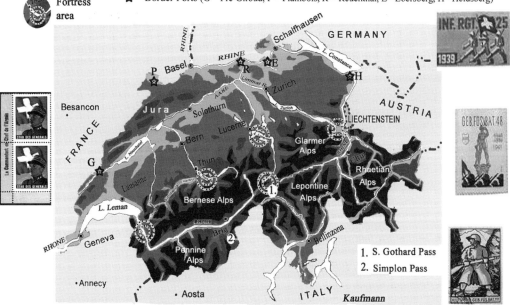

Top map shows the National Redoubt, the Border Defences, and the Army Position. Bottom map shows the major areas of relief in Switzerland (highest elevations are the darkest). Stamp showing General Guisan who as C-in-C determined the strategy and after the summer of 1940 decided to concentrate on holding the National Redoubt. The army units had free postage and issued their own stamps as seen on the right.

throughout the war. The two 75mm guns in Battery Golèze in open positions were replaced in 1940 with a casemate mounting two 75mm Mle 1939 guns. Five men, including a gunner, an aimer, a loader, ammunition handlers and the crew chief served the weapon. A new gallery that ran parallel to the Aiguille ridge replaced Battery Rossignol. On both sides, the gallery included positions for casemates with ten armoured embrasures for three batteries: Battery Buits and Battery Plex with four guns each and Battery Rosseline with two guns. Each battery mounted 105mm Bofors Mle 1935 guns with a range of 18km and had a seven-man gun crew consisting of a gunner, an aimer, two loaders, two ammunition handlers and the crew chief.

A subterranean funicular linked Fort Dailly to Savatan. In other Swiss forts, there were also inclined railways, usually on the surface and/or cable lifts that were especially important in winter. During periods of modernization since the Second World War, many older battery positions could not accommodate the new weapons and their required equipment. At the St-Maurice fortress, especially Fort Dailly, the fortress engineers employed every type of fortress weapon and emplacement they had created between 1892 and the end of the twentieth century. Interlocking fires with Fort Scex and later Cindey, created an almost impassable barrier. The fortress weapons on the other side of the valley could engage enemy attempt to approach any of these forts from the rear.

Fort Scex, built in 1911, occupies the cliff face overlooking the Rhône east of the defile at St-Maurice and on the west side of the valley opposite the Savatan/Dailly complex. Fort Scex mounted four 75mm guns in two of the casemates of 'Gallery Scex'. Other casemate positions mounted Maxim machine guns. By 1913, this gallery not only included the gun casemates, but also a power room with three engines, storage chambers, an infirmary and other facilities. A caponier protected the entrance and there was a searchlight at each end of the fort. An aerial cableway linked the fort to the valley below. Battery Ermitage, a more modern four-gun 75mm battery, was added in 1939 and it was linked by a tunnel to the old facilities in 1942.

Fort Cindey, built during the war between 1941 and 1946, was to strengthen the position held by Fort Scex. It covered the anti-tank barrier formed by the Rhône Canal and the Courset River and newly erected obstacles. It included infantry casemates with machine guns and anti-tank guns in the cliff face, but its armament was not installed until after the war. It was located near St-Maurice and to north and rear of Fort Scex. A gallery of about 50m was excavated to link the fort with the natural caverns of 'Grotte aux Fées', which had been linked to Fort Scex in 1935–6.

Further down the Rhône near Lake Leman, Fort Champex was built in the rock above the right bank of the Rhône. Its construction began in late 1940 and continued on different parts until October 1942 and late 1943. The first two artillery casemates, each with a 75mm gun, became operational by the end of 1942. Two additional casemates, each mounting two 105mm guns, with a range of over 18km, aimed along the Great St. Bernard Pass, became ready for occupation in January 1944. In addition to the casemates, there were three observatories and an emergency exit on the rock face. The entrance at the rear of the fort had road access; its caserne housed 300 men. The fort was located between Yvorne and Corbeyrier at 800m and covered the Rhône valley below. It also anchored the defences covering the avenue of approach into the Rhône Valley from the Dranse Valley to the south of Martigny that leads to the Great St. Bernard Pass and on to Asota, Italy.

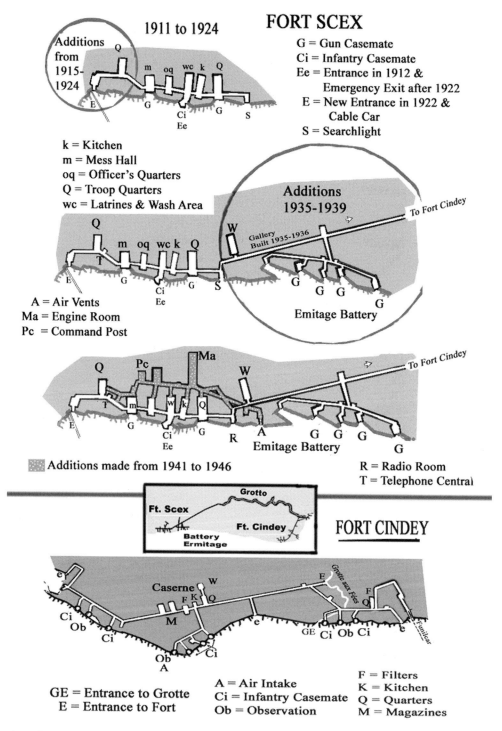

Fort Scex from 1911 to 1946, and Fort Cindey linked to it by a gallery. These forts formed part of the St. Maurice Fortress.

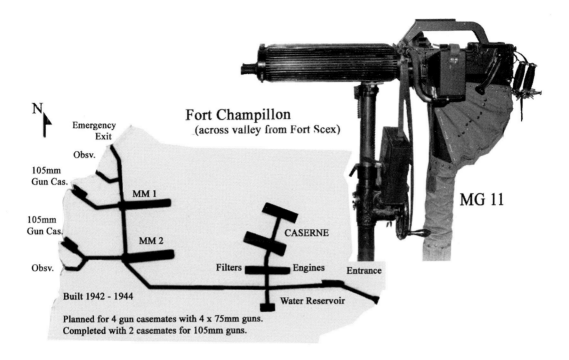

Fort Champillon
(across valley from Fort Scex)

N

Emergency Exit

Obsv.

105mm Gun Cas.

MM 1

105mm Gun Cas.

MM 2

CASERNE

Obsv.

Filters

Engines

Entrance

Built 1942 - 1944

Water Reservoir

Planned for 4 gun casemates with 4 x 75mm guns.
Completed with 2 casemates for 105mm guns.

MG 11

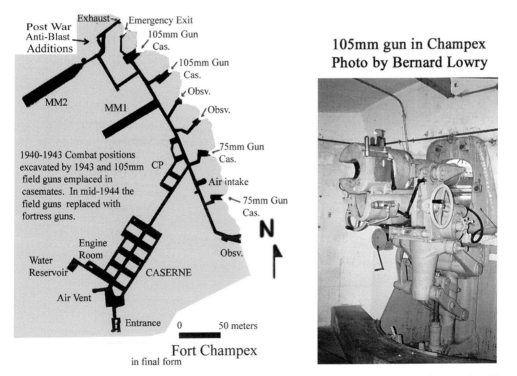

Exhaust

Emergency Exit

Post War Anti-Blast Additions

105mm Gun Cas.

105mm Gun Cas.

Obsv.

MM2

MM1

Obsv.

75mm Gun Cas.

1940-1943 Combat positions excavated by 1943 and 105mm field guns emplaced in casemates. In mid-1944 the field guns replaced with fortress guns.

CP

Air intake

75mm Gun Cas.

N

Engine Room

Obsv.

Water Reservoir

CASERNE

Air Vent

Entrance

0   50 meters

Fort Champex
in final form

105mm gun in Champex
Photo by Bernard Lowry

Plans of Forts Champillon and Champex located at Lake Geneva approach to Fortress St. Maurice. Photo of 105mm gun courtesy of Bernard Lowry.

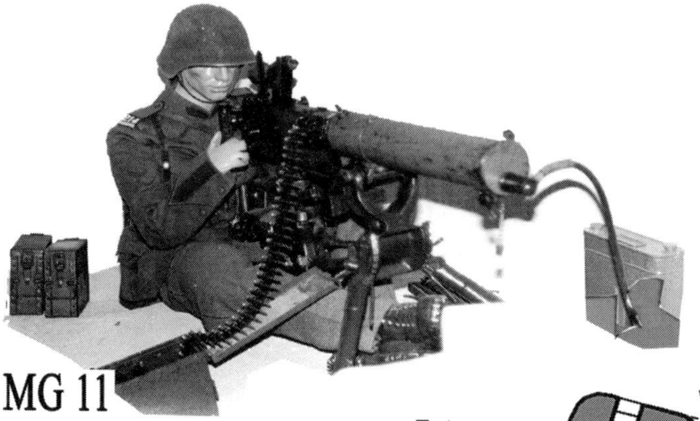

MG 11

Entrance
60°
70°
60°
AT Gun
Ob
MG
WC
Access to Lower Level
Ob
AT Gun
MG
60°
70°
60°

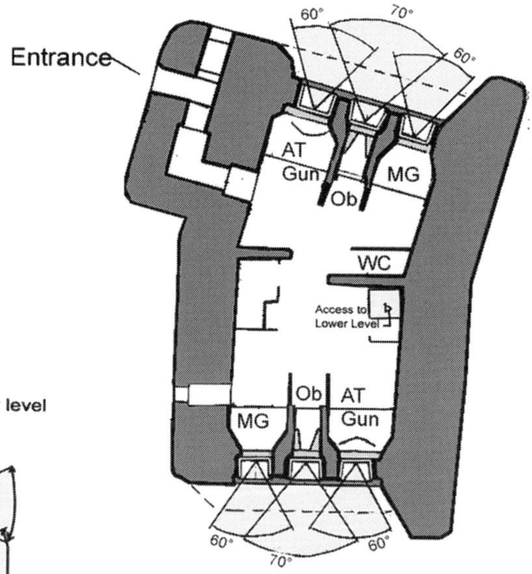

Double Fortins with 2 levels.

Upper Level

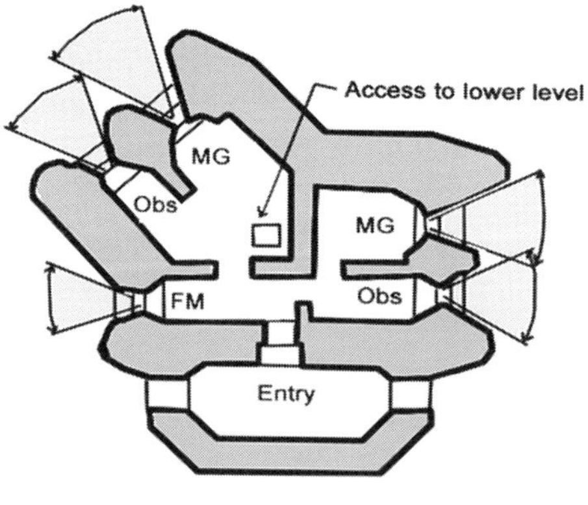

Access to lower level
MG
Obs
MG
FM
Obs
Entry

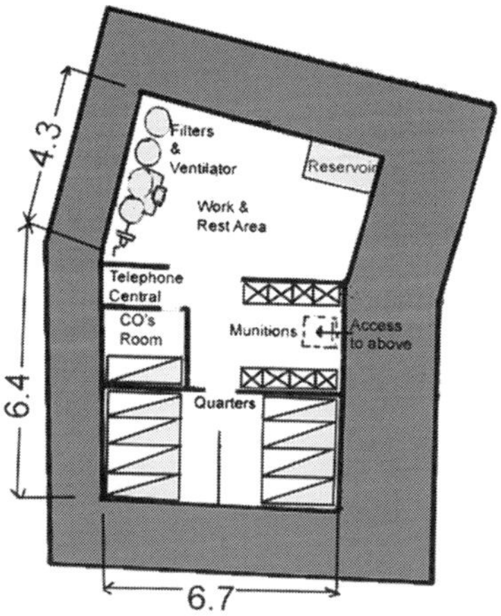

4.3
6.4
6.7
Filters & Ventilator
Reservoir
Work & Rest Area
Telephone Central
CO's Room
Munitions
Access to above
Quarters

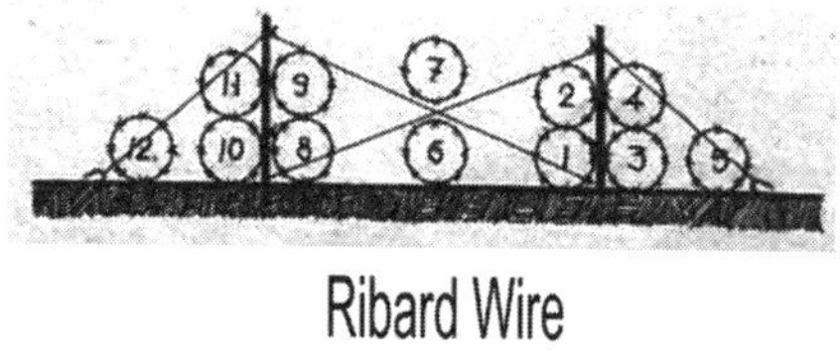

11
9
7
2
4
12
10
8
6
1
3
5

Ribard Wire

Two examples of a double fortin (weapons embrasures on two sides). These were large machine-gun bunkers, sometimes including anti-tank guns. Top: Photo of an MG Mle 1911 with field mount. Bottom: example of Ribard Wire, named after French general who developed it in the First World War. It is similar to concertina wire.

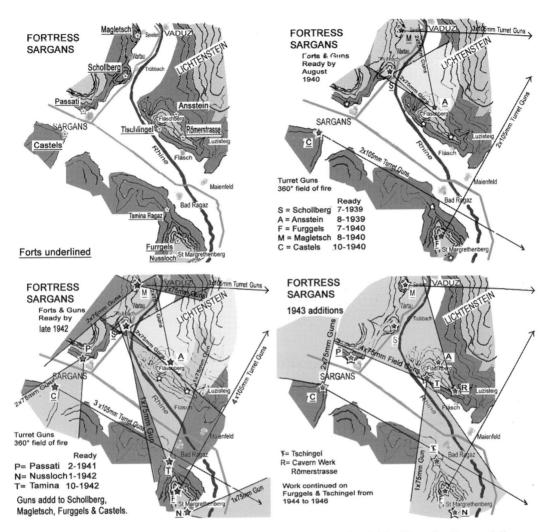

Development of Fortress Sargans during the Second World War showing fields of fire of artillery and diagram of a 105mm gun turret.

In February 1942, the Swiss began the expansion of Fort Chillon, located next to Château Chillon on Lake Leman where the road and the railway to Lausanne ran close to the shore. At this time, six 75mm guns in casemates were added to the position. Previous work around Chillon had consisted of field positions that had been reinforced in December 1940 with six 75mm guns, concrete positions and additional obstacles. The fort's garrison numbered about 130 men. Local defence of the fort came from nine detached bunkers.[34] The fort included tunnels through the steep mountainside. The mission of Forts Champex and Chillon was to stop an enemy advance along the northern side of the lake towards the St-Maurice Fortress.[35]

The Sargans Fortress was given priority for major construction in 1934, but work did not begin immediately. High mountains surround the valley where Sargans is located. The Rhine twists through the valley before flowing north along the border with the western part of Lichtenstein. The fortress was to bar entry into Grisons (Graubunden) from the north and cover the eastern approach to the Gotthard fortress. The main front of the fortress consisted of several forts overlooking the Rhine. Work on the first of these forts finally began in October 1938 and lasted through the war after the annexation of Austria to the Reich. The first fort of this complex, Schollberg, was ready for service in July 1939. It was followed a year later by other forts in the area. Built into the Scholl Mountain, it included three 75mm guns in casemates, a 47mm anti-tank gun and two machine guns with a searchlight position. Schollberg #2, completed later, consisted of a large infantry position with bunkers for a 24mm and three 47mm anti-tank guns and several machine guns and a searchlight position. The fort supported several lines of bunkers and anti-tank and infantry obstacles in the sector. Fort Ansstein formed the first barrier position with Schollberg on the Rhine. It occupied a site on the western flank of Mount Falknis (2,562m/8,405ft) overlooking the old road to Luziensteig in the Steigwiesen Valley.[36] Fort Ansstein had two casemates cut into the rock mounting 75mm fortress guns. They created interlocking fields of fire with Fort Schollberg across the river. The fort did not become operational until August 1940, a year after Schollberg.

The main defensive positions of Sargans were begun in late 1939 and consisted of Forts Furggels, Passatiwand, Kastels and Magletsch. Construction began in November 1939 at Fort Furggels (or Furkels) on the southern side of Fortress Sargans, overlooking the Rhine from its mountain position. In July 1940, its two 105mm cannons in armoured turrets were ready for action. Two turrets added in 1941 became operational in May 1942. In Early 1945, four casemates for 150mm guns were completed, but they were not operational until a year later. Like the other forts of Sargans, it was tunnelled into the rock and it included complete facilities. The fort, known as the 'Mountain Battleship', occupied the northern side of the mountain of St. Margrethenberg at an elevation of 1,250m (4,100ft). It had a commanding position over the eastern approach to Sargans along the Rhine. All the gun turrets on the plateau were carefully camouflaged. The cloches occupied optimal observation points for the forts. The camouflage techniques for casemate embrasures, turrets and all exposed elements were excellent.[37] The fort had two gallery levels spaced about 20m apart and consisting of 7.5km of tunnels. A sloping passageway and lifts linked the two levels. Most facilities of the caserne were on the lower level whereas the upper level included the gun casemates, fire direction and command centres and the engine rooms. The fort, which could accommodate over 500 men,[38] included everything needed for independent operations: engine rooms, fuel storage, food reserves, kitchens, water reservoirs, extensive medical facilities, etc. Like most entrances in the Sargans Fortress, it was able to accommodate trucks. Once inside the entrance, the trucks were unloaded and a turntable reversed their direction so they could head back out.

Fort Magletsch, 'The Hammer', stands on the northern end of Fortress Sargans, north of Schollberg on the west side of the Rhine Valley with Liechtenstein across the river. Its construction began in October 1939 and its upper level and three turret positions with 105mm guns, which controlled the area, were ready by August 1940. Two casemates with 75mm fortress guns that formed Battery East, which and covered the Rhine Valley, were completed in late February 1941. Two additional 75mm gun casemates, which formed Battery West and fired to the southwest, came on line in July 1941. A long gallery linked Battery West to the fort; access to all gun positions was on the upper gallery level. The lower gallery level included the main entrance, medical facilities and two gun casemates forming Battery East. Ten machine-

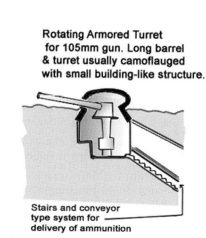

Rotating Armored Turret
for 105mm gun. Long barrel
& turret usually camoflauged
with small building-like structure.

Stairs and conveyor
type system for
delivery of ammunition

T = 105mm Gun in Turret
G = 75mm Bunker Gun (Casemate Mount)
FC = Field Cannon
MG = Machine Gun
LMG = Light Machine Gun
Obs = Observation
S = Searchlight

ME = Main Entrance
EE = Secondary Entrance with Exhaust
c = Communications Room
d = decontamination area
f = Food Magazine
q = Quarters for troops, NCOs, & Officers
fi = Filters and ventilation
h = Hospital
n = Mess Hall
= Stairs
MM = Munitions Magazine
U = Engine Room and Fuel supply
WC = WC and wash areas
w = Water Reservoir

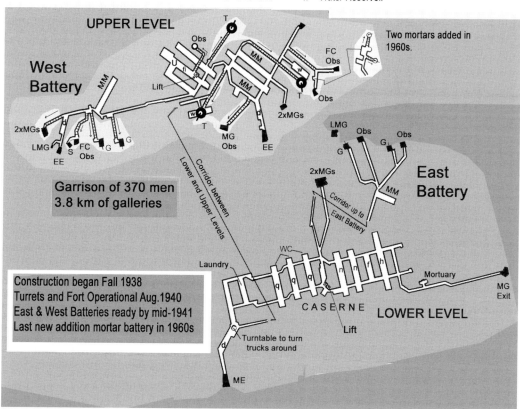

UPPER LEVEL

West Battery

Garrison of 370 men
3.8 km of galleries

Construction began Fall 1938
Turrets and Fort Operational Aug.1940
East & West Batteries ready by mid-1941
Last new addition mortar battery in 1960s

Two mortars added in 1960s.

East Battery

LOWER LEVEL

CASERNE

Laundry

Turntable to turn trucks around

Corridor between Lower and Upper Levels

Corridor up to East Battery

Mortuary

MG Exit

Plan of Fort Magletsch at Sargans Fortress showing the upper and lower gallery levels. This was among of the largest Swiss forts built.

gun positions served for close defence along with nearby bunkers. The combat positions were ready by November 1940 when the army occupied the fort, but it took until 1943 for some of the subterranean sections to be completed, including the large medical facilities on the lower gallery level. In many of the forts, large sections of gallery cut in the rock and left in their natural state, with no concrete lining. The geological configuration at the site of Fort Magletsch included water-permeable layers of rock that delayed its completion because 4km of its galleries had to be lined with concrete. Like Furggels and other forts, it included complete facilities. The garrison numbered 350 to 370 men during the war. A mountain border battalion occupied nearby bunkers and other positions as part of the defensive scheme.

In November 1939 (possibly March 1939), work began on Fort Kastels on the west side of the fortress near Sargans with two of the first 105mm gun turrets with a range of 18km. The fort served as the command centre for the fortress. Between October 1938 and January 1940, a fortress artillery company with four 120mm guns took up positions at the southern edge of Mels, west of Sargans in response to the German takeover of Austria. This company was to hold the area until the army could occupy the forts under construction. Even though these guns were outdated, the army was unable to replace them through most of the war. The armoured turrets and the machine-gun positions at Fort Kastels were not ready until the autumn of 1940. There were plans to cover the anti-tank barrier at the entrance to the Seez Valley (west of Mel) with anti-tank guns and possibly a third turret. However, only the turret was approved and it was completed in July 1941. Two casemates for 75mm guns that fired northwest into the valley leading to Wallenstadt became operational in the summer of 1942. The fort held a garrison of about 340 men.[39]

The construction of Fort Passatiwand, on the opposite side of the mountain from Kastels, began in November 1939. This fort had a couple of 75mm gun casemates and several Maxim Mle 1911 machine guns for defence of the Seeztal Barrier. Passatiwand was ready for its garrison of about 130 men by March 1941 and served with Kastels as part of the fortress' command system.

To defend the barrier formed on the eastern entrance to the valley between Fort Furggels and Fläsch, four small forts were built between October 1941 and March 1942. Fort Tamina Ragaz, begun in early 1942 and finished in October, included a casemate with a 75mm gun with a field of fire north to the town of Fläsch. Near the same town on the other side of the valley, Fort Tschingel became operational in 1940. It covered the barrier obstacles with the Tamina position. It was excavated in the 1,135m (3,632ft) high Fläscherberg. The Lichtenstein border ran across its western end and behind its northern side. It had four levels and included casemates cut into in the bare rock face of the steep mountainside. It mounted machine guns and searchlights to cover the barrier below.[40] A 75mm gun in a casemate position was not ready until early 1943. On the other side of the valley to the east of Fort Furggels, Fort Nussloch Mastrills went into service in September 1942. It had a single 75mm gun casemate that covered the entrances to the valley from the east and another valley across from it. To complete this section of the fortress, the army added cavern Werk Römerstrasse on the Fläscherberg that was ready in 1943 with four 75mm field guns.

Further up the Rhine, Forts Molinära and Haselboden were built between mid-1941 and February 1943 a short distance down the river to the north of the town of Chur. They had two and three 75mm guns in casemates respectively with interlocking fire to close access to the valley.

Fortress Sargans in 1940

Forts	75mm Guns	105mm Guns
Schollberg I	3	–
Ansstein	4	–
Magletsch	4	3
Furggels	–	2
Tschingel	–	–
Kastels	–	2

New weapons were installed at Fortress Gotthard during the war. The small forts of San Carlo and Foppa Grande received 105mm Mle 1939 L52 cannons in turrets between 1939 and 1941. Three of these turrets were emplaced at Fort Guestsch in 1942 and the first turrets were installed Fort Fuchsegg.

Long Range Artillery Turrets

105mm Gun Turrets Installed in Forts	Total	Installed by
Dailly (St-Maurice)	2	1940
Furggels (Sargans)	2	July 1940
	2	June 1941
Kastels (Sargans)	2	October 1940
	1	July 1941
Magletsch (Sargans)	3	August 1940
San Carlo (Gotthard)	2	1941
Foppa Grande (Gotthard)	1	1941
Guetsch (Gotthard)	3	1942
Fuchsegg (Gotthard)	2	1942
	2	1943

Source: Oswald Schwitter, correspondence and http//www.schweizer-festugnen.ch

Construction of Fort Fuchsegg, which was near Andermatt overlooking the road to the Furka Pass, began in 1941. Its artillery covered the Grimsel Pass and the San Giacomo area. Although the first two 105mm gun turrets became operational in 1942, they remained unusable until work on the subterranean facilities was finished. Despite the fact that its four gun turrets and three machine-gun bunkers for close defence were ready in 1943, the fort was not become fully operational until right after the war ended. It took a garrison of up to 450 men. A dozen 20mm Bofors anti-aircraft guns provided additional protection from airborne attacks on this and other forts after 1942.[41]

The Swiss adopted the 150mm Mle 1942 gun with a range of 24km mounted in casemates and requiring a ten-man crew. The first two were installed at Fort Dailly in 1944, but the newer Mle 1945 went to Fort Furggels since its positions were not ready until the war ended. Several other forts including Sasso da Pigna, Grimsel and Wissiflue had older Mle 1942 by1944.

Fort Sasso da Pigna, the largest fort of Fortress Gotthard, had 2.4km of galleries, accommodation for 500 men and a hospital with over eighty beds. Completed in 1943, the fort's four casemates temporarily used 105mm guns until they were replaced in the fall of 1944 with the 150mm Mle 1942 guns. Located at the St. Gotthard Pass, its guns formed Battery East and West. The western one covered the San Giacomo Pass.

Fort Grimsel, a large work near Furka, had six 105mm guns served by ten-man crews that covered Andermatt, the Gotthard Pass and the San Giacomo Pass. Fort Wissifluen the fortress at Lucerne, temporarily used 105mm guns until its four 150mm weapons could be installed in 1944.

Other forts were built in and around the mountain redoubt including the two little mentioned fortress areas at Lake Thun and Lake Lucerne. The first, the Fortress Bernese Oberland,[42] included Fort Burgfluh at Wimmis, Forts Waldbrand and Legi at Beatenberg, Forts Hondrich, Faulensee and Krattigen around Spiez and several others. The large artillery fort of Burgfluh had a garrison of about 450 men and was located in the Bernese Alps south of Lake Thun and above Wimmis guarding the exit from the Simmental Valley.[43] It defended a western gateway[44] into the redoubt. This fort, built between 1942 and 1943, comprised a dozen casemates cut into the rock that mounted eight 150mm Mle 1916 Krupp howitzers and four 75mm guns. According to the Swiss historian Oswald Schwitter, it even had stables for the horses that hauled these field pieces into the fort. On the other side of the lake, opposite Spiez, there were several smaller forts and a position known as the Beatenberg, which consisted of a mountain with three linked forts (Waldbrand, Legi and Schmockenfluh) mounting twenty-two guns in 1944. Fort Waldbrand mounted eight 105mm guns in positions cut into the rock face. Fort Legi stood 90m below, numbered eight 150mm howitzers and had a garrison of about 100 men. Fort Schmockenfluh was near the bottom of the mountain. Construction began in 1941 and local companies carried out the work in great secrecy employing civilians not on military duty. In 1942, it had only two 105mm guns in casemates. Later, it was expanded with additional casemates for two 105mm and two 75mm fortress guns. As a result, this fortress area received less attention than the other fortresses. Apparently, similar procedures were followed throughout the country, which prevented the enemy from knowing much about the Swiss fortifications and what awaited them if they attempted an invasion.

On Bödeli, a strip of land that separates Lake Thun from Lake Brienz and includes the town of Interlaken, a group of five small positions on the heights in the rock face controlled the road between Thun and Lucerne. Each consisted of two casemate positions for a 75mm gun and a connecting gallery with limited facilities. Access to most of the artillery positions was by a ladder up the steep cliff. Other fortified positions and the standard array of anti-tank and anti-personnel barriers also defended this area.

Fortress Stans[45] occupied the northern entrance to the National Redoubt overlooking Lake Lucerne. One of its components, Fort Muesterschwanderberg, which occupied a ridge that rose to 860m (2,752ft) above Lake Alpnacher, was built between July 1941 and 1944. It included three large sections: Zingel overlooking the lake, and Drachenfluh and Blattiberg in its eastern section covering the eastern part of Lake Lucerne. In 1944, like Beatenberg, it mounted twenty-two guns, which covered the lake road from Lucerne to Altdorf that led south to the Gotthard Pass. A subterranean funicular and staircase connected the three sections. Four detached machine-gun bunkers provided close defence. In October 1943, the Blattiberg section consisted of twelve 75mm Krupp Mle 1903/22 guns in three four-gun battery positions cut into the rock. One of

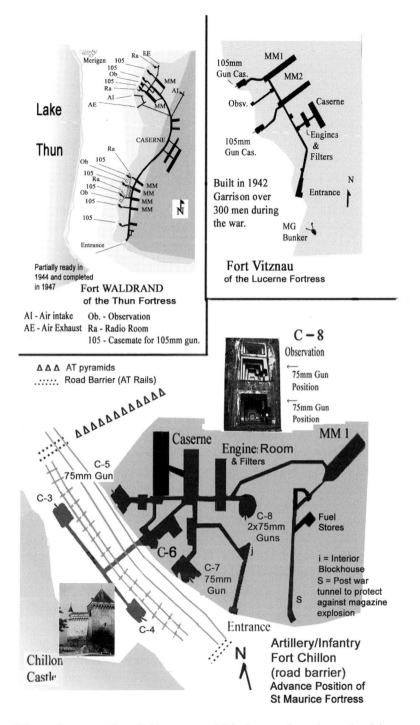

Fort WALDRAND
of the Thun Fortress

Lake Thun

Merigen 105
105
Ob
105
Ra
AI
AE
Ra EE
MM
AI
MM
CASERNE
Ra
Ob 105
105
Ra
105
Ob
105
105
MM
MM
MM
MM
N
Entrance

Partially ready in 1944 and completed in 1947

AI - Air intake
AE - Air Exhaust
Ob. - Observation
Ra - Radio Room
105 - Casemate for 105mm gun.

Fort Vitznau
of the Lucerne Fortress

MM1
105mm Gun Cas.
MM2
Obsv.
Caserne
105mm Gun Cas.
Engines & Filters
Entrance
N
MG Bunker

Built in 1942 Garrison over 300 men during the war.

△ △ △ AT pyramids
.·.·.·.·. Road Barrier (AT Rails)

C–8
Observation
← 75mm Gun Position
← 75mm Gun Position

Caserne
Engine Room & Filters
MM 1
C-5 75mm Gun
C-3
C-8 2x75mm Guns
Fuel Stores
C-6
i
C-7 75mm Gun
i = Interior Blockhouse
S = Post war tunnel to protect against magazine explosion
S
Entrance
C-4
N
Chillon Castle

Artillery/Infantry Fort Chillon (road barrier)
Advance Position of St Maurice Fortress

Forts of three different fortresses. Fort Chillon was established across from the castle of the same name as a road barrier first with 75mm field guns and then later expanded as shown in the plan. It also included an unusual circular block (C–8) with 75mm guns on two levels.

these batteries was at the lower level near the entrance block. The other two were at a higher level with an observation position also cut into the rock. The Drachenfluh section overlooked the Bouchs Airfield with two 105mm Bofors Mle 1935 cannons installed in 1943. The Zingel section was the first ready for action as early as 1941, but it had only a couple of 75mm guns. In 1944, it included two four-gun batteries of 150mm Krupp Mle 1916 howitzers in the rock face. This was one of the largest Swiss forts built during the war. When it was finished, it had room for over 700 men, over half of whom were quartered in the Zingel section and the remainder in Blattiberg. This large fort supported several smaller ones, including Fort Kilchidossen, just to the north of it and Fort Fürigen, both of which were ready in October 1942.

Across Lake Alpnacher, Fort Durren – with two four-gun batteries of 120mm Mle 1882 guns operational by December 1942 – covered Forts Muesterschwanderberg, Kilchidossen and Fürigen. Across Lake Lucerne, was Fort Vitznau with two 105mm Mle 1939 guns whose fields of fire covered the lake road and the Blattiberg section of the Muesterschwanderberg. This fort was ready in the spring of 1943. To the south, Fort Wissiflue received its two two-gun batteries of 150mmm Mle 1942 guns in the summer of 1944. Nearby was Fort Ursprung with another battery of 150mm guns installed in 1945.

Fort Fürigen, typical of many of the small forts cut into the rock, was located along the lake. A lakeside path led to its concealed entrance. Fort Fürigen and nearby Fort Kilchlidossen (four 120mm Mle 1912/39 howitzers), completed in October 1942, were the first forts ready to block the avenue of advance from Lucerne into the National Redoubt. Fürigen mounted two 75mm Mle 1939 fortress guns, three Maxim Mle 1911 machine guns and a searchlight.[46] It was the smallest artillery fort in the area. Its gun crews consisted of seven men and a crew chief. Its entire garrison numbered about eighty men. The two-level caserne included medical facilities and a kitchen on the lower or gallery level and quarters with enough bunks for just over half of the garrison – the men used the bunks in shifts – on the upper level. The fort contained all facilities needed for independent operation. Prepared demolitions would have destroyed the lake access path in case the fort was in danger of assault. Fürigen included standard features like an engine room for power and light, a water pump, ovens (coal, wood-burning and electric), a month supply of food and gas protection. In the firing chambers, the ventilation system for expelling the gases from firing was not totally adequate. There were hand-operated ventilators and gun crews wore gas masks that they could hook into an airline. Above each gun and telescope, a pantograph depicted the terrain in the field of fire. Its pointer and magnifier moved with the weapon indicating where it was aimed. Supposedly, this system increased the accuracy of night firing. Fort Fürigen had only one munitions magazine, unlike larger forts, which had more than one. A radio room was located near the entrance, a telephone central in the upper part of the caserne and latrines and showers in the caserne.

The Army Position, which ran behind the Border Position and was mainly located behind the border, formed a defensive line against Germany. Called Limmatstellung (the Limmat Position), it became the main position in the north in 1939 and 1940 following the river from Zurich to the Aare River. The Army Position was extended beyond the Limmatstellung. It stretched from the Juras to the east of Basel from the Aare River, eastward from Lake Zurich and on to Fortress Sargans. Its construction started after the war broke out using mainly troops who worked with plans to construct bunkers and set up other defences.[47] Some of the sites identified as forts are little more than a couple of bunker positions with a gallery and some facilities for the crews. In 1939, three of the Swiss army corps and seven of the army's nine

Fort behind the rock at edge of lake

Fort Entrance covered by shack

Observation and Gun Embrasures

Main corridor beyond Entrance

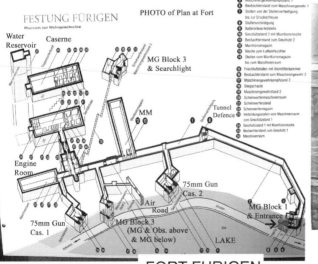

FESTUNG FÜRIGEN
Museum zur Wehrgeschichte

PHOTO of Plan at Fort

Water Reservoir
Caserne
MG Block 3 & Searchlight
MM
Tunnel Defence
Engine Room
75mm Gun Cas. 2
Air Road
75mm Gun Cas. 1
MG Block 3 (MG & Obs. above & MG below)
MG Block 1 & Entrance
LAKE

FORT FURIGEN

Commander's Room

Barracks

An example of a small fort of the National Redoubt, it is located on the lake shore of the Lucerne Fortress. Most of the other forts of this fortress are much larger. Photo of plan mounted on a wall of the fort is annotated. (*Authors*)

infantry divisions held this line (six divisions located between Liestal and Zurich covering access to the Mittelland). A fourth army corps formed in early 1940 so that two corps instead of one held the Limmatstellung.

In front of the Army Position and extending along the French frontier, border brigades held defensive positions that included barriers and prepared demolitions created before the war. Construction of several small forts that became part of the Border Line began before the war, as early as 1937.[48] It continued in 1939 and 1940 with the addition of bunkers and obstacles. The Border Line ran from Vallorbe on the French border to the Rhine, after which it followed the river along the German border to Schaffhausen and Lake Constance to Fortress Sargans. The casemates along the Rhine consisted of two levels with crew quarters, munitions storage and a filter and ventilation system on the lower level. The firing positions for machine guns and anti-tank guns and an observation position were on the top level. The bunkers included a grenade launcher similar to the one used in Belgian bunkers. The exposed concrete walls were 2.1m thick and the roofs 2.0m; additional protection was provided by the rock cover. Similar bunkers were found in the Army Position and elsewhere. The Border Line represented an uninterrupted curtain of machine-gun fire from Basel to Schaffhausen with bunkers spaced 500m to 760m apart. It was protected by a continuous barbed-wire barrier.

Five border forts were built. Fort Pré-Giroud was at the southwest end of the Border Line where it dominated the Joux Valley and the rail tunnel through the Mont d'Or from France. Construction took place between 1937 and 1939. It consisted of an entrance block with an emergency exit and the main air intake concealed in a wooden building. An elevator and stairway gave access to the underground gallery 30m below. An engine room, across from the elevator, contained two diesel engines that provided power. Beneath the floor, there was a storage cistern with a two-month fuel supply. Under the gallery floor, there were conduits for drainage, fresh air and power and phone cables. The combined length of the main gallery and the lower galleries that connected to the combat blocks was 500m. The fort's largest casemate had three embrasures, one for a 75mm gun, one for a 47mm anti-tank gun and one for the observation equipment. Two blocks consisted of three levels. Sand and rock for repairs were stored at the lowest level. The intermediate level housed the ammo reserve and air filters. At each end of the main gallery was a casemate for a 75mm gun. Lower galleries at each end of the main gallery branched off toward two blocks mounting Maxim Mle 1911 machine guns with an observation position and an emergency exit. The machine-gun blocks looked like chalets complete with wooden balconies and painted windows with curtains. Three unconnected bunkers, one of which was located on high ground above the entrance block and two of which were located further down the slope in front of the fort, served for close defence. They mounted two machine guns. The fort could house a garrison of 150 men.

Except for Heldsberg, the other forts were similarly designed and they housed two 75mm guns and had garrisons of about 90 to 100 men. Fort Reuenthal overlooks the Rhine at the point where it meets the Aar near the town of Koblenz. It was ready by April 1939, but an emergency exit and an air intake about 300m behind the fort were added in July. The simple layout included a combination machine gun/entrance block of two levels. From that block, the main gallery ran the length of the fort – about 210m. About 100m down the gallery was access to another machine gun block, the caserne and engine room. Between the two machine gun blocks, there were two artillery blocks, each of which housed a 75mm gun that covered the Rhine valley.

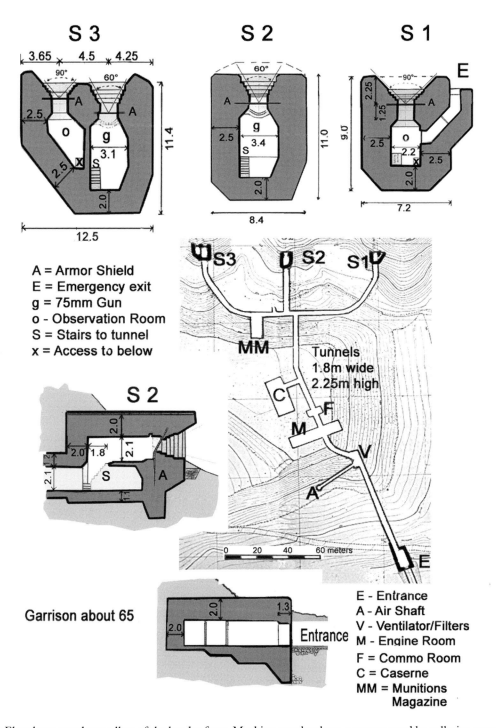

S 3 S 2 S 1

A = Armor Shield
E = Emergency exit
g = 75mm Gun
o - Observation Room
S = Stairs to tunnel
x = Access to below

Tunnels
1.8m wide
2.25m high

S 2

Garrison about 65

Entrance

E - Entrance
A - Air Shaft
V - Ventilator/Filters
M - Engine Room
F = Commo Room
C = Caserne
MM = Munitions
Magazine

Fort Ebersberg was the smallest of the border forts. Machine-gun bunkers, not connected by galleries, occupied positions near the fort to defend it from assault.

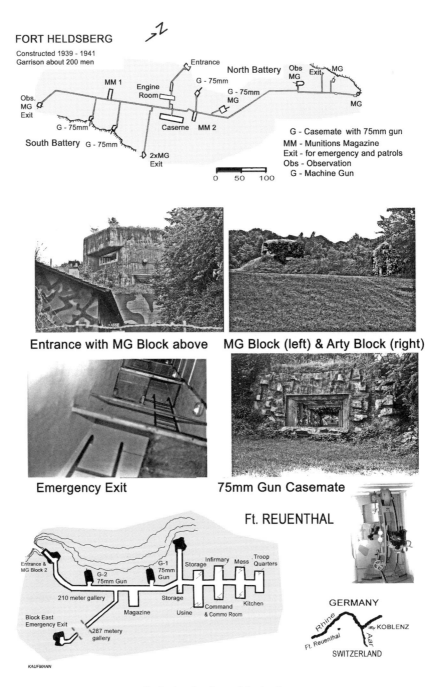

Swiss border forts. (*Authors*)

Fort Heldsberg, the largest of the border forts built between 1939 and 1941, was located at the northeast end of the Border Line. It consisted of four artillery blocks each mounting a 75mm gun. One pair of gun blocks covered one direction and the other pair another. It included seven machine guns and two observations positions. It took a garrison of 200 men.

Close defence was provided by twenty-five bunkers not linked to the fort with 24mm and 47mm anti-tank guns and machine guns.

The other two border forts similar to Reuenthal were Plainbois and Ebersberg. Plainbois was located southwest of Basel at the eastern end of the Jura, within 3km of the French border. It had a 200m long main gallery and four combat blocks, two with a 75mm gun, similar to those at Reuenthal. Ebersberg overlooked the Rhine across from Rüdingen, to the south of Schaffhausen. Built into the sandstone hills of the same name at an elevation of 456m, it consisted of an entrance block and three combat blocks, two with a 75mm gun. One of these blocks was an observation and emergency exit. The garrison was the smallest of the border forts with about sixty-five men. An infantry bunker with a 47mm anti-tank gun stood in front of the fort.

The Army Position, to the rear of the Border Line, included several strongpoints including Festung Dietikon, which consisted of bunkers and obstacles around the town of the same name. Another fort located near Baden was similar to the border forts but was designed as an infantry position. The position also included many bunkers for troops and shelters and anti-tank and anti-infantry obstacles. Plans for at least three artillery forts with gun turrets for the Limmat sector were cancelled after the fall of France when General Henri Guisan changed the defensive strategy to concentrate on the defence of the National Redoubt.[49]

Switzerland had other fortifications as well, including those in the southeast. The construction of Fort Crestawald near the Splügen Pass was delayed until September 1939, so the fort did not become active until July 1941. Fort Crestawald, with a garrison of ninety-five men, had 105mm guns and machine guns. Further south, there was a network of fortifications to the north of Bellinzona in the Riviera district of Canton Ticino where work began in 1940. The code name LONA referred to the defended area between Lodrino and Osogna where the valley walls were 1,300m (4,160ft) high, which consisted of many bunkers and barriers backed by artillery.[50]

In addition to field fortifications, the Swiss built many concrete bunkers throughout the country. Their sizes and shapes varied until the troops received plans in the late spring of 1940, after which these bunkers followed a standard designs that consisted of two levels, the lower one for the crew, equipment and supplies. They usually had three embrasures: one for an infantry gun, one for a machine gun and one for observation. They were similar to the bunkers built in the previous World War, but had thicker walls of 2.0m or more.

Wire obstacles surrounded forts that were easily accessible, like those on the northern border. Anti-tank obstacles of many types were deployed to block roads and possible avenues of advance. Holes were dug in roads and covered with metal caps. In time of danger, the caps came off and troops inserted anti-tank rails to close the road or even bridges, which were also prepared for demolition. Where the terrain allowed the passage of armoured vehicles, lines of anti-tank obstacles – usually Dragon's Teeth – blocked the area. The Swiss used anti-tank rails, anti-tank ditches and walls. The Swiss Dragon's Teeth were similar to the ones the Germans made because they produced them the same way. However, during the war, the Swiss created their own design nicknamed 'Toblerone' after the chocolate bar because of their shape. Some good examples of these obstacles still stand in a 10km sector of the 'Toblerone Line', which runs from the west side of Lake Leman at Prangins to the Bassins in the Jura. This line includes about 3,000 anti-tank obstacles and bunker strongpoints. The country bristled with obstacles and well-concealed forts and bunkers during the war.

Swiss manufacturers produced all the major items for their fortifications during the war, but in the late 1930s, the government purchased armoured plates for the border forts from Krupp,

Left: Post holes with covers
that are removed to emplace
steel rail AT obstacles

The Swiss used a variety of anti-tank obstacles including more traditional-looking Dragon's Teeth. The pictured type were named after the Toblerone chocolates because of the similarity. Road barriers normally consisted of prepared positions in roads for inserting steel rails to from the obstacle. The covered holes can be seen in the bottom photo. (*Authors*)

according to Günther Reiss. Some cloches and machine-gun cupolas came from Czechoslovakia in 1937. Since German deliveries were delayed and uncertain and the Czech state disappeared, the Swiss began to produce their own armour. Swiss industry manufactured 75mm anti-aircraft guns and the turrets for the 105mm guns under license from Schneider Creusot. They also produced 150mm guns and 105mm field guns under license from Bofors. The Swiss developed the 75mm Fortress (casemate) Cannon based on the Bofors 75mm mountain gun.

Swiss Fortress Weapons

Weapon	Range (metres)	Rate of Fire (rounds per minute)	Notes
7.5mm Maxim Mle 1911 MG	1,500	400	
47mm Fortress Mle 1937	6,800	20	Böhler
53mm Mle 1887 QF	3,000	–	Krupp (Grüson)
53mm Mle 1907 QF	4,000	–	Krupp (Grüson)
75mm Mle 1903	–	–	Krupp
75mm Mle 1903 L22 M*	8,700	15 to 20	Bofors
75mm Mle 1939	11,000	–	Used in casemates
84mm Mle 1879	3,000	–	Krupp
105mm Mle 1881	9,500	–	Fornerod-Krupp****
105mm Mle 1935 L42	18,000	8 to 10	Bofors
105mm Mle 1939 L52	15,000 to 20,000**	6 to 8	Thun. Turret gun
105mm Mle 1942	18,000 to 22,000**	6 to 8	Turret gun
120mm Mle 1882 L25	9,000***	1 to 4	1881 Krupp gun modified at Thun for casemates and turrets. Turret at Bäzberg and disappearing mounts at Dailly
120 Mle 1891 How.	5,900	–	Used in 5 turrets of Savant, 1 of Dailly and 1 of Bühl
150mm Mle 1877	8,500		Krupp. 'Gros Fritz' at Dailly
150mm Mle 1942 L 42	24,000	4	Thun. Casemate gun.
150mm Mle 1915 L14 Fortress How.	8,000	4	Thun. Casemate howitzer.

*Mountain gun.
** Ranges for steel shell and pointed shell.
*** Increased to 10,500m with new shell after First World War.
**** Lt. Col. Auguste Fornerod-Stadler (1839–79) served in the Swiss army and was involved the planning for the defence of Switzerland in the 1870s and improvement of Swiss artillery. He was responsible for the Fornerod 150mm bronze/steel cannon built in Switzerland also the design for the 105mm cannon Krupp built to his specifications after his death.

[Source: Lt. Col. Jean de Montet, *L'Armement de L'Artillerie de Fortresse de 1885 á 1939* (Edition ASMEM 1984)].

Gotthard Fortress

Fort (Built)	Elevation (approx)	Offensive		Close Defence		
		105mm Guns	120mm Guns	Guns	MG	Notes
Bühl (1890–2)	1,400m	–	2 in T	2 (120mm mortars)* 2 (84mm) 3 (53mm in T)	–	
Bäzberg (1889–92)	1,850m	–	3 in T	3 (84mm) 4 (53mm in T)	–	Rotating Obs T
Battery Fleuggern (1911–13)	1,900m	–	4 in T	–	–	
Battery Rosemttlen (1911–12)	2,100m	–	6	–	–	
Stöckli (1894–8)	2,460m	–	–	2 (120mm How) 2 (53mm in T)	1	MG casemate added 1915
Battery Grossboden (below Ft. Stöckli)	–	–	2	–	–	
Gütsch (1890s) (1941–2)	2,300m	3 in T	12	–	5	5 MG Bunkers
San Carlo (1939–41)	2,050m	2 in T	–	–	–	MG Bunkers
Hospiz (1893–4)	2,100m	–	–	2 (120mm How) 2 (53mm in T)	2	Obs cloche
Sasso da Pigna (1941–5)	–	4 **	–	–	–	
Battery Motto Bartola (1888–90)	1,550m	1 in T***	4	4 (84mm)	–	Reconstructed 1914 – 4 x 120mm guns
Stuei (1892–93)	1,500m	–	–	2 (84mm)	–	
Foppa Hill positions (1895)	1,400m	–	–	2 (120mm How) 2 (53mm in T)	–	1907 Obs cloche.
Galenhütten (1890–2)	–	–	2	1(120mm Hw T) 2 (84mm)	–	
Airolo (1887–9)	1.350m	–	2 (both guns in one T)	5 (84mm) 12(84mm bronze guns) 4 (53mm in T)	–	3 Obs cloche
Grimsel (1941–3)	–	6	–	–	3	1945 105mm replaced with 150mm

*Replaced with 120mm How. in 1904.
** Replaced in 1944 with 4 x 150mm guns.
***Added in early 1940s on Foppa Grande.
T = Turrets (single gun turrets, except if noted otherwise)
Source: Oswald Schwitter correspondence and data posted on the internet.

German Plans for Switzerland[51]

Nazi propaganda of the mid-1930s claimed that most of Switzerland ethnically belonged to Greater Germany. In Switzerland, many of the German speakers at first appeared to sympathize with Germany, but most were disheartened by the lies and activities of Hitler's Reich. The annexation of Austria and the destruction of Czechoslovakia spurred a rapid expansion of the Swiss defences with the main emphasis along the border of the Third Reich. Swiss strategy was to mass their forces along this area and to cooperate with the French.[52] Secret meetings took place between representatives of the French and Swiss military just before and during the war. The French planned to send troops to back the Swiss in the event of a Nazi invasion. The Swiss had even begun building positions according to French specifications on the heights of Gneppen overlooking Basel so the French artillery could use them if need be.

After Dunkirk, during the final German offensive in the West, Panzer Group Guderian raced toward the Swiss border to cut off French units retreating from the Maginot Line in June 1940.[53] General Henri Guisan (1874–1960), promoted to that rank in August 1939 when the crisis began, knew the situation was bad and as the French sought an armistice, he ordered the destruction of all the secret documents concerning Swiss cooperation with the French. Unfortunately, the Germans had captured French copies of these documents. Hitler was incensed. On 18 June, Hitler met with Mussolini and planned to encircle Switzerland. Ironically, he had previously warned his Italian ally against an offensive in the French Alps because it would be costly. Now, he intended to isolate Switzerland completely after the fall of France. On 20 June, the Italians advanced a short distance across the French border only to be beaten back by the troops in the Little Maginot Line in the Alps. This was only a foretaste of what the Germans could expect if they invaded Switzerland. The armistice left the Swiss with a common border with unoccupied (Vichy) France, which allowed them a trading outlet that displeased the Führer.

Goaded by the fact that the small Swiss Air Force of only about 200 aircraft, with only fifty modern German Me-109s, had engaged and destroyed a few German aircraft that had overflown their airspace and by the secret cooperation with the French before May 1940, Hitler ordered the elaboration of 'Case Switzerland'. Captain Otto Wilhelm von Menges from the General Staff's Operations Division began drawing up the plans on 24 June 1940. The objective was to occupy Switzerland rapidly and prevent the destruction of key facilities and lines of communication. The Swiss were estimated to have six infantry divisions, three mountain divisions, three mountain brigades and three light brigades with seventy-five battalions of territorials. They deployed six to seven of these divisions along the north and northeast border and only one division faced the French border. The remaining forces were in the southeast covering the National Redoubt facing Italy. The plan was rapidly to occupy Berne, Lucerne and Zurich[54] in the first two days, take control of the Mittelland and prevent the Swiss from retreating south. Menges ruled out attacking the Sargans area because of the fortifications and terrain. He also considered using airborne troops near Berne to take control of the mountain passes and near Olten and Solothurn to block a Swiss retreat through the

Mittelland. The Italian army's mission was to attack through the difficult terrain of the Chur-Davos area. Planning continued as German divisions took up positions along the Jura. These forces included four corps of the Twelfth Army of General Leeb's Army Group C. The 73rd and 21st Divisions were near Basel and, to the southwest of them in the Belfort area, there stood a corps with the 23rd and 260th Divisions. Another corps consisting of the 6th and 1st Mountain Divisions at Pontarlier and Salins-Morez respectively along the border and the 52nd Division in reserve near Vesoul. Finally, near Dijon, another corps with 5th and 15th Divisions was in reserve. Opinion remains divided on whether this plan was just ruse or a serious scheme. Menges' plan, which became known as Operation 'Tannenbaum' and was completed in October 1940, called for about twenty divisions. However, some of the divisions had already moved towards the Channel for Operation 'Sea Lion', including the 1st Mountain Division which left on 24 July and the 6th Mountain Division. Thus, by October, the invasion of Switzerland was no longer viable.

While he waited for the Germans to strike, General Henri Guisan revised the Swiss strategy. He asked his officers to take an oath to fight to the death that summer after the fall of France, but he was not going to allow the Germans the advantage. After mobilization in 1939, seven of his nine divisions concentrated along the Army Position, mostly in the Limmat sector. His revised plans for July 1940 called for border brigades to fight to the death to delay the enemy along the frontier while the majority of the army was to hold the National Redoubt where the Germans would be unable to use the element of surprise once more

Meanwhile, the Germans came up with a modification to their invasion plan on 12 August 1940. Now, the 20th and 29th Motorized Divisions were to strike in the vicinity of Geneva and advance around both sides of Lake Leman. The 5th Division supported by the 4th Panzer Division was to advance from the vicinity of Pontarlier, penetrate onto the Mittelland between Lakes Leman (Geneva) and Neuchâtel and advance on Berne and Thun. The 73rd Division was to advance near Basel, supported by the Leibstandarte Adolf Hitler SS Regiment and take Solothurn, then Lucerne. Along the Rhine, the 276th Division was to attack south towards Zurich and the Mittelland and advance into the Lake Constance area. The 1st Mountain Division was supposed to penetrate the Jura between the 73rd and 5th Divisions. On 26 October, General Erwin Witzleben formed Army Group D taking control of German forces in the West. At this time, German divisions were withdrawing from the West. On 11 November, the Army High Command (OKH) dropped Operation 'Tannenbaum'. General Franz Halder, Chief of the German General Staff, wrote that the Jura mountain frontier, where most of the German divisions were concentrated, was not favourable to an attacker.

Earlier, in July 1940, the Swiss army demobilized many of its troops, leaving only about 200,000 men on active duty. Soon an additional 50,000 returned to civilian life. At the time the National Redoubt was not ready to take the fully-mobilized army. On 20 July 1940, General Guisan issued Operations Order No 20 directing the army to concentrate in the National Redoubt to defend the main approaches in rough terrain. The frontier units were to maintain their fortified positions and covering forces would use the Army Position (including the Limmatstellung) as an advanced point from which to block enemy penetration and create a defence in depth in front of the National Redoubt. The new Swiss strategy made a Blitzkrieg impossible, at the cost of sacrificing the Mittelland within a day or so. The National Redoubt would be ready to fight with supplies for civilians and soldiers that would last for almost half a year. The Swiss took measures to deal with paratroopers in any possible landing zone in the mountainous terrain. In July, the Federal President advocated appeasement, but changed his tune later. The risk of the new Swiss strategy was that it would leave the families of many of the soldiers in occupied territory.[55] On the other hand, nothing would stop the Swiss military and local units from destroying bridges, roads and other facilities that had been prepared for demolition in the fortress area even before the war had begun. These operations would close down the main railway lines through the Gotthard and Simplon for years and with them, the routes that were critical to the success of the German/Italian war effort. According to the terms of an international treaty of 1909, the Germans and Italians were allowed to use these facilities for hauling non-war materials. There was no question of the two Axis powers using a Trojan Horse type of action like in the Netherlands because the trains were closely inspected at the border and there were too many key points along each line that had to be secured.

The historian Willi Gautschi uncovered a document from apparently the autumn of 1940 stating that the Swiss government would request the British RAF fly in 100 aircraft to help hold the National Redoubt with some additional troops and equipment. They hoped that the British could provide continued air drops to sustain their resistance.[56]

By the summer of 1941, all nine Swiss divisions in the National Redoubt had sufficient provisions to last five months. Meanwhile, both German and Italian diplomats and leaders warned the Swiss to maintain their neutrality and maintain an embargo on trade with the Allies. The Swiss had only one route from Geneva through Vichy France to conduct trade outside of occupied Europe. Despite supplying the Germans with optical equipment and other products for their military, the Swiss helped the Allies. They were able to deliver many small precision devices such as time fuses that were easily carried out of the country in large numbers in small suitcases. Neither belligerent wanted to lose these assets, but a German invasion would most likely result in the loss of these industries for both sides.

In the summer of 1942 and again in the spring of 1943, the possibility of a German invasion loomed again. When Hitler publicly complained on 26 August 1942 that Switzerland was 'a pimple on the face of Europe' that 'cannot be allowed to continue', tensions flared again, but the Wehrmacht had its hands full fighting on all fronts. Nonetheless, the Germans still held on to their invasion plans. After May 1940, the German generals and military logic no longer influenced Hitler's decisions, which seemed increasingly to be guided by his whims and desires. As Italy's future looked progressively bleaker due to Allied operations in North Africa in the spring of 1943, Hitler ordered his generals to review once again the plans for a takeover of Switzerland. At the end of 1943, SS General Herman Böhme drew up a plan that required twelve divisions and three mountain divisions. The main force coming from the north was to occupy the Mittelland and capture the key Swiss industries intact. The second part of the invasion plan required troops in the east to take on the Sargans fortress. The mountain divisions and other units were to attack in the south towards Brig, St-Maurice, Geneva and Lausanne. To breach the National Redoubt, airborne units would land inside the fortress area in the vicinity of St Gotthard, Brig, Thun and Lucerne. Although Böhme expected stiff resistance and heavy casualties, he believed that German overall superiority in aircraft and armour would prevail. However, his plan was overly optimistic since this was not 1939 or 1941 and a Blitzkrieg against a nation whose army occupied a strong position was unrealistic. A winter operation was not advisable. In the spring of 1944, Allied troops were preparing another offensive in Italy, while the seaborne invasion from England was expected at any time. Based on their experiences with the Polish Home Army during the Warsaw Uprising of August 1944, the Germans could expect many weeks of Swiss resistance at best. If the invasion succeeded, most of the vital transport routes would be wrecked, forcing their military in Italy to depend entirely on the Brenner Pass and non-military supplies no longer able to use the Swiss rail system.

A further complication arose when the Western Allies landed in France in 1944. It was possible that they might want to use Switzerland as a back door into the Reich. This situation would have seriously confounded the Swiss because they knew that if the Allies invaded, the Germans would have a pretext to rush in to their 'aid.' In this case, the Swiss would resist the Germans but it was questionable how to handle the Allies since they were obligated to resist them in this situation.

Timeline of Swiss Fortifications

1st Construction Period: 1830 to 1860
- Construction at St-Maurice
- Some fortifications built at St. Luziensteig
- Line of fortifications at Bellinzona

2nd Construction Period: 1880 to 1920
    1882–92: Forts Bühl & Bäzberg (FG)
    1887–91: Fort Airolo (FG)
    1890–4: Fort Galenhutten (FG)
    1891–4: Fort Stuei (FG)
    1894: Fort Hospiz (FG)
    1892–4: Forts Savatan & Dailly (FsM)
    1911: Fort Scex (FsM)
    1913–20: New defences in Canton of Tessin

3rd Construction Period: 1930 to 1945
    1937–9: The five Border Forts
    1939–40: The Border Line
    1939 (late)–40: The Army Position
    1938–40: Forts Schollberg & Anstein (FS)
    1939–42: Forts Magletsch, Kastels, Fugels & Passatiwand (FS)
    1940–3: The LONA Line north of Bellizona.
    1941–3: Forts Molinära & Haselboden (FS)
    1941–3: Fort Fuchsegg (FG)
    1941–3: Forts Tschingel, Nussloch & Tamina Ragaz (FS)
    1941–4: Fort Muesterschwanderberg (Lucerne fortress)
    1941–4: The Beatenberg forts (Thun fortress)
    1941–1945: Fort Cindey (FsM)
    1942–3: Fort Champex

FG= Fortress Gotthard, FsM =Fortress St-Maurice, FS = Fortress Sargans

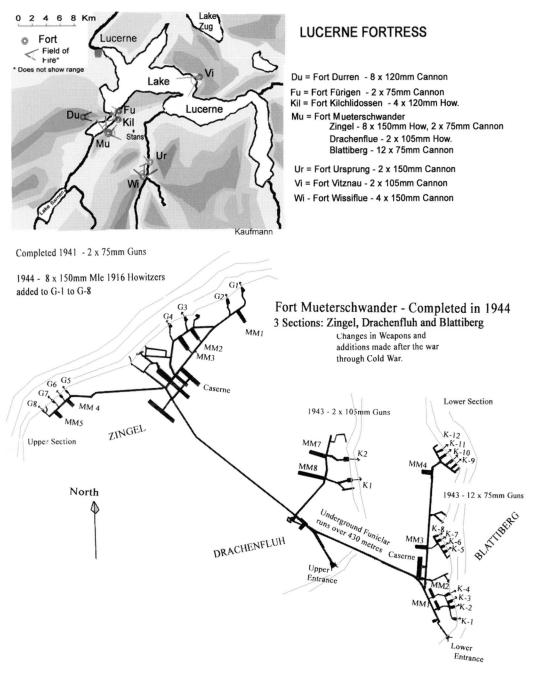

LUCERNE FORTRESS

Du = Fort Durren - 8 x 120mm Cannon

Fu = Fort Fürigen - 2 x 75mm Cannon
Kil = Fort Kilchlidossen - 4 x 120mm How.

Mu = Fort Mueterschwander
       Zingel - 8 x 150mm How, 2 x 75mm Cannon
       Drachenflue - 2 x 105mm How.
       Blattiberg - 12 x 75mm Cannon

Ur = Fort Ursprung - 2 x 150mm Cannon

Vi = Fort Vitznau - 2 x 105mm Cannon

Wi - Fort Wissiflue - 4 x 150mm Cannon

Completed 1941 - 2 x 75mm Guns

1944 - 8 x 150mm Mle 1916 Howitzers
added to G-1 to G-8

Fort Mueterschwander - Completed in 1944
3 Sections: Zingel, Drachenfluh and Blattiberg
Changes in Weapons and
additions made after the war
through Cold War.

1943 - 2 x 105mm Guns

1943 - 12 x 75mm Guns

North

Plan of Fort Mueterschwander, the largest fort in the Lucerne Fortress. A map showing the area of the Lucerne Fortress including the artillery forts and the weapons they mounted between 1942 and 1945.

Chapter Seven

Conclusion

In late 1929, France became the first country to build a major new line of fortifications with large underground positions. As the French began to build their Maginot Line along the border with Germany and on the Italian frontier in the Alps, other nations followed suit. Since there were limited options for such subterranean fortifications, many of the new defences mushrooming up in Europe wound up having similar characteristics. These new works may be called 'Maginot Imitations' only because they served a similar purpose, had underground facilities and had weapons positions with minimal exposure on the surface. In the German East Wall created in the mid-1930s, the largest positions consisted of several large but relatively lightly-armed combat blocks placed in groups and linked by underground galleries. After 1936, the Germans also began the construction of the West Wall, which originally was to include large forts somewhat similar to those of the Maginot Line 'ouvrages'. However, they eventually decided to switch to a more modern type of defence in depth using a deep line of bunkers backed with obstacles and the first large-scale anti-personnel minefields.

The countries that lay between France and Germany adopted the role of neutral buffer states. Belgium did not join the Netherlands and Switzerland in the neutral bloc until 1936, when its king tried to avoid war once more after a similar effort had failed in 1914. The Dutch had a late start in fortification building because their politicians were deadlocked for decades on the matter of defence. No decision was taken until it appeared that Germany would not honour their neutrality in the looming war. Belatedly, they started to improve their defences, but the Grebbe Line and their other fortifications could not include subterranean features because of the high water table. The Dutch built only two new forts on the Afsluitdijk, restored some old ones and launched a massive bunker-building program on the eve of the war. Their Belgian neighbours, on the other hand, restored old forts and began to prepare a new defensive line in the French style at about the same time as France. This new line in the vicinity of Liège comprised a few forts with subterranean facilities whose designs were very distinct from the Maginot ouvrages. Like the French, they used twin-gun artillery turrets, but they mounted a heavier 120mm gun in some of them. They used three-gun artillery casemates like the French, but their 75mm guns were not angled for flanking fire. The guns had a 70° field of fire instead of 45° and faced in the direction of the enemy, leaving the façade of the casemate exposed. Fort Eben Emael, considered the lynchpin and flagship of their defences, had the weakest passive defences of the four new forts and it did not compare favourably with the ouvrages of the Maginot Line. The Belgians could not avoid war because Liège, and later the Ardennes, were on the path of German forces intent on outflanking the Maginot Line, which they preferred not to take on. Eben Emael fell quickly and the remainder of the Belgian fortifications and fortified lines proved inadequate in stopping the German advance. Both Belgium and the Netherlands succumbed in record time to the German invaders who used new methods – including vertical envelopment – to neutralize their fortifications.

The Swiss occupied a virtual mountain fortress with potential enemies on every border. They continued to improve their fortifications in the 1930s and maintained contact with French military engineers. The only similarity between the Swiss Border Line and the Maginot Line was that its few forts looked much like miniature Maginot ouvrages. The key position in the Alpine Redoubt, on the other hand, did not resemble in the least the Maginot forts of the Alps. Although they were never tested in war, the Swiss Alpine fortresses probably would have held up as well as the Maginot Line of the Alps, which, although held with troops heavily outnumbered by the enemy, crushed every Italian offensive effort in the summer of 1940. Switzerland was the only one of the three neutral states to avoid being sucked into the World Wars thanks to its terrain and fortifications, which made invading it too costly.

What all three of these perennial neutrals had in common at the time of the Second World War was that their defensive systems relied heavily on National Redoubts. The effectiveness of a National Redoubt is dubious. Such a defensive strategy may have even contributed to the early defeat of The Netherlands and Belgium, which are made up mainly of low-lying terrain. The defences relied heavily on inundations and water barriers with access to the sea as a possible lifeline for foreign aid. During the First World War, Antwerp and the Scheldt served this purpose, but even with the arrival of British troops the defences of the city were overwhelmed. Belgian troops, on the other hand, were able to cling on and resist in Western Flanders, but almost all of the country was occupied and suffered for the remainder of the war. During the next conflict, the Belgian military leaders were divided on how to use fortifications. Some concluded that it was best to plan a retreat to the coast where the army would have a better chance to hold out, a strategy Belgium implemented in the 1930s. A National Redoubt, based again on Antwerp, was re-established and extended to include the Ghent Bridgehead. Even if the Belgian army had concentrated on holding this line between 1939 and 1940 instead of spreading its scarce resources and manpower on fortifications elsewhere in the country, it is doubtful that the outcome would have been much different from that of the Great War.

In the Netherlands, Fortress Holland was, in fact, the National Redoubt. This position actually incorporated large and relatively effective water barriers some of which consisted of deliberate inundations. By the turn of the century, the Amsterdam Ring had become the last stand position or National Redoubt and the New Water Line in front of it was the main line of defence. After the Great War, the Dutch changed their defensive strategy and the Amsterdam Ring no longer played a major role in Fortress Holland. The New Water Line was improved and the front was pushed further east to the Grebbe Line, forming the main land defences of the National Redoubt. Fortress Holland enfolded a large part of the Dutch population and much of its industry whereas the Belgian redoubt area enclosed a smaller part of its population and only part of its industrial capacity. To be fair, most of the population centres and concentrations of economic resources in Belgium were more widely scattered than they were in the Netherlands. Despite this, the enemy breached both of these National Redoubts within a few days during the Second World War. Other factors also contributed to the two nations' rapid downfall.

Switzerland, unlike the Netherlands and Belgium, successful avoided invasion in both World Wars. After the fall of France in 1940, the Swiss military leadership headed by General Guisan concluded that their country could not resist an invasion and changed their strategy to defending a National Redoubt, which was very different from those in the Low Countries.

Switzerland has no access to the sea and extremely mountainous terrain. The Swiss redoubt relied on the mountains and only protected a few population centres and a small part of Swiss industry. It was much like the Belgian National Redoubt in this respect. Between June 1940 and September 1944, Switzerland had little chance of surviving if it was invaded by the Axis Powers. Its National Redoubt strategy worked only because a conflict on its territory would have closed the main north-south routes between Italy and Germany for many years if key bridges and tunnels had been blown up. This possibility more than anything else probably discouraged the Axis powers from invading.

The National Redoubt strategy also failed the Germans who tried, albeit half-heartedly, to establish an Alpine Fortress in many ways similar to the one in Switzerland.[1] Even if they had succeeded, after the Allied armies occupied most of Germany in 1945, this Alpine Redoubt would have been unable to prevent the final defeat of Hitler's regime. In twentieth-century warfare, reliance on static lines of defence like a National Redoubt generally failed to prevent nations from becoming embroiled in conflicts and even led to defeat. The only exception was Switzerland, which thanks to its unique topography, was able to avoid the vortex of war.

In 1915, an anonymous German writer, known as simply as 'C', published an article entitled 'The Value of Permanent Fortifications' in *Kriegstechnische Zeitschrift*[2] magazine, in which he explained,

> The best defense of the Fatherland is a rapid and well-sustained offensive by a strong and thoroughly trained force. Such a defense requires no land fortifications. Other countries have built land fortifications on the theory that they would furnish points of support for forces acting on the offensive. This theory is not borne out by the operations of 1870 in the recent operations in Belgium [1914].
>
> France has always built extensive permanent fortifications, but the Germans have placed little confidence in such works. The present conflict may upset many of our ideas and it may not be amiss to outline the fortification problem. A land fortress may be considered 'modern' when the works and their grouping meet the tactical requirements of their locality; when the guns and engineering features are superior to those which the enemy can bring against them; when they possess sufficient defensive power to withstand a siege; and when they are proof against assault prepared by any artillery that can be taken into the field.
>
> None of the existing fortifications are modern in this sense, even disregarding the 42 cm Howitzer. Siege artillery is now superior to the means of defense and modifications in type of fortifications must be made to meet this superiority. The modifications will be expensive, but the expense must not be spared or the result may be failure. Battleships go to the scrap heap in 20 years and we must recognize that fortifications are similarly of limited life. It may be argued that fortresses are obsolete and that improvised trenches will answer but it is not the French and English trenches that have stopped the German offensive …
>
> The conclusion from the above is that permanent fortifications still remain a factor to be reckoned with…. The modern fortress will be feared by an enemy and form a staunch bulwark of the defense of the country.

This anonymous German officer was mistaken when he claimed that fortifications, like battleships, are good for only about twenty years. Many of the Swiss fortifications of the 1940s remained in service until the end of the century. This was also the case for some of the Maginot Line forts and positions in several other countries. As a matter of fact, some American battleships from the 1940s saw combat in the 1990s.

Notes

Introduction
1. They began their empire long before their independence was recognized.
2. Hugo Grotius, a Dutch jurist of the early seventeenth century, laid the groundwork for international law. The Hague became the site of two international peace conferences in 1899 and 1907.
3. This area, part of Limburg, has coal deposits mined by the Dutch for centuries. Thus, the economic importance of the Maastricht Appendage made it unlikely that the Dutch would ever voluntarily give it up for more secure borders.
4. Vauban used the term *Pré Carré* in reference to two lines of fortified towns he would build in French Flanders based on the theory that a square, resulting from two lines, would be easier to defend than a circle.
5. The French did not adopt the Carnot Wall even though it was an idea proposed by the French engineer Lazare Carnot (1753–1823), Napoleon's Minister of War in 1800. His older contemporary, the Marquis René de Montalembert (1714–1800), came up with a polygonal system with guns in casemates. The Germans (Prussians) adopted both of their ideas in the nineteenth century.
6. The French term 'Fence of Iron' was used to describe the *Pré Carré* in James Falkner's book *Marshal Vauban and the Defence Louis XIV's France* (Barnsley: Pen & Sword, 2011).
7. Throughout history most moats were dry since many locations were not adaptable for wet moats.
8. Montalembert's ideas were not popular with the French. He did much of his work with the tenaille system that was mainly a zigzag trace without bastions or curtains and consisted of salients with re-entrant angles between them.
9. The French finally adopted the system after seeing the results achieved by rifled cannon.
10. The term, coined by the French, was inspired by the shape of the shell.
11. These would not be the first armoured forts.
12. In the 1930s the famous Oerlikon 20mm anti-aircraft gun began to appear in many nations' arsenals and later two- and three-barrelled versions were produced during the war. These weapons remained in service until the 1990s. After 1942, with the occupation of Vichy France, the Swiss could only sell these weapons to the Germans. The Swiss field army emplaced many of these weapons around their fortifications during the war.
13. These new forts were to guard the St. Gotthard Tunnel.
14. A foreshadowing of most of these changes in all fields of warfare occurred during the American Civil War (1861–5). Many technological advances had already begun in the eighteenth century and early in the nineteenth century, but they resulted in the most dramatic effects on strategy and tactics during and after the Civil War and the Franco-Prussian War.
15. Swiss optics and precision instruments were of value, but not worth an invasion.

Chapter 1
1. Beginning in the seventeenth century, the Netherlands had been one of Northern Europe's first Republics. The French Revolution resulted in the creation of the Batavian Republic between 1795 and 1806. The Kingdom of Holland under Louis Bonaparte replaced the republic and it was annexed in turn

by Napoleon in 1810. In 1815, with the end of Napoleon's empire, the Netherlands became a monarchy under William I of Orange.

2. One method of breaking the ice was to lower the water level slightly to cause it to collapse.

3. Antwerp, which had been part of the Spanish Netherlands, economically declined when it the Treaty of 1648 cut off its access to the sea. It rose to prominence again after the French invasion in the 1790s. When Belgium was part of the Netherlands from 1815 until 1830, Antwerp was the leading city for much of that period.

4. The alliance with the French was in the Second Anglo-Dutch War (1665–7) in which the Dutch lost their American colony to the British, but the Dutch were victorious.

5. The Third Anglo-Dutch War (1672–4).

6. The ruling family of Brandenburg acquired Prussia in 1618. In the next century, it was common to refer to both Brandenburg and Prussia simply as Prussia, but the famed Prussian army originated in Brandenburg.

7. William III's mother was Mary Stuart, the daughter of King Charles I of England. Mary II was the daughter of King Charles II of England. The English Parliament invited them as legitimate heirs to the throne to replace James II after the Glorious Revolution of 1688.

8. Rudy Rolf informed the authors that Blanken's dry dock was based on a French model, with a boat door as a closing element. It remains *in situ* in Hellevoetsluis.

9. In addition to working on the water defences and designing forts, he built the North Holland Canal and invented the first dry dock (at the naval base of Hellevoetsluis and Den Helder) using a steam pump to drain it. He purchased the pump from James Watt's company. He designed the North Holland Canal, built between 1819 and 1825, for merchant ships and 55-gun frigates. Construction of the main dike of Helder and the fortifications had begun during the French occupation. The 75km-long canal runs from Amsterdam to Den Helder on the North Sea. It eventually became inadequate for larger shipping and later the construction of the shorter North Sea Canal from Amsterdam to Ijmuiden replaced it.

10. The excavation of a canal around the lake began in 1839. The earth removed formed a dike. In 1848, engineers added pumping stations and by 1852, the lake was pumped dry with three steam engines instead of windmills.

11. The reduit (also known as a redoubt) served as a last-stand position.

12. Muiden is a medieval castle. A bastioned earthwork surrounded it centuries later as part of the bastioned enceinte that turned the entire town into a fortress. Adjacent to the bastions to the northwest of the castle is a Napoleonic Era fortified sluice with rifle embrasures. In the last half of the nineteenth century, the army added a tower fort further to the northwest where few remains of the fortress still exist. Also, an artillery position to the south on the southeast of the castle formed part of the fortress. Weesp is a seventeenth-century fortress.

13. The city of Maastricht was first fortified in the early thirteenth century. During the centuries leading up to 1815, the city changed hands several times, becoming part of the Spanish Netherlands and ending as part of Napoleonic France before 1815. The Spanish, Dutch and French took turns putting it under siege. The Napoleonic Wars ended with the Congress of Vienna, which allotted the city and region to the Netherlands. When the Catholic Belgians revolted in 1830, the city remained under the control of the Dutch even though the population largely preferred to be part of Belgium. The 1839 Treaty of London awarded the city and most of the province of Limburg to the Netherlands.

14. Dambenoy was prime minister for part of the year of 1857.

15. Landwehr (Landweer in Dutch) referred to troops who had been trained and placed in reserve for several years subject to being called to active duty. The system varied from country to country. The one the Dutch adopted was less effective than the German model. The Dutch army also copied some other aspects of the victorious German army such as the creation of a General Staff. In 1887 and in 1901, the

government corrected flaws in the Dutch system of conscription through legislation intended to create an army of a higher calibre and increased size.

16. The Scheldt is spelled Schelde in Dutch and Flemish. The French call the river the Escaut. The source of the river is in northern France and it runs for the greater part of its 350km through Belgium with the river's mouth in the Netherlands allowing the Dutch to control access to Antwerp in Belgium.

17. Weitzel served again as Minister of War from 1883 to 1888, which was also an important period in the next phase of fortification construction.

18. René Ros: http://www.stelling-amsterdam.nl/stelling/index.html

19. The Germans built eleven ships of this class between 1876 and 1881. The Dutch were afraid that these shallow-draft armoured gunboats could enter the Zuider Zee and come close enough to Amsterdam to bombard it. Each vessel mounted one 305mm gun. However, they proved unseaworthy and only satisfactory for operations in German coastal waters. By 1911 all of these gunboats had been taken out of service.

20. These numbers vary since some sources classify forts as batteries and vice versa.

21. Actually, much of the area of the Amsterdam Ring of forts and along the New Water Line consists of large sections of peat.

22. We use his classifications since they now appear elsewhere and help give a better understanding of what was built. No such classifications existed a hundred years ago for these forts so these do not represent official designations.

23. Many of these forts were five-sided and included a Right Front, Left Front, Right Flank, Left Flank and Gorge side.

24. The Dutch and Germans often refer to these as 'Alert Rooms' whiled the English call them 'Guard Rooms'. This is also what the Dutch refer to on these forts as the 'Frontal Building'.

25. The Dutch use the German method of rounding off the numbers of the calibres of their artillery. Many sources, especially German sources, list these weapons as 6cm or 60mm for a 57mm gun, 7cm or 70mm for a 75mm gun and 10cm or 100mm for a 105mm gun.

26. The Germans and Austrians used the terms Flusseisen and Flussestahl. Both were a form of steel. The first was also known as soft or low carbon steel, or ingot iron. The German term 'eisen' indicates it was classified as 'iron'. Many of the Austrian cupolas were classified in German as 'iron' but some included steel components. Thus, there is confusion as to whether these cupolas should be identified as either iron or steel.

27. A number of these Grüson observation cupolas rotated.

28. Chilled cast iron in German is known as Hartguss.

29. As previously noted, the Austrians classified most of these turrets and cloches as iron.

30. The Kromme Rijn or Crooked Rhine once was the northernmost branch of the Rhine Delta. It is located in the province of Utrecht.

31. This arrow-shaped caponier was also surrounded by water.

32. The road that runs through the centre of this fort was built in 1930, resulting in the removal of the reduit since it passed between the two frontal bastions and through the location of the reduit.

33. The Merwede is formed where the Maas and Waal rivers meet.

34. See Sidebar: Fortifications Act of 1874

35. Ij refers to the waterfront at Amsterdam, i.e. Ijsselmeer.

36. In 1840, the province of Holland was divided into North and South Holland both of which formed Fortress Holland.

37. One turret remains mounted today and the other is on display outside Fort Hoek van Holland.

38. See Note #19 on the *Wespe*.

39. The closing of the Zuider Zee resulted in its name being changed to Lake Ijssel becoming the largest fresh water lake in Western Europe. The Great Dike, about 32km long, is actually named the Afsluitdijk (Enclosing Dike).

40. Guardhouse is often a confusing term. In eighteenth-century forts, they are often a position that supports, like a caserne, a small garrison and is not a simple sentry post.
41. In Dutch, this type of bridge is known as a 'Kraanbrug', or crane bridge. The term is derived from the shape of its swiveling supports. It was designed by the Dutch railway engineer Frederik Willem Conrad (1800–69) and used on railways. In the late 1870s, some of these bridges were added to Fortress Naarden and later to Fort Ronduit.
42. Artillery referred to as 'rifles' in that era were simply cannons with rifling as opposed to smoothbores.
43. This was an Austria weapon produced under license beginning in 1904.
44. The American Colonel Isaac Newton Lewis in 1911 designed the Lewis machine gun. After retiring he attempted to produce it in Belgium in 1913, but soon gave a British company the license to produce it using a .303in round. This was the first machine gun used on aircraft.
45. It has also been described as triangular, but the gorge side is semi-circular.
46. The First House of the bicameral Dutch legislature (States-General) is the Senate.
47. Haringvliet is the main inlet leading from Hollands Diep into the North Sea. Hellevoetsluis is near the near the end of this channel. Another important channel leading from the Hollands Diep is Volkerak that connects to the Grevelingenmeer that leads into the North Sea. This is all part of the huge Meuse (Maas-Rhine-Scheldt) Delta.
48. The author of the article appears to have overlooked the Scheldt naval shipyards at Vlissingen (Flushing).
49. After HMS *Dreadnought* was built, all new battleships became known as dreadnoughts while the older ones were called pre-dreadnoughts.

Chapter 2

1. Maartje Abbenhuis points out that the 1901 Landweer Law replaced the ineffective militia. Most conscripts went directly into the Landweer rather than serving time in the regular army. One problem was that these troops only had six days of training a year by 1914. In addition, the majority of Landweer troops served near their homes so more than half of these battalions were mobilized inside Fortress Holland. Thus, it was practical to assign most of those battalions to the fortifications even though the skills of the troops were lacking. The Landstrom was composed of men who avoided conscription and had little to no training. Although it was considered a reserve force, it was rather a fictional force of no value during the Great War.
2. Source: Theo Rothstein (1871-1953), 'The German "Menace"', *Justice: Weekly Newspaper of British Social Democracy*, 18 February and 25 February 1911. Rothstein, who was born in the Russian Empire, wrote for the newspaper *Justice* at the beginning of the twentieth century. He was a communist and returned to Russia after the Revolution having served as an interpreter for British intelligence. Of interest in the same 18 February 1911 article is his comment, 'In case a war with France, Germany would undoubtedly attempt to turn the left flank of the French army by forcing a passage through Belgium, in which case it would be the duty of England' to enter the war as a guarantor of Belgian neutrality.

   In addition, Erskine Childers' *The Riddle of the Sands* (1903) was one of several pre-war novels that heightened British fears of a possible German invasion of Great Britain.
3. Fort Kijkduin was also supposed to have been armed with two of the Krupp turrets for two 280mm guns, but when of the war ended the government scrapped those plans.
4. According to M.M. Abbenhuis, author of *The Art of Staying Neutral*, the Dutch prepared chemical weapons in April 1918, but production of gas masks was limited so that they only had one for every eighty soldiers. However, by November there were enough masks for the field troops only. During the same month, Dutch factories produced sufficient helmets to equip only one out of every forty soldiers. Dutch industry was unable to meet the demand and imports of foreign raw materials and equipment were limited due to the war.

5. These were old fortresses with limited value. In some cases, new works went up near them. Gorinchem and Woudrichem occupied important positions along the Upper Merwede. Gorinchem stood on the north shore. Fort Vuren was built to the east of it in the 1840s. On the south side of the Merwede, Woudrichem, a sixteenth-century fortress town surrounded by a moat, is located at the point where the Waal and Maas (Meuse) Rivers meet to form the Upper Merwede. In 1815, these positions became part of the New Dutch Water Line, which also included Fort Loevestein, a three-bastion fort that surrounded a fourteenth-century castle of the same name. The castle was turned into a bombproof reduit during the nineteenth century. Its last improvement consisted of a concrete shelter built in 1883. The fortifications on the south side of the Merwede and Waal lost much of their strategic value after the First World War. Forts Sabina Henrica and Frederik, near Willemstad, dated from the Napoleonic Era; they were modernized in the 1880s and later received Krupp 240mm coastal defence guns. They formed part of the Willemstad Position. However, by the end of the Great War, both positions and their guns became obsolete.

6. Den Brielle was an old fortress on the island of Voorne-Putten at the mouth of the Nieuwe Maas. Together with Hellevoetsluis, it formed the 'Stellung' or Position at the Mouths of the Maas and Haringvliet. Between Hellevoetsluis and Brielle stood the small forts of Penserdijk and Noorddijk, which formed a defensive line across from Voorne with the help of inundations.

7. Some source consider the area north of Amsterdam's fortifications of North Holland as not part of Fortress Holland and identify the Amsterdam Ring as forming the North Front. In practical terms North Holland should considered part of Fortress Holland.

8. The province of South Holland included the South Front of Fortress Holland and Utrecht province had much of the New Dutch Water Line.

9. This effectively turned the Zuider Zee into the Ijssel Meer (lake), although the former term remained in use.

10. He compares this density to the Ijssel and Maas forward defence lines where the number of casemates was about three per kilometre, although it was always much greater at river crossings sites and blocking points on road and railway routes.

11. Although General Voorst was the likely choice for the position, Dijxhoorn had to take into consideration that Vorst and his two brothers who served on the General Staff were Catholics. Appointing a Catholic to such a position in this Protestant nation would not be politically acceptable.

12. Winkelman gave up on the Peel–Raam line in March 1940 when the Belgians decided not to maintain contact with the border positions.

13. The *Marten Harpertzoon Tromp* was a pre-dreadnought built in 1904. It mounted two single gun turrets with 9.2in guns and four single gun turrets with 5.9in guns. The navy decommissioned the ship in 1927.

14. Their bunkers were of interest to post-war scavengers who plundered their interiors for teak wood imported from the former Dutch East Indies. The teak was used to line the ceilings to prevent flaking of the concrete when under bombardment.

15. Concrete standards varied from one country to another as did the quality of the concrete. In the French Maginot Line, 3.5m of concrete was the thickest protection and able to resist 420mm artillery rounds, while 2.75m was able to resist 300mm rounds. The French considered 2.25 metres sufficient to resist 240mm rounds. Thus, these Dutch forts could resist most German artillery and dive-bombers.

16. The Waal is the largest channel of the Rhine Delta.

17. The periscopes had not been installed before the German invasion.

18. The railway bridge dated from the previous century, but the road bridge was built in 1936; both were 1500m long.

19. The doors included a rifle embrasure to cover the entrance.

20. Major Colbern's estimate of the location of the II and IV Corps was correct. There were no A and B Divisions, but there were Brigades A and B located in these positions.

21. He correctly identified the I Corps, but no sources identify a Division C or D.

22. Japan did not sign the Tripartite Pact forming the Axis powers until September 1940. Relations with Germany were probably close enough that the attaches would pass on the information since they had signed the Anti-Comintern Pact in 1936.
23. Colbern's measurements do not fit any type of Dutch bunker, although he most likely was making an estimate and probably only from the side with the entrance. He probably could not determine the size or actual shape of any bunkers relied on his guide for the type of weapons and crew size. What he seems to have described were mostly S Type bunkers.
24. Since the Brandenburger Special Forces were controlled by the Abwehr, Colonel Oster must have warned Major Sas that this type of operation was planned. In addition, the early war directives also mentioned that the 7th Airborne Division was assigned to the assault on the Netherlands so he must have warned him about this too.
25. In 1939, the French High Command and General Maurice Gamelin favored Plan E, the Escaut Plan in which they would advance only to that river since the Belgians were intent on remaining neutral until an actual German invasion. In 1940, Gamelin formulated Plan D believing the Belgian defences between Antwerp and Namur had been significantly improved for the Allies to defend them.
26. The term 'Fifth Column' comes from the siege of Madrid in the Spanish Civil War when Franco's Nationalists surrounded and attacked the city with four columns and a fifth column rose up inside the city.
27. The containers had concrete sides 2m thick to withstand bombardment. The bottoms of the containers were only 20cm thick so the explosives could blow them out to drop their contents.
28. The main road was blocked by one of the large gates and the other blocked the path of a future road. At either end of this gap, two smaller gates blocked the cycle paths. According to Casper Vermeullen, since the seal was not watertight, the local farmers were expected so supply horse manure to seal the gates. The gates were only used in practice drills and the sealing procedure was never performed.

Chapter 3
1. Flanders is the Flemish region of Belgium. The main population centres of Wallonia, such as Liège and Namur, are on the northern part of Wallonia which is also north of the Meuse.
2. That is why nothing is left of their Vauban-era fortifications today.
3. Termonde is located on the south bank of the Scheldt between Ghent and Antwerp.
4. All Belgian armoured turrets were made of iron as was the turret blocks' glacis armour (avant-cuirasse).
5. The Cockreill (or Cockrell) Company of Liège began producing turrets in 1906 for the forts of Antwerp and continued manufacturing turrets and armoured components for the forts of the 1930s. John Cockreill founded the company in 1834 and had it producing rifles by the 1850s.
6. Rolling bridges were inside the entrance way and slide into the wall exposing a pit.
7. Fort Chartreuse barracks complex could accommodate 2,000 to 3,000 troops, but it lost importance in the late nineteenth century. The Germans used it as a prison during the First World War. The Belgians refurbished it as a barracks in 1919, a function it continued to have until 1945.
8. See *The Forts and Fortifications of Europe 1815-1945: The Central States* (Pen & Sword) for a detailed description of the German Feste.
9. In trapezoidal forts, the gallery crossed the ditch and joined a gallery leading to the double counterscarp and single counterscarp casemates. When an additional counterscarp casemate was in the gorge, it was linked to the counterscarp section of the caserne.
10. According to some historians, construction began in 1888 and others insist it goes back to 1881, but the latter date is very unlikely because it predates the invention of the high-explosive shell and Brialmont's writings on the need for the forts.
11. Different mixtures are used with Portland cement, which does not give the same results when making concrete. The Belgians, being the first to build concrete forts, did not come up with the ideal concrete mixture.

12. Brialmont's standards were sufficient until the twentieth century when the Germans and the Austrians developed 305mm and 420mm howitzers.

13. 'Reinforced concrete' was patented by a Frenchman named Joseph Monier in the 1870s, but it did not include rebar like the reinforced concrete used to build bridges and buildings in the late 1880s and 1890s.

14. The latrines were inaccessible in combat.

15. During the next war, infantry did not form part of the garrison of the forts since the army felt its positions on the forts had been too vulnerable.

16. It took up to thirty-six hours to assemble these weapons. Recent research indicates that the Skoda 305mm weapons and their Austrian crews were not at Liège but at Namur.

17. According to General Leman's report, only Forts Pontisse and Loncin had been targeted by the Big Berthas. The big guns fired between forty-three and fifty-one rounds at Pontisse and twenty-five at Loncin, scoring thirteen hits. The causes of surrender were low morale at Forts Barchon and Hollogne, detonation of magazines at Chaudfontaine and Loncin and gases from enemy shelling, defensive fire and the poor sewage system at Pontisse and Fléron. Evegnée, Embourg, Liers, Boncelles, Lantin and Flémalle also suffered from ventilation problems. According to Commandant Mozin at Fléron, the 420mm rounds that hit his fort came from the Plateau of Belleflamme, although this is unlikely since by this time the battery would have been moving from its firing positions at Mortier to new location for firing on Loncin.

18. Like his son Leon, a noted anthropologist who worked extensively in Africa and formulated racial theories for his perceived inferiority of the Black Africans, he is largely forgotten today. Herman Frobenius was so well known at the time that only his last name was used in many sources. His ideas were not as outmoded as his son's were.

19. For more detailed information on the campaign against the Belgian Forts see Clayton Donnell, *Breaking the Fortress Line 1914* (Barnsley: Pen and Sword, 2013).

20. Captain Karl Becker was later promoted and worked in the development of weapons after receiving his doctorate in 1922. By 1933, he was a general of artillery. Early in the Second World War, Hitler blamed him for munitions shortages, which led him to commit suicide in April 1940.

21. Erdmann had the most important mission, but his full name is not documented and he seems to have remained in obscurity.

Chapter 4

1. For over a century, the British tried to maintain the balance of power in Europe through alliances. The Versailles Treaty may have convinced them that Germany was no longer a threat. The Russian Empire appeared to be coming apart in a major civil war. New countries appeared in East and Central Europe following the breakup of the German, Austrian and Russian empires. Thus, in 1920, it seemed to the British that only France and Italy remained as major European powers, but both had suffered heavily during the war. There was, therefore, no further need to become involved in what might prove to be costly alliances as far as Great Britain was concerned.

2. He was Prime Minister from 1911 to 1918. In 1911, he advocated preparing the army to prevent German aggression and during the war he was in conflict with the king since Albert wanted to negotiate peace with the Germans. After the war, he became Minister of Interior from 1918 to 1919 and Minister of Defence from 1926 to 1930. In 1932, he became Prime Minister again and served until 1934.

3. The Maginot Line was not given its name until after its construction began early in the 1930s.

4. The fort was completed in 1935. The canal was begun in 1930 and not ready for use until 1939.

5. The French eventually extended the Maginot Line further along the Belgian border, but the last group of large fortifications was at Maubeuge and none of them was as impressive as the fortifications of the Maginot Line in Alsace and Lorraine. The French, convinced thanks to Marshal Pétain that the Belgian Ardennes were impassable to a modern army, only planned to send light forces into the Ardennes and major elements of their field army into Belgium north of the Meuse.

6. The plateau is bounded on the west by the Meuse valley. Here on the outskirts of Liège are some of the forts of PFL 2. On the east, it reaches the German border with the high points between Liège and Aachen. The Vesdre (German Weser) River borders it on the south and the Dutch border on the north.

7. Many historians consider Eben Emael as part of PFL 1 and in that case there are three large forts.

8. Months earlier, on 7 March 1936, German troops reoccupied the Rhineland, so this decree of neutrality gave the appearance of Belgium backing away from the threat of a resurgent Germany. On 30 January 1937, Hitler guaranteed the neutrality of Belgium and the Netherlands after repudiating the Treaty of Locarno of October 1925. The treaty – actually several agreements – signed by Germany, had fixed its western borders and included the commitment that the Rhineland would not be militarized. Hitler had already violated the section dealing with the Rhineland in March 1936. One of the agreements was that disputes with Czechoslovakia and Poland would be settled through arbitration and not warfare.

9. Plan D included an expanded version, the Breda Option, which had French forces sent by land and sea to assist the Dutch. This option overextended the Allied forces and achieved nothing other than placing additional French divisions further north of the Ardennes. In both plans the Ardennes was left only a few cavalry divisions to meet what became the main German thrust.

10. Mount St Peter is a ridge that runs between Maastricht and a point just short of Liège. The Caster Cut – 1.3km long and 65m below Mount St Peter in addition to the depth of the canal – sliced through the ridge so that the Albert Canal would reach the Meuse. The cut created a perfect position for the construction of the fort.

11. These water-cooled machine guns were connected to a water reservoir in the firing chamber.

12. Standard ammunition storage was 500 rounds per weapon.

13. This is not to be confused with the lance grenade used in some turrets (described in this chapter) that had a similar grenade, but included attached fins and a cartridge to launch it from a spigot-type mortar.

14. The French grenade launcher was slightly more complex and usually dropped the grenade into a small diamond fossé (a small angular ditch) that was in front of the embrasures of most French combat blocks. The Belgians seldom used this type of fossé. In many bunkers, the Belgians used a cage to catch the grenade so it would explode just above ground level.

15. The three artillery observation cloches were identified as Eben 1, 2 and 3. Eben 1 was on Block O1 overlooking the canal area and to Visé. Eben 2 was on Block Mi-Nord with a view along the Albert Canal and Kanne. In addition, there were several artillery observation posts outside the fort and over a dozen two-man rifle pits on the surface of the fort for observers.

16. The reason the northern corner of Eben Emael only had dummy turrets is that the terrain was unsuitable for heavy works. In 15 January 1932, the Director of Fortifications, Lieutenat Colonel Lauwers, received a report from the Chief of the Geological Service that indicated that the north end of the site consisted of layers of sand mixed with layers of clay underlying the gravel on the surface, making it prone to solifluction.

17. Most of these details come from the series of books *La Position Fortifiée de Liège* by Coenen and Verier. See their books for additional details and plan.

18. The diesel engines at Eben Emael were 160hp and the other forts had engines of 115hp.

19. The larger forts received engines of 175 CV and the smaller forts 130 CV.

20. The French did not use the same size of diesel engines in each fort. Instead, some large forts might have four engines of 100 CV and other forts four engines of 250 CV. The idea was to have no more than four engines and that was why the size varied, with the exception of Hochwald, which was like two forts, and the Alpine forts.

21. Turrets and cloches of nickel-chromium steel were common since the nickel gave the steel added strength and the chromium in proper proportion made it stainless steel so they did not rust away.

22. Only seven were made and used on entrance blocks and air intake blocks.

23. Only two of these were built and found on Block W and Block J.

24. The French used mixed garrisons of infantry and artillery troops with specialists from other services.
25. According to initial plans, 105mm guns and not 120mm weapons were to be used.
26. This information comes from correspondence between the authors and Jean Puelinckx and contradicts the more unrealistic claim that the fort was beyond the range of German heavy artillery.
27. Despite variance in mixtures, most concrete mixes between nations had similar resistance strength with only minor variations.
28. The French also had to face budgetary cuts on their Maginot Line forts, but, instead of weakening the resistance of the combat positions, they eliminated features such as surrounding anti-tank ditches and some positions in the forts or leaving them for a later phase of construction
29. These measurements are for the 120mm turret at Battice. It is assumed the one at Eben Emael may not have been as thick. Each of the steel layers was attached to a 40mm-thick piece of sheet metal. Between the two sections of steel and the sheet metal, there was a 50mm layer of a felt-like material to reduce the vibrations from hits. The 75mm turrets consisted of one piece of steel with two 25mm metal sheets under it.
30. No agreement exists on exact numbers for any of these forts in relation to garrisons.
31. The French standard for the Maginot Line was 30m depending on the type of soil and rock layers above the gallery.
32. Usually this was a shower or something similar.
33. The wooden peacetime barracks buildings at the Belgian forts were designed for rapid removal in time of war. See *La Position Fortifiée de Liège*, Vol 4 by Coenen and Vernier for additional details on the 'slide' entrance.
34. In the Belgian forts, all artillery blocks had monte-charges for hauling ammunition from the gallery below. Other types of blocks may have had smaller versions that were not large enough to carry personnel.
35. This was similar to those the French used to protect most of their weapons embrasures.
36. Coffre is a French term for a counterscarp gallery or casemate
37. Several sources state the surrounding ditches for the four new forts were 6m deep and 8m wide. However, an American intelligence report from 1937 gives measurements of about 6m depth and 15m width for Battice. According to Coenen and Vernier, all three forts east of the Meuse had ditches 5m deep and 15m wide.
38. The lance grenade was a German grantenwerfen taken after the war. They were a type of short-range spigot mortar with a range of 320m when installed in the turrets at a 55° angle. The weapon's short barrel was 120mm calibre, but the grenade was much smaller. The tube was wide enough to accommodate the grenade's fins. Its main purpose was to make certain the projectile passed through the side of the turret roof. The grenade came with five charges that gave it a range of 75m to 354m. Each turret had between two and four of these weapons (two at Barchon, two at Evegnée, four at Chaudfontaine and four at Flémalle). There were none in the other Liège forts according to the German Denkshrift of 1941, which reports that Fléron had two 81mm mortars, but it is not clear if this is correct. At the Namur forts, the lance grenades were mounted in one of the old 120mm gun turrets and the reversible machine guns in the other. They were mounted along the turret wall with the barrel projecting through the side of the turret roof at 55° as at Liège. However, they were also mounted in the embrasures at a 35° angle. The last type of mounting increased the range to 354m. The Denkshrift lists four lance grenades at Maizeret and Marchovelette, three at Andoy, two at Dave and Malonne and none at Forts St Héribert and Surlée. The reversible Maxim machine guns and mounts were the same as used in the new forts.
39. The French also stopped using open infantry positions on their forts, but they included infantry troops in their garrisons, unlike the Belgians who assigned only artillerymen and technicians.
40. Fort Hollogne had the cast iron glacis armour of one of its 57mm turret positions sent to Fort Chaudfontaine and the armour of two other 57mm turrets sent to Fort Embourg. Some sources give it a range of 5.7km and other 6.0km.

41. Some sources give it a range of 5.7km and other 6.0km
42. Some latrines were connected to a sewer system, but others were not and had to be emptied. They were placed throughout the fort including in the blocks and coffres.
43. Referred to the quadrilateral, located below the central citadel, because of the pattern it created with its connecting passages.
44. Fort Boncelles did not have one of these 'bombardment galleries'.
45. These doors could only be locked from the inside. A padlock secured the bunker on the outside door when the position was not occupied
46. The new forts used manufactured metal decoy turrets to create dummy positions.
47. These were designed by French General Léon Edmond Cointet for the Maginot Line. Known as the Cointet Device or Element C (for Cointet) , they were more popularly known as Belgian Gates because of their shape.
48. Today this is known as the Antwerp Anti-tank Ditch which, with its bunkers, is largely intact.

Chapter 5

1. See previous chapter.
2. Based on the operations that took place in Belgium on the German Sixth Army front in May 1940, the old plan might have also resulted in a decisive victory. Manstein's plan reduced the Sixth Army's role to engaging the Belgians and Allies north of the Meuse with two panzer divisions and about fifteen infantry divisions and was more of a diversion. At Hannut on 12–14 May and in the Gembloux Gap on 14–15 May, Sixth Army's two panzer divisions engaged French armour of the Cavalry Corps. Both sides took heavy tank losses. Although these encounters are considered tactical victories for the French, they were covering a retreat. The Manstein Plan allowed seven additional panzer divisions to race through the Ardennes. If the Belgian chasseur divisions had not withdrawn and the French had sent in a more a substantial force to take advantage of the terrain, they might have blunted the German thrust. If the original plan had been implemented, most of the panzer divisions would have used the same line of advance as the Sixth Army. Based on the results of the previously-mentioned engagements, they would have overwhelmed the Allies north of the Meuse. Even at the battles of Hannut and Gembloux, the Luftwaffe dominated the air. In addition, the airborne operations at Eben Emael and in the Netherlands and the deployment of the Brandenburgers had spread the fear that a Fifth Column was behind Allied lines.
3. Named after the contractor hired to do the construction. The barriers, which included doors, were placed along the French and German borders.
4. These generators were replaced in 1939; see previous chapter for more details.
5. Two years later, the Belgians decided that the distance between positions was too great and that additional bunkers must be added in 1939/40. Over 200 bunkers were built on these lines by 1940.
6. These were the only paratroopers to participate in this operation and they did not to arrive by glider.
7. The 400 volunteers of the battalion commanded by Captain Walter Koch came from the 1st Parachute Regiment. The unit also included a platoon of combat engineers from the same regiment commanded by Lt. Rudolf Witzig that was assigned to land on the fort. The unit was divided into Assault Group Granite (eighty-six men) to attack Eben Emael, Assault Group Steel (ninety-two men) to capture the Veldwezelt bridge, Assault Group Concrete (134 men) to take the Vroenhoven bridge and Assault Group Iron (ninety men) to grab the Kanne bridge.
8. Troops were warned against opening ammunition boxes during previous training because it had to be protected from the elements until needed. This brings to mind the British defeat at the hands of the Zulus at Isandlwana in 1879. When the Zulus attacked, the British quartermasters strictly controlled distribution of ammunition leaving most of it sealed in its boxes as the Zulus overran the British troops.

9. German intelligence indicated that there were two large gun turrets on a section of Eben Emael where the Belgians did not normally place them on other forts. This section would logically be the most exposed if the Germans attacked through Dutch territory. The Belgian planners had intended to build some type of positions for this part of the fort, but the geological structure of the subsoil made it impractical.
10. Heavy pressure from the Germans or not, the Allies had advanced as the Germans wanted since this was still only a diversion to draw them into northern Belgium as the main thrust came through the Ardennes.
11. The information on the damage at Battice and the events that took place at the fort comes from a single source, *Ceux de Battice en 1940*, produced by Amicale des Anciens du Fort de Battice. Presently, this book is the main source of details about the fort's battle history based on accounts of the survivors.
12. The Germans captured the commander of the fort and several others during their escape from the doomed fort.
13. Some of the data in this section on the PFL 2 comes from the German denkshrift on Belgian fortifications (1941) and internet site La Position Fortifiée Liégeoise at : http://users.skynet.be/jchoet/fort/index.htm.
14. This left the fort with only two 75mm howitzer turrets in operation.

Chapter 6
1. Most Europeans viewed the army of Louis Napoleon (Napoleon III) as the most formidable in Europe until its defeat in 1870.
2. C.W.B. Bell, *The Armed Strength of Switzerland* (London: War Office, 1889).
3. Sonderbund refers to a special or separate alliance the cantons were prohibited from forming by the 1815 constitution. The Catholic cantons formed such an alliance anyway because of the government's anti-Catholic policies.
4. Dufour took command of the army again in 1856. Neuchâtel revolted and broke away from the King of Prussia in 1848. He put down a pro-Prussian revolt in 1856. The crisis ended in negotiations between the great powers. Neuchâtel was both a Swiss canton and a Prussian principality since 1814. Prussia mobilized 150,000 against 30,000 Swiss troops, but backed down. At a conference in 1857, the canton's status as a Prussian principality ended. Dufour also presided over the 1st Geneva Convention in 1864 that dealt with the treatment of wounded during time of war.
5. Sargans was a creation of the late 1930s even though plans for it had been under consideration for many years previously.
6. Work began in 1857.
7. This would be the site of the Sargans fortress. Little more than a tower and small works were built in Dufour's time.
8. Dufour built three of these towers. A second tower at Luzisteig reinforced the defences of the Rhine Valley and the third at Bellinzona covered the entrance of the Leventina Valley leading towards Gotthard. All three towers remain to this day. They are of made stone and masonry and circular with long vertical firing slits in each of the three levels for musketry.
9. Liechtenstein dissolved its army in 1868 and it remained neutral until the end of the First World War even though it had been economically aligned with Austria. The tiny nation then aligned itself with Switzerland and again remained neutral during the next World War.
10. The rank of colonel is the highest in the Swiss army, except in time of crisis when the Federal Parliament in Berne elects an officer to the rank of general to command the army. That officer holds the title of general for the remainder of his career. Herzog was a young artillery officer during the Sonderbund war and was elected in July 1870 because of the Franco-Prussian War that resulted in another mobilization of the Swiss Army to defend the nation's neutrality.
11. Germany, Austria-Hungary and Italy formed the alliance, while France on the western Swiss border worked to create its own powerhouse alliance ten years later.

12. In 1888, the Italian army prepared plans to invade this southern region of Switzerland in support of their alliance in a future war.
13. The army scrapped these two guns in the 1960s, but the turret remains.
14. New ammunition increased the range of the howitzer to 7km in 1937.
15. In 1867, Joseph Monier, a gardener in France, patented his method of adding metal pieces to create reinforced concrete for small objects. Ernest L. Ransome patented a type of ferroconcrete using twisted iron rods in 1884 and built a couple of bridges in San Francisco with this method in 1886. It is not clear when forts were first built or reinforced with ferroconcrete because most construction details were considered military secrets for many years. From the limited data available, it appears that the French and Germans did not use reinforced concrete until they built the forts at Verdun and Metz, mainly in the middle of the first decade of the twentieth century. In many cases, they were using it to strengthen existing positions and build turret blocks. By the 1930s, ferroconcrete fortifications were standard except in countries like Italy where iron and steel was in short supply and seldom used for concrete reinforcement. See Appendix I.
16. The 1,874m-long Furka tunnel was not completed until 1925 and opened in July 1926. The tunnel is at an elevation of 2,160m (6,912ft).
17. The city was a strongpoint between Basel and Geneva in Western Switzerland.
18. Günther Reiss, 'Fortification in Switzerland from 1860 to 1945', *FORT* (1993).
19. The Urseren Valley is located between the Furka Pass and Oberlap Pass and the Rhine and Rhône rivers.
20. Günther Reiss, 'Fortification in Switzerland from 1860 to 1945', *FORT*. 1993.
21. The positions of the Central Group are rarely mentioned and probably had little significance.
22. These are little-known positions except for the two forts.
23. This was similar to a disappearing gun, except that it included an armoured shield for some overhead protection.
24. The E1 and E2 trenches connected and they may have been single-gun batteries until another gun was added to each of them later in the decade.
25. Some sources identified the 105mm gun batteries as C10 and Battery Aiguille, instead of C10 South and C10 North respectively.
26. Exact type of weapons not specified but some sources claim 120mm guns in open positions.
27. The first bridge was of wood from the thirteenth century and replaced by a stone bridge in the sixteenth century. In 1820 work began on a new bridge that took ten years to complete. This bridge was a key link on the route to the St. Gotthard Pass and made commercial trade through the pass possible.
28. W.G. Fitzgerald, 'Military Manoeuvres Above the Clouds', *Pearson's Magazine* (July 1902).
29. Italian Alpini, French Chasseurs Alpins and the Austro-Hungarian Landesschützen werer formed in 1907. The German Alpen Korps formed later in 1914, eventually becoming the German Gebirgsjäger. However, the Swiss probably had the most skilled mountain troops even though they had not been tested in war.
30. Colonel Maxime Weygand, Foch's chief of staff, was sent to Berne to work out arrangement for having the Swiss prepare the needed lines of communication so French forces could rush to their aid.
31. Eric Margolis 'Inside Switzerland's Secret Forts' for www.Resnse.com, 2002.
32. French General de Lattre de Tassigny when meeting with an envoy of General Guisan in the autumn of 1944 referred to the National Redoubt in these terms, although this might well refer to the entire country.
33. They remained in service until 1994.
34. The Swiss often refer to large bunkers and sometimes a pair of connected bunkers as 'Fortin', especially if they have the ability to operate somewhat independently. A Fortin is therefore not to be confused with an actual fort. This is also true of many 'Artillerie Werks' which may be a fort or something more like a 'Fortin'.
35. The amount of literature available on these forts recently opened is limited and often contradictory in regards to dates an installation of weapons. Most of the data is on internet sites and the few books

available. The former are often updated, while in the book were written when much information was still classified.

36. Steig means 'steep' and Steigwiesen means 'the steep way'.
37. Swiss camouflage methods continued to improve during the Cold War.
38. Normally the garrison numbered about 400 men, about seventy of whom were in the fortress infantry.
39. In April 1944, two types of 150mm guns were tested at the fort.
40. A battery of 105mm howitzers was added to the fort after the war.
41. A quarter of the garrison operated the anti-aircraft weapons positions.
42. Neither the fortress areas around Lake Thun and Lake Lucerne had names found in the literature until after the 1990s. If the military had an official name for them, it has not been found by any researcher at this date. Recently the terms used to describe these two fortress zones and Fortress Bernese Oberland for the area around Lake Thun and Fortress Stans for the Lake Lucerne area.
43. The Simmental Valley widens from Lenk to Boltigen and includes the main road from Wimmis to Aigle.
44. Fortress St-Maurice traditionally covered the western gateway into the National Redoubt. The creation of Fortress Bernese Oberland leaves St-Maurice covering the southwest gateway with the redoubt expanded.
45. As mentioned, Fortress Stans is a relative recent term for this position. Most of the forts are clustered near the historic town of Stans while the city of Lucerne, like Thun, is actually outside the fortified area. Stans was also the home of national hero Arnold von Winkelried.
46. One machine-gun position was part of the entrance and another between the two gun positions with an observation post and the third located with the searchlight at a higher level (30m up) and accessed by ladder.
47. Willi Gautschi in *General Henri Guisan* notes that the Swiss troops, like many French troops during this time were not able to conduct training exercise since they had to work on the defences. It was not until May 1940 that they finally received plans to work to create standard types of bunkers. In addition, in the Limmatstellung, because of a lack of demolitions, explosives had to be removed from half of the Simplon tunnels mine chambers. The Germans referred to the Limmat Position as the 'Guisan Line' until 1942.
48. In 1940, the *New York Times* referred to the Border Line as the 'Winkelried Line' after a Swiss national hero. Swiss sources do not use this name for the Border Line, so it may have been an invention of the media in the same way the German West Wall became the 'Siegfried Line'.
49. Gautschi states in his book that it was in May 1940 that General Gusian decided on establishing the main defences in the National Redoubt. He also wrote that actually the conception of the National Redoubt is not even mentioned until after the war began. The Gotthard Fortress was initially considered the central point until Gusian's staff concluded it was not satisfactory for manoeuvre and could only be considered a blocking position. His staff at one point considered using Sargans as an advanced base and St-Maurice to be independent of the National Redoubt, but eventually decided to include them as part of the fortress. On 10 July 1940 Guisan issued the order creating the National Redoubt. At first, it was to be used for training, but soon the construction of new fortifications was authorized.
50. Early in the war consideration was given to abandoning the border positions in the south and pulling the troops back to the National Redoubt.
51. Sources for this section included: Schwarz, *Eye of the Hurricane*; Halbrook, *Target Switzerland*; Urner, *Let's Swallow Switzerland*. More details on invasion plans can be found in these books.
52. All three army corps when mobilized concentrated in the north on either side of the Limmatstellung and in it, with a fourth corps added in 1940. By the spring of 1941 all the divisions and mountain brigades were moved into the National Redoubt.
53. Guderian's 29th Motorized InfantryDivision reached the border at Pontarlier on 16 June.
54. General Guisan and his staff had alrady decided that Zurich would not be declared an 'Open City'.

55. This was the type of situation resulting in most French soldiers outside of France giving up ideas of resistance and refusing to join the Free French. About two-thirds of Switzerland's population would be abandoned.
56. This was an optimistic view of British capabilities after the fall of France.

Chapter 7
1. See *The Forts and Fortifications of Europe 1815-1945: The Central States* (Pen & Sword) for details on the German Alpine Fortress.
2. A translation of the article appeared in English in *International Military Digest Quarterly*, Volume 1 (1915), pp. 133–4.

Bibliography
1. Note that internet sites only remain as long as someone maintains them. Thus, unlike a book which will last either in print or digitalized form for many years, these sites can disappear soon after a book is published. Fortunately, an internet search will produce similar new sites that will replace these. We have listed some of the most useful sites for the most updated information.

Bibliography

Abbenhuis, Maartje M., *The Art of Staying Neutral* (Amsterdam Univ. Press, 2006)*

Andrey, Brigadier Dominique, 'Secteur fortifié de Saint-Maurice: Le fort de Dailly – Agir dans deux directions' (Association Saint-Maurice d'Études Militares. 2006). *tp://www.asmem.ch/2012/2012-01-29-13-29-29/secteur-fortifie-de-st-maurice/secteur-de-dailly/60-le-fort-de-dailly.html*

'Anti-Gallican Bulwarks', *The United Service Journal and Naval and Military Magazine* (London: December 1835), p. 254

'Armor and Fortifications', *Scientific American* (Dec. 26, 1896), pp. 457–8

A.S.B.L [Association for preservation] Fort Aubin-Neufchâteau, *P.F.L. Aubin-Neufchâteau* (Belgium: Privately published by Jean Puelinckx, 1997)

Balace, Francis, 'Description détaillée des forts de la Meuse en 1914', *Liège 1000 Ans de Fortifications Militaires* (15 December 1980 to 16 January 1981)*

Beach, Lt. Lansing, 'Turrets in the Forts on the Line of the Meuse' (translation of article 'Die Panzerthürme der Forts der Maas-Linie' by Josef Fornasari Edler von Verce), *Journal of the Military Service Institution of the United States* (1894), pp. 1046–57

Becker, Captain (German Army), 'The 42-cm Mortar: Fact and Fancy', *The Field Artillery Journal*, Vol. XII (1922), pp. 224–30

Bell, Colonel C.W. Bowdler, *The Armed Strength of Switzerland*, prepared for Intelligence Division of the War Dept (London: HMSO [printed by Harrison and Sons], 1889)

Bevaat, Dr. V., *Nederlandse Defensie: 1839-1874* (The Hague: Sectie Militaire Geschiedenis 1993)

Brassey, Lord, *[Brassey's] Naval Annual, 1886* (London: J. Griffin & Co., 1886)

Browne, Captain C. Orde. 'Development of Armour and its Attack by Ordnance', *Journal of the Royal Artillery* Vol 20 (Woolwich: Royal Artillery Institution, 1893), pp 48–68 and 84–106

C., 'The value of Permanent Fortifications' (extracted from *Kriegstechnische Zeitschrift*, Jan–Feb 1915), *International Military Digest Quarterly* Volume 1 (Princeton University: Cumulative Digest Corp., 1915), pp. 133–4

Califf, First Lieutenant Joseph M., 'The Development of Armor', *The Railway and Engineering Journal* (September 1890), pp. 411–12, (October 1890), pp. 458–60

Carden, Lt. Godfrey L., 'Gruson Coast-Defence Turrets', *Harper's Weekly* Vol 45 (19 Jan. 1901), pp 387–9

Ceux de Battice en 1940 (Belgium: Amicale des Anciens du Fort de Battice, 1989)*

Ceux du Fort D'Eben-Emael (Belgium: Le Comité de l'Amicale, 1978*

Clarke, George Sydenham, *Fortification: Its Past Achievements, Recent Developments and Future Progress* (London: 1907 (reprint))*

——, 'The Lydd Experiments of 1889', *Professional Papers of the Corps of Royal Engineers*, Vol 15 (Royal Engineer Institute, 1889), pp. 97–114

Coenen, Emile and Franck Vernier, *La Position Fortifiée de Liège* Tome 1-5 (Belgium: Editions de Krijger. 2002)*

Tome 1 *Les abris de la Position Avancée*

Tome 2 *Les abris de la P.F.L. 1*

Tome 3 *Les abris de la P.F.L. 2*

Tome 4 *Les nouveaux forts*

Tome 5 *Les forts de la Meuse Modernisés*

Collon, Lt. A., 'Commentaries on Contemporaneous Art of Defense', *Journal of the United States Artillery*, Vol. XVII (Ft. Monroe (VA) ; Artillery School Press, 1902), pp. 120–30

Cdt au Fort 13. 'Armement de Savatan et Dailly à la fin de le 3ème période de construction (1910)', St-Maurice 6.2.1990. internet site: http://www.box.net/shared/ocrt1arkb2

Deguise, Captain Victor, *Cours de Fortifications Permanente* (Brussels; Polleunus et Ceuterick, 1896)

Dijk, Kees van, *The Netherlands Indies and the Great War,1914-1918* (Lieden: KITLV Press, 2007)

Doorman, Col. P.L.G., *Military Operations in the Netherlands from 10th-17th May, 1940* (London: George Allen & Unwin Ltd for The Netherlands Government Information Bureau, June 1944) (internet at: http://www.ibiblio.org/hyperwar/UN/Netherlands/Ops-1940/index.html#A2)

Douglas, General Sir Howard, *Observations on Modern Systems of Fortification Including that Proposed by M. Carnot and a Comparison of the Polygonal with the Bastion System* (London: John Murray, 1859)

Engineering Mechanics , Vol 14 (Philadelphia: October 1892) p. 271

Encyclopaedia Britannica: A Dictionary of Arts, Sciences, Literature and General Information, Eleventh Edition (Cambridge University Press, 1911)

Fiebeger, Colonel Gustav Joseph, *Permanent Fortification*, prepared for the use of the Cadets of the United States Military Academy (West Point (N.Y.): United States Military Academy Press, 1900 and 1916 editions)*

Fischer, Karl (ed), *Die Wehrmacht 1940: Der Freiheitskampf des großdeutschen Volkes* (Berlin-Charlottenburg: Oberkommando der Wehrmacht, 1940)

Fitzgerald, W.G., 'Military Manoeuvres Above the Clouds', *Pearson's Magazine* Vol XIV No. 79 (July 1902)

'Fortification and Siegecraft', *Encyclopaedia Britannica* 11th edition, Vol X (New York: 1910), pp. 696–700

Frobenius, Colonel Herman, 'Permanent – Experience With Europes War' (extracted from 'The Fortress in the Present War', *Kriegstechnische Zeitschrift* [Jan–Feb 1915]), *International Military Digest Quarterly*, Vol 1 (Princeton Univesity: Cumulative Digest Corp., 1915), pp. 134–5

Fuhrer, Hans Rudolf, Walter Lüem, Jean-Jacques Rapin, Hans Rapod and Hans Senn, *Die Geschichte Der Schweizerischen Landesbefestigung* (Zurich: Orell Füssli, 1992)*

Gautschi, Willi, *General Henri Guisan* (New York: Front Street Press, 2003)*

Hogg, Ian V., *The History of Fortification* (New York: St. Martin's Press Inc., 1981)

——, *Allied Artillery of World War One* (Ramsbury: Crowood Press Ltd., 1998)

Hopkins, Albert A. (ed), 'Description of the Famous Gruson Armored Turret Used in European Fortifications' by Major A.G. Piorkowski, *Scientific American War Book: the Mechanism and Technique of Warfare* (New York: Munn & Co., 1915), pp. 61–5

Howe, Henry Marion, *The Metallography of Steel and Cast Iron* (New York: McGraw-Hill Book Company, 1916)

Intelligence Division of the War Office, *The Armed Strength of Belgium* (London: HMSO, 1882)

Jaques, Lt William Henry, *Modern Armor for National Defence* (London: G.P. Putman's Sons, 1886)

Jeram, Charles S., *The Armies of the World* (New York: New Amsterdam Book Company, 1900)

Johnson, Douglas W., *Topography and Strategy in the War* (New York: Henry Holt and Company, 1917)

'The Land Defenses of Holland' translated by Charles Junken from an article in the *Internationalen Revue uber die Gesamten Armeen und Flotten, Beihft*, No. 130 (June 1911), *Journal of the United States Artillery*, Vol. 37 (Artillery School Press: January 1912)

——, 'Professional Notes' (Vol. 40. Ft. Monroe (VA); Coast Artillery School, 1913)

Kaufmann, J.E., and H.W. Kaufmann, *Maginot Imitations* (Westport (CT): Praeger, 1997)

——, *Fortress Europe* (Conshohocken, PA: Combined Publishing, 1999)

Klinkert, Dr. Wim, *Het Vaderland Verdedigd; Plannen en opvattingen over de verdediging van Nederland 1874-1914* (S-Gravenhage: Sectie militarie geschiedenis, 1992)

Ley, Willy, 'German Siege Guns of the Two World Wars', *Coast Artillery Journal* (Jan/Feb 1943), pp. 14–20

Liège: 1000 Ans de Fortifications Militaire (Liège: Centre Liégeois D'Histoire et D' Archéologie Militaire, 16 Dec. 1980–16 Jan 1981)*

Lombaerde, Piet (ed), *Vesting Antwerpen: De Brialmontforten* (Netherlands: Snoeck-Ducaju & Zoon, 1997)

Lüem, Walter and Andreas Steigmeier, *Die Limmatstellung im Zweiten Weltkrieg. Baden: Baden-Verlag* (1997)

Lüem, Walter and Max Rudolf, *Wehrraum Sargans/Die grossen Artilleriewerke Furggels und Tschingel* (Wettingen (Switz): Gesellschaft fuer militaerhistorische Studienreisen, 2001)*

Mallory, Keith and Arvid Ottar, *The Architecture of War* (New York: Pantheon Books, 1973)

Mercur, James, *Mahan's Permanent Fortifications* (2nd edition, New York: Wiley & Sons, 1889)

Montet, Lt. Col. Jean de, *L'Armement de L'Artillerie de Forteresse Suisse de 1885 à 1939* (Association Saint-Maurice, 1984)*

The Penny Cyclopaedia of the Society for the Diffusion of Useful Knowledge (London: Charles Knight & Co., 1839)

Professional Papers, Fourth Series, Vol 1 – Number 7, 'Fortresses and Military Engineering in Recent Literature' (Royal Engineers, 1907)

Reiss, Günther D., 'The Development of Fortification of Swiss Territory from Post-Napoleonic Period up to the Second World War' for Fortress Study Group tour of Swiss fortifications in 1990.

——, 'Fortification in Switzerland from 1860 to 1945', *FORT* Vol. 21 (1993), pp. 19–53

——, 'Daniel von Salis-Soglio – Innovative Fortress Designer', *FORT* Vol. 26 (1998), pp. 143–68

Rolf, Rudi, *A Dictionary on Modern Fortification* (Middleburg: PRAK Publishing, 2004)*

——, and Peter Saal, *Fortress Europe* (Shrewsbury: Airlife Publishing Ltd., 1988)

Rothstein, Theodore, 'The German Menace', *Justice: Weekly Newspaper of British Social Democracy* (18 Feb. and 25 Feb. 1911)

Sakkers, Hans, Johan den Hollander and Ruud Murk, *De Holland Stellung* (Antwerp: Witsand Uitgevers, 2011)

Schwarz, Urs, *The Eye of the Hurricane: Switzerland in World War Two* (Boulder, Colorado: Westview Press, 1980)

---

* Recommended

Steenbeck, Wilhemina, *Rotterdam: Invasion of Holland* (New York: Ballantine Books, 1973)

Stehlik, Eduard, *Lexikon Tvrzí: československého opevnění z let 1935-38* (Prague: Fort Print, 1992)

Thuillier, Henry Fleetwood, *The Principles of Land Defence and their Application to the Conditions of Today* (London: Longmans, Green & Co, 1902)

The Times History of the War: The Battlefield of Europe (New York: Woodward & Van Slyke Inc., 1914)

Trotter, Major J.K., *The Armed Strength of the Netherlands and Their Colonies*, complied by the Intelligence Branch of the War Office (London: Eyre & Spottiswoode, 1887)

Urner, Klaus, *Let's Swallow Switzerland* (Lanham, Maryland: Lexington Books, 2002)

Verbeek, J.R., *Kazematten Op De Afsluitdijk: Den Oever, Kornwerderzand, Wons, Breezand* (Netherlands: privately published, 2012)

Veve, Thomas Dwight, *The Duke of Wellington and the British Army of Occupation in France: 1815-1818* (Westport: Greenwood, 1992

Wehranstrengungen im Raum Nidwalden 1935-1995 (Stans: Officers Association Nidwalden, 2007)

Wieringen, J.S. van, 'The Grebbe Line: a long defence line with a long history', *FORT*, Vol. 19 (1991), pp. 73–92

Newspapers

Vlissingsche Courant: 11 Feb. 1914, 13 Mar. 1914, 29 Jul. 1914, 13 Oct. 1919, 29 Mar. 1919 and 4 Jun. 1925, 30 Jan. 1935, 15 Feb. 1936

American Military Attaché Reports

Barnes, Major G.M., 'Seacoast Defenses of the Netherlands – G-2 Report', Berlin: Military Observer, 2 Dec. 1922

Colbern, Major William H., 'Land Frontiers and Interior Defense System', The Hague, Military Attaché Report No. 4552, 15 Feb. 1940

——, 'Land Frontiers and Interior Defense System', The Hague, Military Attaché Report No. 4578, 19 Apr. 1940

Fuller, Lt. Col. H.H., 'Land Frontiers and Interior Defense Systems. Northern Defense of Belgium', Belgium: Military Attache Report No. 24, 106-W, 14 Mar. 1938

Kroner, Major Hayes A., 'Belgian Defense Works', London: Attaché Report No. 36536, 26 Oct, 1934.

Waite, Lt. Col. Sumner, 'Land Frontiers and Interior Defnense System. Eastern Defense of Belgium', Paris: Military Attaché Report No. 23,413-W, 11 May 1937

German Documents from the 1930s to 1945

Befestigungen und Geländehindernisse in Ostbelgien und den südlichen Niederlanden, Abteilung Fremde Heere West, 20 Oct. 1939

Die Ijssel-Linie wassertechnisch ausgewertet, Abteilung Fremde Heere West, 3 Dec. 1939

Denkschrift über die belgische Landesbefestigung, Berlin: OKH, 1 Oct. 1941

Denkschrift über die niederländische Landesbefestigung, Berlin: OKH, 1 Oct. 1941

Denkschrift über die jugoslawische Landesbefestigung, Berlin: OKH, 1 Oct. 1942

Technische Angaben über die niederlädischen und belgischen Befestigungen, Abteilung Fremde Heere West, 1 Nov. 1939.

Verbesserung der Rheinufer – Stande, Heeres Gruppenkommando 2, 22 Feb. 1939

US National Archives

Miscellaneous Documents from the US National Archives found on Microcopy No. T-78, Record Group No. 242/ Roll 542, Part 1 and 2, listed as *Records of HQ, German Army High Command (Oberkommando des Heeres – OKH)*. Items included: 'Befestigungen und Geländehindernisse in Ostbelgien und den südlichen Niederlanden' 20 Oct. 1939, 'Die Ijssel-Linie wassertechnisch ausgewertet' 3 Dec. 1939, 'Technische Angabe über die niederländischen und belgischen Befestigungen' 1 Nov. 1939, 'Sperren in Osterreich' 8 Jan. 1937–Feb. 1938, 'Akten des Servcie Geologique de Belgiuqe über das Festungsbiet "Lüttich". Forts: "Eben Emael", "Flemalle", "Fleron", "Hollogne", "Lantin", "Liers", "Loncin" and "Pontisse"', 1928–1932.

Internet Sites:[1]

'Amsterdam Position'
http://www.stelling-amsterdam.nl/english/common/enquiry/index.html
'Dutch Forts'
http://www.mverhoeks.com/Overzicht_verdedigingslinies/Forten-SvA.html
'Fortifications in Switzerland'
http://www.schweizer-festungen.ch/
'L'index de la fortification belge de 1830 à 1914' http://www.fortiff.be/ifb/
"War over Holland." http://www.waroverholland.nl/index

Index